Science and Golden Ratios in Maṇḍala Architecture

Contours of Indian Art & Architecture

1. The Panorama of Jaipur Paintings; by Rita Pratap; (ISBN 978-81-246-0068-9)
2. Islamic Tombs in India — The Iconography and Genesis of Their Design; by Fredrick W. Bunce (ISBN 978-81-246-0245-4)
3. Feminine Beauty in Indian Art and Literature; by T.N. Mishra (ISBN 978-81-246-0387-1)
4. A Socio-Economic Study of Company Paintings (CE 1757-1857); by T.N. Mishra (ISBN 978-81-246-0571-4)
5. Pahari Paintings of an Ancient Romance: The Love Story of Usha-Aniruddha; by Harsha V. Dehejia, Vijay Sharma (ISBN 978-81-246-0561-5)

Contours of Indian Art & Architecture, no. 6

Science and Golden Ratios in Maṇḍala Architecture

Rekha Rao

D.K. Printworld (P) Ltd.
Publishers of Indian Traditions

Cataloging in Publication Data — DK
[Courtesy: D.K. Agencies (P) Ltd. <docinfo@dkagencies.com>]

Rao, Rekha, 1951-
Science and golden ratios in maṇḍala architecture/
Rekha Rao.
p. cm. — (Contours of Indian art & architecture ; no. 6.)
Includes bibliographical references (p.) and index.
ISBN 13: 9788124605875

1. Mandala. 2. Hindu symbolism. 3. Hindu art. 4. Golden ratios. 5. Proportion (Art) 6. Composition (Art) 7. Hindu temples — India — Karnataka — Designs and plans. I. Title. II. Series: Contours of Indian art & architecture ; no. 6.

DDC 294.537 22

First published in India, 2011
ISBN 13: 978-81-246-0587-5 **ISBN 10: 81-246-0587-4**

Published and printed by:
D.K. Printworld (P) Ltd.
Regd. Office: 'Vedaśrī', F-395, Sudarshan Park
Ramesh Nagar Metro Station
New Delhi – 110 015-11
Phones: (011) 2545 3975; 2546 6019; *Fax*: (011) 2546 5926
E-mail: indology@dkprintworld.com
Website: www.dkprintworld.com

Preface

DURING my work on the *apsaras*es of Belur temple, my attention was drawn towards the *bhuvaneśvarī* — the central ceiling of the assembly hall of the temple, which had not caught my attention in the past. I was amazed at the volume of work and wondered why it was placed so high, even though fixing such a wonderful piece of art, in a dome shape, was a Herculean task for the sculptors. My curiosity made me observe the diversity of patterns in the *bhuvaneśvarī*s of other temples, which, though looked beautiful, did not reveal any information about the purpose in installing such beautiful art forms of geometrical patterns, so high in the ceilings. In spite of being a student of history and culture, the unfamiliarity and lack of understanding with these varied designs in the *bhuvaneśvarī* aroused my interest to know more about them. The superficial curiosity, followed by enquiry, led me to the quest of finding the data associated with the circular designs, *maṇḍala*s as they are called, carved in the *bhuvaneśvarī*. It was amazing to study the intricate and different patterns in each circular design — *maṇḍala*s in temples, as each one appeared like a model for cosmic diagram, concealing vast knowledge of the organisational structure of life. Most of the books on *maṇḍala*s said that *maṇḍala*s had something to say on the cosmos, but it was not clear in what way the *maṇḍala*s were associated with knowledge of cosmos. It was on the advice of Dr S.R. Rao I was instigated to work on a scientific orientation to these circular designs, the *maṇḍala*s of the *bhuvaneśvarī* in the pillared hall of the temples, as art, science and spirituality, all three appeared to be merged into one. He also motivated me to study the book, *Synthesis of Science and Religion*, a compilation of 32 essays by renowned scientists and philosophers, which made me realise that relation between science and spirituality is like part and a whole. Religion ultimately leads to spirituality, so also science. Science and spirituality are the two ways of looking at same things; both are with the approach to truth. One is subjective and the other is objective. Science leads by logic, and spirituality by intuition, both adding dimension to the knowledge of the supreme power. Science proceeds in part by observation, giving clues to what is real, true and ultimate with matter that is visible, without giving a slightest thought to the idea of God's existence. But religion and spirituality deal with the supernatural, based on natural world-considering reality as a whole. The development of the knowledge of science decays in the absence of spirituality. Hinduism with its practical wisdom understands the reason, yet retaining its tradition.

The common question that arises is — why should there be science involved in *maṇḍala* designs of temples. In the early and medieval period of Indian history, temples were not merely places of worship but they were also an indispensable part of society with various responsibilities. They were centres of education, fine arts and promoted the cultural heritage among the masses, especially the younger generation.

Our ancestors were eager to understand the world and they also knew that the scientific approach was the most powerful and elegant way to know about the cosmos. Science interprets nature through reason and experimentation. Kṛṣṇa says in *Bhagavad-Gītā* that he is the reason in knowledge which helps to conclude that science is one form of divine manifestation. Ancient philosophers knew that scientific laws pervaded nature, the nature of earth, sky and also the way the world worked. The

Upaniṣads say — *padārtha jñānāt mokṣam* — the knowledge of cosmos, even in a fraction, leads one to *mokṣa* (liberation). According to *Muṇḍaka Upaniṣad,* two kinds of knowledge need to be known, by the *jijñāsus* (the seekers of knowledge of *Brahman*). They are the lower knowledge (*parā vidyā*) and higher knowledge (*aparā vidyā*). *Aparā* is the knowledge of the four Vedas, six Vedāṅgas, to understand the field of *nakṣatra gati* (the science of astronomy), and *gaṇita* (the science of mathematical calculations including arithmetic, algebra, and geometry). *Parā* knowledge was beyond this and focused on the attainment of *Brahman.* A rigorous study of Vedas and Vedāṅgas revealed the approach to the attainment of ultimate truth (the *Brahman*), which was the goal of life. Science deals with *aparā vidyā* — the material knowledge, whereas spirituality deals with *parā vidyā* — the knowledge on the spirit that is enduring and maintaining the equilibrium of the universe. If the knowledge of one's body, its components up to the atoms and molecules, gained through sensory perceptions — is *aparā vidyā,* the knowledge of the conscious living being (*ātmā*), transcendent life, and God is *parā vidyā,* which is experienced through the discipline of *yoga.* The science of *aparā vidyā* studies the nature of an atom outwardly, proving its existence by experiments, but *parā vidyā* or the theology explains how to become an atom and experience the oneness with the nucleus, that is, the vital centre. *Aparā vidyā* is much like the scientific knowledge of calculation — the *gaṇita śāstra* and engineering skills involved in building a long-lasting and huge temple that houses God — the soul within. Science develops on logic satisfying the physical body and senses while spirituality develops intuition satisfying the mystic experience of soul. One can see God through science.

As explained by Swami Vivekananda, we can go to the limits of this universe, but we shall still find God spread out beyond.

We can dive deep into the heart of each atom of matter, only to discover that we have entered a greater realm of his power and glory. The manifest universe is a very small part of his glory and power. We try to grasp this truth with our puny little mind and senses, and all that we can clasp is a pebble as nature does not reveal glories once and for all.

*Maṇḍala*s in the *bhuvaneśvarī* of the *navaraṅga* hall of temples, like flashes, bring to light the hidden truth existing around the governing laws of nature, which can now be considered as the documentations, recording the scientific achievements of our ancestors in an ornate and artistic expression. The mystery of science deepens, as we advance and dwell in this field — so also in spirituality. There is an unending mystery in both science and spirituality. The more we try to know about this world, or self, the better is our understanding as to how little we know about it. A fusion of facts and dreams are in *maṇḍala*s. The purpose of installing the *maṇḍala*s in temples was for upliftment, and to pass on the knowledge of how things are in cosmos.

*Maṇḍala*s were probably like the medium, to fill the ignorance gap by explaining the concepts that everyone needs to understand. It is intended to encompass the mainstream fields of not only spirituality but also physics, mathematics, architecture, biology and so on. One can feel that the complex scientific details are condensed and simplified into an artistic looking design that even non-scientific people can appreciate the scientific concepts that rule the universe. *Maṇḍala*s can be seen as an attempt to make science look like a series of ideas and not a complicated body of facts — with the intention that as many people as possible should have a basic knowledge of science. But, just like the map of a country will not represent the whole truth, but will faithfully represent some aspect of it, *maṇḍala*s indicate some aspects of the science as understood during that period, because in ancient times the study of physical sciences was neither formalised nor separated from other branches of knowledge. The underlying scientific principles of the way the world worked was amalgamated with the spiritual thoughts and the *maṇḍala*s of temples thus became an approximate awareness of science. However, the application of the laws of physics and an insight into the branches of science as per the ancient rational treatises can be seen practically documented in the *bhuvaneśvarī*s of Hindu temples. They are no doubt crucial to humanity to compare with the present stage of knowledge in the fields of physics, chemistry, botany and other physical sciences. As an example, when the *maṇḍala* of Belur Cennakeśava temple was considered, the central deity was Lord Narasiṁha, a deity of "Tejas" when presented in a *maṇḍala* (or the *cakra* (wheel) of Viṣṇu in symbolic form) it is read as a *sudarśana yantra*. A study on *sudarśana yantra* revealed that there are two varieties of it like *jyotirmayī* and *vāṅgmayī sudarśana yantra*, that bear a relation to the faculties of sight and sound. When the properties of light was studied, it matched quite well with the pictorial form of *maṇḍala* of Belur in a subtle way. Similarly the shape of petals and progression in the number of petal divisions of the Keladi Vīrabhadra temple tallied quite well with the properties of sound, which reinforced the logic that the temple *maṇḍala*s are the representations of the aspects of science in a hidden form.

Through this study, I would like to present a few thoughts on the relationship that was existing between spiritual ideas and the ideas of scientific advancement, co-exhibited in the *maṇḍala*s of ancient temples. It is an attempt to trace the scientific advancement of ancient period that lay hidden in the *maṇḍala*s and draw the parallels between laws of physics to metaphysical ideas. Science is an ongoing process that never ends. There is no single ultimate truth in science that is achieved, after which the scientists can retire. It operates under the guidance of paradigms — the structure of the scientific revolutions and the progressive knowledge that is taught to the new generation of scientists. The advances in technology solve many problems of the world during calamities, but are unable to help in solving some of the personal problems of man that cannot be explained on material basis in the abstract thoughts like beauty of love, compassion, self-sacrifice, and so on. It is this aspect of life and consciousness that theosophy helps to explain where methods of science lead to chaos in the deeper and inner aspects of truth. Both science and spirituality are aimed at satisfying the inquisitiveness of humans on the three planes of consciousness like the body, mind and spirit. But spirituality gains an upper hand, as the knowledge of *Brahman* (*Ātman* and spirit) is an experience that is beyond the domain of logic and proof, whereas science orients more towards the gross and physical body with logic and proof. Einstein, prophet of the redemption of matter, declared that there is no logical way to the discovery of these elementary laws and the only way is by intuition. Ancient Hindus adopted a scientific approach to discover the supreme power *Brahman* in self.

This book is an attempt to refer to science as understood by the people of ancient times. The analysis is based on the symbolism and significance of the sacred numerology of Hindu traditions. In temples, the *maṇḍala*s in the *bhuvaneśvarī* observe a dome shape with three-tier or three-level wave pattern usually. Even though the intention is to give a continuity of the designs with the three levels of the body, it is because of the architectural treatment that a huge circular design is presented at three levels with the purpose of giving strength to the *maṇḍala* structure. It gives an illusion of a two-dimensional picture to the human eye.

The inscriptions of the temples speak about the gods that were installed, provisions made for the services in the temple, grant of revenues and the titles of the king. There is hardly any information about the ceiling panels, even though some temples had more than 10 or 12 designs, each different from one another. Inadequate documentation of the ceiling designs in books dealing with archaeology no doubt posed an obstacle, as the personal photographs of the *bhuvaneśvarī maṇḍala*s did not do justice for the lack of light in the zone of the *maṇḍala*s. The choice of *maṇḍala*s is at random, but based on geographical preferences of Karnataka state of southern India.

The *maṇḍala*s in some of the temples of early Cāḷukya, late Cāḷukya and Hoysaḷa periods are analysed with both the philosophical and scientific perspectives in this book.

I express my thanks to Dr Paniveni Udayashankar, professor and H.O.D. of department of physics, NIEIT, and visiting research scholar, Indian Institute of Astrophysics, Bangaluru, for reviewing the physics aspects of the manuscript.

My sincere thanks to Varun Eshwer, a computer engineer, for the computer graphics in this book.

I am greateful to the Archaeological Survey of India, Bangaluru and Dharwad for providing me photographs to illustrate my presentation.

Rekha Rao

World of Maṇḍalas

The word *maṇḍala* is from Sanskrit language meaning circular. It is derived from the root word *maṇḍa* meaning the essence and *la* a short syllable in sanskrit prosody used to mean container, a container of the essence, the centre. The circular design of a *maṇḍala* is associated with the centre in its composition and the centre point is equated at a microcosmic level with the central power that is existing and nurturing the cosmos. *Maṇḍala* is a sacred design as the body of it contains the knowledge of the physical, psychological or the spiritual aspects of the cosmos. The journey from creations to the creator, concised as the theories of the *maṇḍala*, originated in India, the allegories and the implications were conveyed in well-designed symbolic expressions.

Even though etymologically the term *maṇḍala* can be traced to Indian roots, the concept is a universal logo.

*Maṇḍala*s are popular both in the eastern or Asiatic part and the Western or the Europian countries. In the Eastern cultures, *maṇḍala*s are categorised into the Buddhist and Hindu *maṇḍala*s, where both are structured with a spiritual theme of the centre.

The Hindu *maṇḍala*s are big, mostly carved on a permanent material like stone or metal. They also have the central dot or *bindu* as it is called representing the central deity and the body consisting of concentric circles in numbers of three, five or seven, and protected by the square boundary — the *bhūpura*. Sacred geometry (which is considered sacred when geometric figures of triangle, square or octagon, etc. symbolise the five elements of nature) and number symbology plays a major role in the Hindu *maṇḍala*s. The purpose behind is with a goal of enlightening one about the higher level awareness and to experience ourselves and the universe as the totality of God's absolute nature. The geometric designs are symmetrical and radiating from the centre towards the outer circles. It is essential to decode the symbolic designs to understand the theme of the *maṇḍala*, that is related to the knowledge of cosmos in a microcosmic form. Mostly Hindu temples, including the cave temples, are adorned with one or many *maṇḍala*s in the ceilings of the temple assembly hall.

The Buddhist *maṇḍala*s are visual representation of Buddhist scriptures, are very picturesque, colourful, and painted on a soft material of any size. The central figure is of Buddha or any god of that religion and the body part of the *maṇḍala* contains various aspects of Buddha's life, or the stories from Jataka tales or about the path of *dharma* — the righteousness, all-encompassing as an aid to meditation.

The art of painting the inside of domes or the cupola of prayer places, churches, cathedrals, basilica in the European countries can be seen with the themes of Jesus Christ, the stories of Bible, or the symbol of cross painted on the domes of the big halls that look like parallels to the concept of *maṇḍala*s of the eastern countries.

Islamic monuments also contain mandalic designs with sophisticated geometric patterns. The Islamic art developed a unique character of indicating Allah's infinite power and perfection, invoked by designs with the name of Allah or quotes from Qur'an in script along with perfect geometric designs.

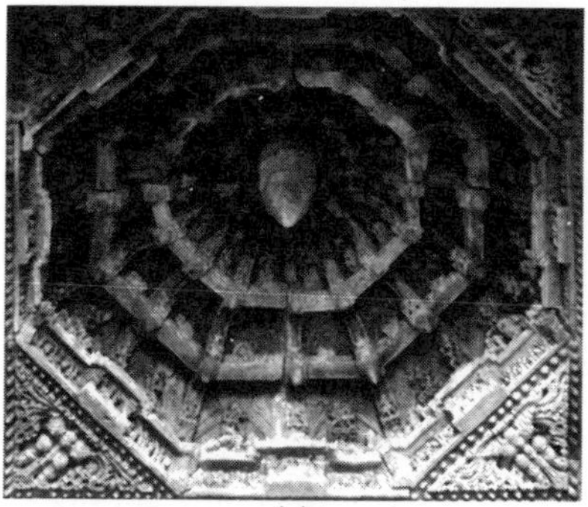

(a)

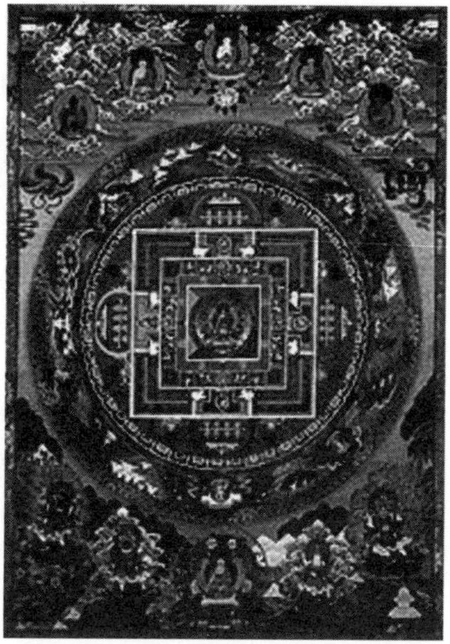

(b)

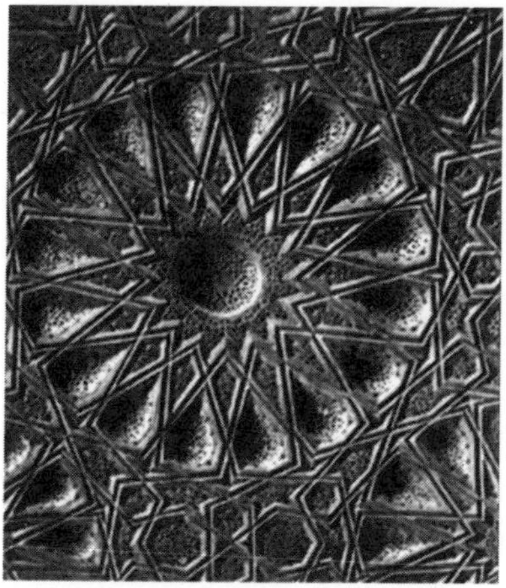

(c)

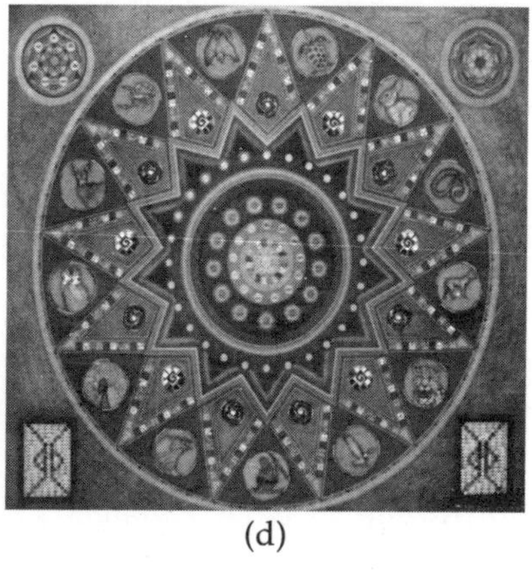

(d)

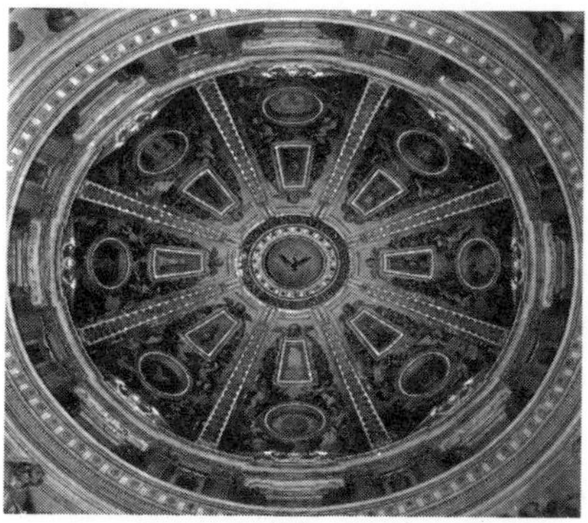

(e)

PL. 1: Images of Hindu, Buddhist, American, Islamic, and European *maṇḍala*s

Since the use of human and animal forms were discouraged in Islamic art, the motifs of foliage and flowers, conceived as the essence of nature, and perfection were used frequently in a simplified and symmetric pattern in the decorative art that embellished the interiors of mosque.

The concept, composition and purpose of drawing a *maṇḍala* is slightly different in the *maṇḍala*s of native Smericans where it is used as a healing ritual and transforming art. The purpose of drawing a *maṇḍala* is more with a healing purpose where the mental focus is shifted from physical suffering to the art of mirroring or magnifying the sacred thoughts or peaceful forces.

The Hindu and Buddhist *maṇḍala*s and their techniques appear more conservative and traditional when they are compared with the creative and liberal concept of the *maṇḍala* art of the Western world.

This book is focused on the Hindu *maṇḍala*s, and the spiritual aspects of cosmos that are associated with it, through illustrations of *maṇḍala*s found in the temples of Karnataka region, in southern India. The symbolic designs are difficult to understand as the language of ancient *maṇḍala*s is obsolete and not much information could be gathered about the *maṇḍala*s from the inscriptions found in the temples. An attempt has been made to decode the significance of the symbols used and interpret the theme of each *maṇḍala* for how they relate to the various mysteries of cosmos.

I was amazed when I noticed the Golden ratios or the Phibonacci ratios as it is popularly called, in the ceiling decorations of Halebid Hoysaleśwara temple. When I tried to know more about golden ratios, I came across an article where Leonardo da Vinci's famous painting of Mona Lisa having the golden rectangle inscribed on it for a better understanding of facial proportions. I made an attempt to find out the golden ratios — the astonishing ratios of nature, hidden in the very famous Hindu divine sculptures like the Idol of Tirupati Venkateswara, the Nataraja Idol of Chidambaram and the world's biggest monolithic sculpture, the Jaina God, Gommateswara of Sravana Belagola, which attract millions of devotees all through the year. I came out with an easy way to understand the proportions of Hindu divine sculptures, without going through the prescribed texts on iconometry of Hindu divine sculptures, according to which these sculptures are carved. Divine sculptures are an anthromorphic manifestation of *maṇḍala*s which are used for focusing the mind in meditation or prayers. Hence the inclusion of devine sculptures is appropriate while studying *maṇḍala*s.

Contents

Introduction

TEMPLES in India were centres of art, places of religious exposition, cultural and educational centres. Even though an individual or a single family was responsible for financing the temple construction, it was not considered as their private property but it belonged to the entire community where people assembled for religious services. They were huge establishments, co-ordinating all aspects of religion and social interactions, of economic and local life. They were like art galleries, and many incorporated a hall for concerts, and lectures and transactions of local affairs as forms of art were believed to gain access to spiritual ideas. Because of the expanded responsibilities, temples often got associated with *maṭha*s which played a role in the expansion of a temple into an organisation. Since temples also played a role in educating the students in the field of Vedic studies, grammar, science and related subjects other than the cultural subjects like dance, music, and the art of carving sculptures, temples got evolved. The area of the pillared hall got expanded in the plan to accommodate more number of devotees; number of pillars in the assembly hall also grew in numbers, involving different and intricate patterns. And the domical ceiling of the hall, the *bhuvaneśvarī,* was used to bring out the various aspects of the cosmos in an artistic way. The soul of God was conceived to be present in the idol of the deity in the *garbhagṛha*. The whole cosmos was presented through geometric and symbolic form in the *bhuvaneśvarī*. Since it was sacred knowledge, it was placed high in the domical ceiling — the sacred space — and also it served the dual purpose of not only decorating the roof of the pillared hall but also as montessori designs to enlighten the viewers about the various aspects of the laws of nature. Area of the outer walls was changed to a stellate design so that more area was created to carve the sculptures of Purāṇic stories and the dancing sculptures of *apsaras*es.

Though a temple was the house of God (Devālaya) they were centres which mirrored the Hindu philosophy in brick and stone. A temple usually consisted mainly of

Jagati	—	the platform,
Mukhamaṇḍapa	—	the veranda,
Navaraṅga	—	the assembly hall, and
Garbhagṛha	—	the *sanctum sanctorum.*

In the inner *sanctum sanctorum*, the deity was installed and worshipped. The *vigraha*s or the figures of worship (the *vigraha*s of worship) were in two forms, viz. *sarūpa* and *arūpa*. In *sarūpa* form, divinities were manifestations of the unmanifest eternal, figurative and carved/shaped after the human anthropomorphic form. The sculptures of Viṣṇu, as Anantaśayana or Padmanābha are the typical examples of *sarūpa* form. They are often projected with one or more unnatural or impossible factors such as four hands or multiple hands and heads or half human body with the head of a lion or an elephant to indicate that they stand for something other than material objects and superior power as they are apparently seen. *Arūpa* was perceived as the formless symbols of an iconic non-anthropomorphic form, where the *śakti* of the supreme power was conceived to be present in a *śāligrāma* or *liṅga* (phallic symbol of Śiva), or were abstract, with geometric patterns as seen in the power diagram of *yantra* — the *Śrī-yantra*, where *puruṣa* and *prakṛti* were conceived in an undifferentiated form.

*Yantra*s and *maṇḍala*s are the power diagrams of a particular configuration with the elementary geometrical designs that function as thought forms about the inherent forces and the nature of the cosmos. *Maṇḍala* — a Hindu word meaning a sacred circle is composed around a central point, which is the point of unmanifest primordial energy, and has to be visualised in the mind while contemplating and meditating. *Maṇḍala*s in stone in the domical ceiling are symbol of forces, thought to exist within inanimate matter. God is beyond human imagination, but the omnipresence of God was visualised in any form. In ancient culture, qualities of permanence, strength, and integrity were heightened and given sacred significance in an individual standing stone or stone amulets as durable symbols of life forces. Stones were used to mark sacred places and a focus place for worship or meditation.

In general, the diagram of a *yantra* and a *maṇḍala* has three components.

1. The central point or the *bindu*.
2. The concentric circles called *valaya* around the point *bindu*, constituting the body of the *maṇḍala*.
3. The protective square boundary around the *maṇḍala* called the *bhūpura*.

The central point called the *bindu* is the symbol of purity, a source of positive energy and the residence of God. It is also seen as the "Life" — from which, for which and around which all things manifest. It is symbolic of the eternal potential and inexhaustible source of power, from which all seeds grow, develop and realise their function. It can be compared to the nucleus of an atom without which even the atom does not exist. The body of the *maṇḍala* is an expansion of the central point, represented as concentric circles, in which are some divisions, manifestations of the five elements and fractal representations (ref. ch. 1/11 for fractals) of the central point indicated by the geometric patterns. All these are designed at a definite distance from the centre, observing a well defined, bilateral order with symmetry and equilibrium. The concentric circles are covered by a protective square boundary — the courtyard and the palace of the inner being, called *bhūpura*. In all *maṇḍala*s, the first principle of *bindu* is constant; the body varies according to the nature and theme of the particular *maṇḍala* and the square boundary is again constant.

The *yantra* also contained the sacred circle or the *valaya* of *maṇḍala*s, in which the *guṇa*s or the aspects of God were conceived in geometrical forms like a circle, triangle, square, hexagon, octagon, or like a lotus with the petals in varying numbers. Any aspect of the supreme principle is bound to the central spot through the geometrical contrivances. Even though structurally both *yantra*s and *maṇḍala*s resemble, the basic difference between them is that the *yantra*s are small in size, are worshipped as they are believed to be effective only when worshipped. *Maṇḍala*s are mostly on permanent material, big, larger than *yantra*s, with the representation of whole cosmos and are beneficial when drawn, recollected or just visualised. Pictorial representations are also seen in *maṇḍala*s but in *yantra*s it is mainly symbols and the *mantra*s (seed syllables). *Yantra*s can be moved from place to place whereas *maṇḍala*s are not moved. Unlike *maṇḍala*s a *yantra* may or may not have the central point. The *Suprabhedhāgama* explains that a mere viewing of the *maṇḍala* cleanses one from all sins. The concept behind is that it is for the *darśana* — viewing of the exterior form of God who inhabits a *maṇḍala*.

Our ancestors were eager to understand the world. The cosmic creator, nameless and formless, was seen as far back as Ṛgvedic days as a great stream of cosmic energy. Over a period of time, human mind preferred to anchor to an anthropomorphic form of God for his prayers and meditation, on which he could concentrate. All aspects of the unseen cosmic power, which was infinite in nature was expressed in an anthropomorphic figure or was represented as *maṇḍala*s — the sacred circles with various geometric shapes. Ancient Hindu literature stressed that God is one but his aspects are many. As it was impossible to worship him in all his glory and fullness, some aspect or the other of the lord was chosen to approach the divine power. Certain symbols, material, verbal or mental were taken up either singly or jointly to glorify God. The symbols, though not a reality became just a means of remembering the lord through the association of ideas. No doubt, God as supreme power was seen in both *arūpa* and *sarūpa* forms. If the soul of cosmic power was seen in the sculpture of God, the body was seen in the *maṇḍala*s. Like any other physical body, the organs and limbs were seen in the *tattva*s associated with it. *Maṇḍala* gave the representation of the universe, highlighting the cosmic and divine powers, as the universe is believed to be the manifestation of the deity. *Viṣṇu Saṁhitā* (9.69) states that all constituent parts of the universe are the manifestations of the deity. *Maṇḍala*s were thus the sacred circles, which revealed the eternal and universal law in which the order of the universe worked, in an abstract and symbolic way. Understanding the nature of the *maṇḍala* was the key to the understanding of ritual as a universal process and the art of *maṇḍala* was intended to uplift the mind to spiritual levels. Though the *maṇḍala* is a universal constant, it is also an act of faith and an integral part of a personal vision quest.

Each *maṇḍala* in temples is venerated for what it represents. The devotee looked upon the divine form as an embodiment of the attributes that reveal the supreme principle in some way or the other. This divine idea further became a symbol of reality that is at the root of everything. Image worship kept within the limit, whether in *sarūpa* or *arūpa* form, can serve a very useful purpose of stimulating devotion, prompting religious art, creating mythological literature and as symbols of spiritual ideas. Unless these forms are seen with the required consciousness, the figure of deity and the symbols of a *maṇḍala* are reduced to a mere design.

*Maṇḍala*s are for focusing the attention of the aspirants. Visualisation is also an aid or a tool in meditation and spiritual teachings, helping to deepen the levels of one's awareness about the ultimate. Most of the circular *maṇḍala*s in the *bhuvaneśvarī* are in low domes of saucer shape. The saucer-shaped structure, a feature of the interior design, plays an important role in places of worship, as it is symbolic of heaven not only in Hindu but in Islamic as well as Christian places of worship. When viewed from below, it resembles the shallow concave shape of a saucer. The shallow dome is often contained in the space between the ceiling and attic and decorated by ornate work. The place of *maṇḍala* is high in the ceilings of the hall because the sacred diagram that is believed to be a source of mystical power enhanced the levels of peace, tranquillity and positive energies in the devotees who assembled in the hall of the temple and hence was revered for its contents. Traditional Hindu rituals observed certain social practices of emphasising on the abstinence of devotees during the inauspicious periods from liturgical ends and human interactions like touching the power diagram were to be declined during these periods. The roof of the pillared hall was thought to be one of the ideal places to install the big designs. The other reason being that the dome has a great deal of structural strength. The components of a dome are held together by compressive force and they can withstand the shocks of the natural calamities to a great extent.

1

The Basics of the Maṇḍala

1.1 The Central Axis of the Temple

GODS have always been attributed to mountains because of the enormous size and commanding nature. The abode of God — a temple — is symbolised like a mountain. All temples have a *vimāna,* the superstructure, to symbolise Mount Meru or the Kailāsa. Often they were also painted in white colour to imitate the snow-capped mountains. The Kailāsa Temple at Ellorā is interpreted architecturally to symbolise Mount Kailāsa — the abode of Lord Śiva. The movement of spirituality is vertical, which is indicated by the mountain-like *vimāna* directly above the image of God.

The earliest Hindu temple was constructed consisting merely of a small, flat-topped *garbhagṛha* to house the God, whose presence was marked in the form of an image or a sacred symbol, representing the deity, and an attached veranda for the worshippers to assemble. In the next effort *garbhagṛha* was given architectural eminence and was topped with tall tapering roof called the *vimāna,* topped by *śikhara* (the peak of the temple) and the veranda was enlarged into a large square space called the *maṇḍapa* (a decorated pillared hall). The entire complex was raised on a paved rectangle, intended to represent the cosmos in miniature — thus making the temple analogous to heaven. From this, temples got developed into a flamboyantly ornate structure, and architectural schools got associated with temple complex.

Gradually, the *vimāna* got elevated to soaring heights, looking like a mountain range, topped by a bold spherical vault, the cupola, also called *āmalaka* supported on an octagonal or polygonal base on which *kalaśa* — the *harmya* and the top of the pinnacle, the finial — called the *stūpikā*, with flying buttresses were designed. The centre of the temple — the *brahmasthāna*, coincided with the *garbhagṛha* and the central deity was installed on this point. The superstructures — the *vimāna, śikhara, āmalaka, kalaśa* and *stūpikā* were aligned on the imaginary axis, rising above the roof of *garbhagṛha*. The *āmalaka*, the dome of *kalaśa* and the *stūpikā* represented the cosmic emperian by way of their positioning. The finial (*stūpikā*), with its point (*bindu*), above the *kalaśa* and *āmalaka*, rose from the centre of the central pillar or shaft of the temple that is compared to the shaft of light.

The upward movement of the central pillar of light is linked to the idea of enlightenment, liberated from the conditions of space and time, and is identified with the crowning finial of the temple. *Āmalaka*, the cogged ringstone, at a high point of the temple denoted the celestial world. The ringstone was the symbol of passage of exit from this world and entry into heaven. *Amala* means without impurity in Sanskrit, from which spotless rays, represented as the lotus petals emanated. Above this was the golden jar the *kalaśa*, denoting the high seat, where the mid Sun rested. The *kalaśa* is linked to the seat of the Sun and the *vimāna* to the Mount Meru, which is the body of the temple (*Śatapatha Brāhmaṇa*, vi, 7.1.17). The finial on the *kalaśa* is the top point of the *axis mundi* manifest, is represented as a lotus bud which opens out to infinity, and connects to the central point on the floor of the *garbhagṛha* along the vertical axis. The flag flying on this point is indicative of weightlessness. The celestial and cosmic power, drawn through the *śikhara* gives the deity effulgence and the metaphysical power. The vertical axis that leads to the highest point is not visible from outside. The top point or the *bindu* of the *stūpikā*, graphically represented as the point of lotus bud, was conceived as the supreme power, was probably represented in the central point of the lotus bud of the *maṇḍala* that was designed in the *bhuvaneśvarī* (the central dome inside the *navaraṅga* hall). The figure of the temple top, and a cross-section/plan of the *āmalaka, kalaśa,* and the *stūpikā* clearly supports this logic of the structure of *maṇḍala*, to be resembling the top structure of the temple. The central axis, exposing to upper world as the lotus bud signifying infinity is represented as the central *bindu* of the lotus bud of the *maṇḍala*. The section of the region of the

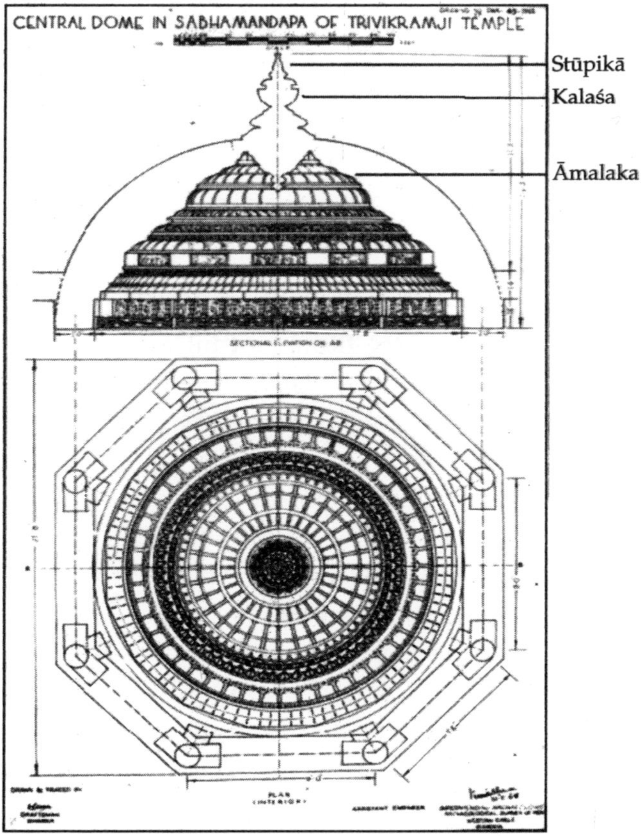

Pl. 2: Figure of the plan and cross-section of the *śikhara,* with *stūpikā.*

āmalaka and the *kalaśa* containing ambrosia of "*ānanda* (bliss)" corresponds to the body of the *maṇḍala*. This central axis point with the *stūpikā* or the *kalaśa*, designed as a lotus bud, signifies the unblossomed state of the creation, which is also seen as a pendant lotus bud hanging down from the central part of the *maṇḍala*. The supreme power is concealed in the core of the bud but one has to uncover the sheaths of *māyā* (illusion) to visualise the core. The three-dimensional lotus bud is represented in an inverted form at the centre of the *maṇḍala*s that are carved in the pillared hall of the temple as a fractal representation. The concept can be observed when the figure of the lotus bud in the temple top (*stūpikā*) and the central conical lotus bud structure of the *maṇḍala* are compared. The cupola along with the *kalaśa* and the *stūpikā* is repeated at various levels as fractal representations in the body of the temple.

1.2. The Purpose, Structure and Meaning of a Maṇḍala

The circular pattern with a centre is a fundamental design occurring in nature as the phenomenon of life in all its forms. The structure of an atom, the flower, a fruit when cut into halves, a cross-section of the stem of a plant or the tree, some of the sea animal forms, geological forms and crystals, solar system, ripples of expanding waves on water surface all are maṇḍalic in structure. Hurricane, cyclonic storms, tornadoes also observe a spiral pattern of *maṇḍala* pointing to the centre. This aspect of nature inspired the humans from the beginning to translate their physical and metaphysical thoughts into forms of art finding an expression in both permanent and non-permanent medium. The structure of places of shelter like a bird's nest inspired man to build his hut in a circular design in his earlier efforts which got extended even to the places of worship and prayer later.

Maṇḍala is a generic term in practice for any plan, chart or geometric pattern that represents the cosmos metaphysically or symbolically, more a microcosm of the universe from a human perspective. The form of Hindu temple, according to ancient architectural traditions of Sthāpatya Veda (Indian traditional architecture) symbolised the model of cosmos. Hindu temple and its traditional architecture had more symbolic meaning than other cultures. It was a fusion of archetypes consciously combined and skilfully crafted into structure of abstract geometry and specific numbers. The geometric figures in temples are characteristically the Hindu religious vision of cosmic order. In the category of geometric figures were the *maṇḍala*s with the symbols of Indian art that echoed the fundamental truth about the cosmic order. *Maṇḍala* means a sacred circle, the magic circle.

All temples had a sacred place, with huge concentric circular patterns, with geometric patterns in its body and enclosed in a square boundary — the courtyard of the *maṇḍala*. This was fixed in the *bhuvaneśvarī* in a dome shape and the central circle, hanging down like a conical pendant. A temple had one or many *maṇḍala*s and each one was focused on philosophical ideas expressed through sacred geometry. They looked very artistic and decorative circular diagrams, in which *Brahma Prakṛti* or the *śakti* of the absolute was represented in a diagram form. *Maṇḍala*s were intended to symbolise the universe and hence were symbols of wholeness — a circle of eternity. The three components of the *maṇḍala* — the *bindu, valaya* and *bhūpura* — are also the symbolic representations of the structure of earth like the core, the mantle and the crust. Sacred geometry was used by archaeologists and geometricians to encompass religion, philosophical and spiritual heritage that have sprung up around geometry in various cultures, during the course of human history. Though *maṇḍala* means a circle, *maṇḍala*s in the shape of square or a rectangle, filled with images or geometric shapes are also seen often to represent the forces of individual and collective psyche.

The *maṇḍalas* are not a special feature of Hindu temples only. They can be seen in places of worship of all religions all over the world, throughout man's history. Even though the purpose was same as tools of meditation for better awareness levels, and symbols of integration, harmony and transformation, the mode of execution differed. The Tibetan *maṇḍalas* came out more figurative and colourful making it easier to understand, while those of Hindu traditions were abstract with the elegance of geometric patterns as symbols. They were more like the revelatory symbols and they could be understood only after realising what the symbolism stood for.

The term *maṇḍala* in Sanskrit also means the whole world, represented as a circle and centre in its general use. Its traditional design often utilises circle — the symbol of cosmos in its eternity — and the square symbolising the man-made world, the earth. *Maṇḍala* in Kauṭilya's *Arthaśāstra* (Book 6) also means a special configuration of the states, from the viewpoint of a king. Etymologically the word *maṇḍala* can be divided into components *maṇḍa* — meaning the essence, and *la* — to take from, the verbal root. A *maṇḍala* is a place in which the practitioner beholds the deities who have been invoked into it and they become an integral part of the structure. A place where a deity can be invoked can be a statue, geometric form with specific design, vessels with water or fire. The shape and the structure used for invoking the deity, in a statue and a circular or square diagram, had to be beautiful, pure and decorative. As explained in *Kulārṇava-tantra* (17.59):

> *maṅgalat, vāc, ca, ḍākinya, yoginī gaṇa, samśrayat* ।
> *lalitat, vāc, ca, devesi, maṇḍalam, pari kīrtitam* ॥

> *Maṇḍala* is auspicious (*maṅgalatva*), it is the abode of a group of *yoginīs* of goddess *Ḍakinī* (who are associated goddesses of levels of awareness). It is beautiful (*lalitat*) and sacred as it is the abode of goddess.

*Maṇḍala*s symbolise spiritual, cosmic and psychic order. Through the concept and structure, man is projected into the universe and the universe into man, viewing both at microcosmic and macrocosmic levels of mutual interpretations to experience a mystical sense of oneness with the cosmos in all its manifold forms. The pattern of circular *maṇḍala*s, with a central point (*bindu*) is used as a focus and guide for meditation. They convey the flow of knowledge/spirituality in a symbolic way. The square represents the frame of the chosen field, a prerequisite much like a filter, segregating the mind from the choices of mundane existence, and the entry can be made from any one of the four gates of *bhūpura* — the gates of knowledge. After an entry into the zone of knowledge, the mind moves in the field amassing knowledge which is compared with the design of the *vīthi* — the plain zone called roads for movement, in the body of the *maṇḍala.* The mind then shifts into the focusing mode from the outer bigger concentric circles to the inner and smaller ones, culminating in the centre — the source of knowledge.

Each *maṇḍala* in a temple represented the mystery of universe pictorially. The worshipper imaginatively enters the *maṇḍala,* focusing successively on each of its stages and absorbing the logic of its form, while approaching the centre. Every *maṇḍala* has its own individual characteristics, regarding the concept and theme. Sometimes a *maṇḍala* houses a number of deities as the *abhimānī devatā*s, who were conceived as guardians associated with protective sphere, the *rakṣā cakra,* (the troop of the main deity). Regardless of the number of deities involved, representations are arranged symmetrically. The essential purpose of all this was to invoke the ever-lasting divine presence. Most common form of a *maṇḍala* appeared in concentric circles, though square grids were also seen. Each *maṇḍala* had a resident deity housed in the centre. The geometric patterns in the body of the *maṇḍala* thus became a connector, something like the "yoke" that connects the ox to a cart. One of the methods for understanding the truth that existed in the order of the universe was to comprehend it visually and meditate upon its symbols. *Maṇḍala* is thus a cosmic framework, with a system of symbols, attributing meaning and establishing powerful, pervasive and long-lasting moods and motivations formulating conceptions of general order of existence.

The structure of *maṇḍala* is an important device for representing the hierarchy of deities within a system. The hierarchy can even include the deities of cosmic order. *Maṇḍala*s mostly follow the common pattern of a concentric arrangement of deities, in concentric circles of lotus petals in varied shapes, with a centre, which is a substitute of a prominent God. It is like the innermost nucleus of an atomic structure, or the farthest region of space, that is bound by the constant flow of life and rhythmic energy creation. The dot in the innermost circle, can be considered in its concentrated form as *bindu*, and its numerical counterpart, being the zero (*śūnya*). The *bindu* is the gathering of forces, and the circle around it is the expansion of the central point.

The centre, with its concentric circles of lotus petals, giving the form of a lotus blossom, is one of the physical props to symbolise the universe and associated with creation myths. Since the earliest times, lotus has been a symbol of the citadel of heart, the seat of self. The heart, which is the spiritual centre of a body, is often represented, symbolically as a lotus. The *Chāndyoga Upaniṣad* (VIII.1.1-3) states that within the physical body — compared to the city of *Brahman* — is the heart, and within the heart lies a little house in the shape of a lotus, within it resides the cosmic power — that which is to be sought after and realised. It is the *Brahman* who resides in the lotus of the heart with all his glory. Though old age comes to the body, the lotus does not grow old nor die as it is untouched by the reality of everyday living.

1.3. Wave Pattern in a Maṇḍala

It is interesting to note that almost all *maṇḍala*s in Hindu temples observe a wave pattern in the basic structure irrespective of the

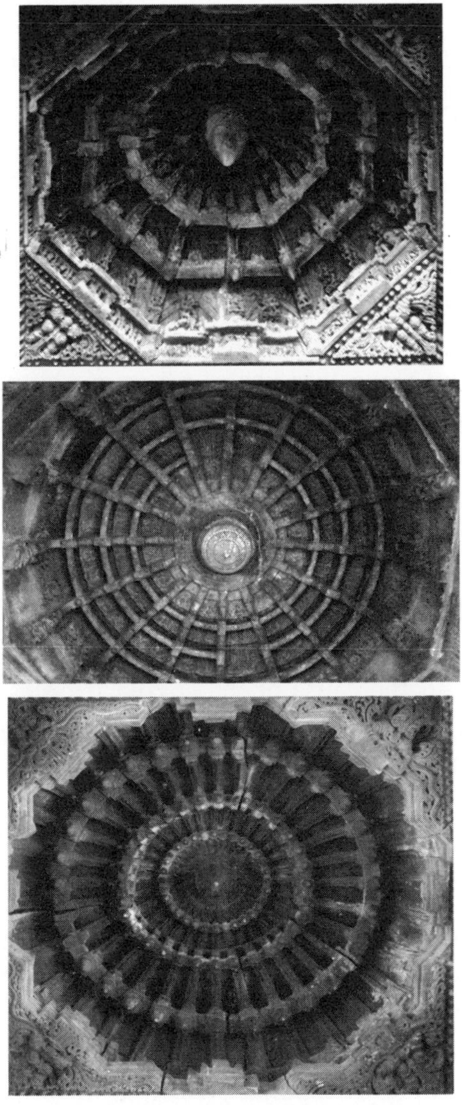

Pl. 3: Wave pattern in the *Maṇḍala*s.

theme or the contents. Even the simple looking *maṇḍala* in the *bhuvaneśvarī* of the *navaraṅga* hall of temple, like the lotus petal design in three or five concentric circles, basically observes the concept and structure of the circular ripples of wave pattern that are formed in a pond when there is some disturbance. Wave is a basic symbol of the activity and expansion in life patterns.

Wave can be defined as a ridge on a surface of a medium containing particles that move across the surface. Waves in the medium of water in a pond may be circular waves which originate from one point, where disturbance occurs. In this, waves travel across the surface in all directions, or waves may be plane waves, which travel together as a front in a straight line direction, perhaps towards the sandy shore. These mental pictures of water waves are useful for understanding the nature of waves. The concentric circles expand following the wave pattern and merging to infinity can be the best analogy for the transmission of the complete knowledge of "God" that spreads out expanding in the universe. The concept of circular ripples in a wave can thus be correlated both philosophically and scientifically. Philosophically, it signifies that every wave has a centre, around which the expansion takes place because centre is the creator and the cause of the circular ripples. It starts from a point — philosophically explained as the cosmic centre that expands infinitely to merge into the cosmos. The centre can be compared to "life" around which and for which all things manifest. Concentric circles represent the expansion of mind, an outcome of which is joy and bliss, that is infinite in nature.

The universe is made up of energy and the language of energy is understood through waves and frequencies. Scientifically wave pattern is the basic design that explains the propagation of sound or light, or any energy form, highlighting the diminution of the intensity of energy as it expands, which is the law of nature. The ripples of wave with its crests and troughs were thought to be the perfect design to explain many scientific and spiritual thoughts.

Waves are everywhere. Whether we recognise or not, we encounter waves on a daily basis, like the sound waves, light waves, radio waves, seismic waves and so on. In addition to waves, the innumerable phenomena of the physical world resemble waves so closely that they are often described as "wave like." The mathematical specifications of waves derived by scientists are unalterably fixed being the equivalent of formulae of quantum mechanics. But the details of physical picture of various wave patterns are not unalterably fixed. Even though waves are everywhere in nature, the patterns are used as an effort of humans to understand nature. The waves of the undulatory theory of light, sound or magnetic forces are just imaginations and an expression of efforts to have a better understanding of the mechanism of energy forms and pictured as waves. The designs on the concentric circles of the *maṇḍala*s was a powerful medium to explain the mysteries of the universe in a method called science to make the grandeurs of the universe accessible to human understanding, and ultimately realise that man is a part of the cosmos.

Nevertheless all waves tend to spread like the ripples on the surface of pond irrespective of whether the wave packet is large

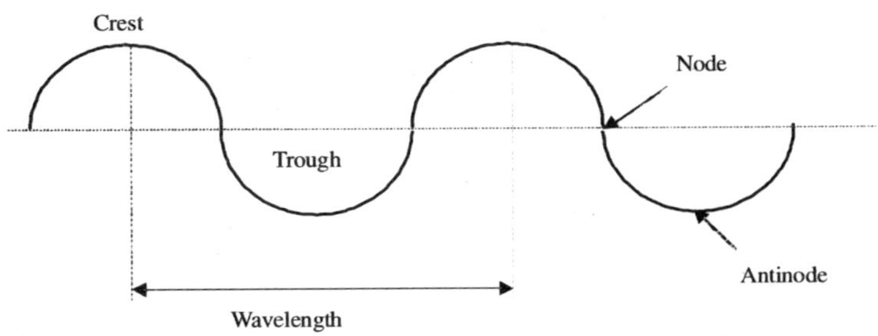

Pl. 4: Figure of crest, trough and wavelength in a wave.

or small. It is essential to know some of the phenomena of wave patterns as the pictures of some *maṇḍala*s are correlated with it.

CREST AND TROUGH

While water waves travel from one location to another, they form crests and troughs. Crest is the high point — the maxima of the wave and trough is the low point — the minima of the wave. Crest is followed by a trough, which in turn is followed by the next crest.

When the crests and troughs of two waves coincide, they result in a stronger wave.

WAVELENGTH

The distance between two successive similar points on an alternating wave, like the distance between two successive crests or troughs.

NODES

The point at which the curve of wave cuts itself at a point of zero displacement.

WAVE FRONT

The continuous locus of points which are in the same phase of vibration.

FREQUENCY

Number of waves that pass a point in unit time.

WAVE GUIDE

A hollow rectangular conductor within which high frequency energy can be transmitted efficiently.

WAVE MOTION

The undulatory movement in waves.

TRANSVERSE WAVES

The movement of the medium is at right angles to the line of advance, as seen in sea waves.

LONGITUDINAL WAVES

The vibrations of the particles of medium are in the direction of advance, parallel to the direction of energy transport as in the case of a vibrating tuning fork.

The designs on the *maṇḍala*, which observe a wave pattern, have the constituents of wave aspect at different capacity. For example, if the *maṇḍala* is related to sound waves, the longitudinal wave pattern can be traced. On the other hand, when it is related to light, transverse wave pattern is used.

The wave guide pattern is used in *maṇḍala*s to depict a continuum of the flow of energy, etc.

The ideas about waves in *maṇḍala*s are mainly speculative and unable to explain the new facts or advancement that have taken place currently. Probably the wave pattern was chosen by observation as a conceptual scheme adopted to explain the facts of nature.

1.4. Graphic Symbols and Geometric Patterns of the Maṇḍala

The art of communication is made with symbols, pictures or words in a *maṇḍala* or a *yantra*, translating concepts that emanate from the inner being. Beyond the inherent and captivating beauty, the sacred art of *maṇḍala* is thus a container of the formal aspect of a system of symbols. Vedas, especially the *R̥gveda*, in Sanskrit language have always been lauded as containing secrets of cosmogenesis. The scientific and spiritual knowledge, based on Vedic knowledge, is hidden in ancient monuments in a coded form. The understanding of these codes conveys a powerful message that transforms our perceptions and understanding of ancient period. *Maṇḍala*s in temples played a role to satisfy the *jijñāsu*s (seekers of knowledge). Further, knowledge, like the rays of rising sun, melts the block of ice (can be compared to ignorance) and then, one does not feel God as a person, nor does one see God's forms. Certain symbols are used in *maṇḍala*s, where the grandest concepts are represented in simplest graphics. They help to convey the knowledge contained in texts in a precise and concise form, which would otherwise take ages to understand. For example, the study of *aṣṭadikpālaka maṇḍala* (refer section 2.12 Marale Siddheśwara Temple, *Pl.* 24) gives the knowledge of the significance of cardinal directions, that is essential for any type of constructional work, be it a house, palace, or temple, as well as city planning. Likewise, the *maṇḍala* at Halebiḍ temple (refer ch. 2, *Pl.* 26) signifies the importance of golden ratios, a numerical constant that exists in nature and how it can be incorporated in the field of art and architecture. Symbols thus give form to the intangible. They are the containers of various levels of knowledge, and relate to far more than what they superficially embody.

Śrī Kṛṣṇa in *Bhagavad-Gītā* (VII.16) explains that four types of persons worship God — the distressed, the seeker of knowledge, the seeker of wealth and the "wise." The seekers of knowledge and understanding, the *jijñāsu*s, from a mere curiosity, try to study and understand the nature of God and thus invoke the grace of the supreme spirit. In the other three, emotions play a role.

In Hindu religion, the personalistic conception of divinity and the symbols attached have played a great part in matters of worship. As explained by Ādi Śaṅkarācarya, human mind knows things through the limiting adjuncts of mind, bound by *kāla, deśa, nimitta* (time, space and causation). In other words, we are bound to the domain of finite, of symbols, which point to the truth — but are not able to express it fully. Since information acquired by the five sense organs are limited, one has to transcend from the inputs of sense organs to experience the subtle aspect of God.

Symbols may be higher or lower. The cosmic process is expressed in an image pictorially. The image of God is also a symbol of a name or sound, a symbol of thought, which becomes a reality that is expressed but inadequately expressed. In Hinduism, the worship of personalities, through the domain of symbols is vast and existed from Vedic times down to the present day, with a view to realising God in some aspect or the other.

Symbols are that which by custom or convention represent something more than the obvious. Every perception has a unique counterpart as space-time code form in the brain. They are the coded expression to something that is underlying or fundamental. In the communication of larger ideas, they can be considered to predate even writing. Symbols are like typographical models, should not be considered to be ultimate truths, but allowing access to the imaginative realms. Hindu gods are highly symbolic in their representations. As it is impossible to worship God in all His fullness and glory, some aspect or the other of God is chosen and with the help of different symbols, Lord is remembered through the association of symbols, sacred geometric designs, numerology and ideas. The term "sacred" is used as the study of numbers could reveal the principles of creation and the laws of space and time. Numbers were believed to be used by gods to regulate the world, and each number had a particular significance. Similarly the geometric designs are based on the features of the visible universe and its natural forms which are also based on ancient human psychic response to the natural world. They also reflect the mystery of God and the dimensions of the universe at the practical level. The grandest concepts are often represented by simple geometric shapes or graphics. For example, the point is an ancient symbolism of infinitely compressed energy, and origin of life. Squares and cubes conveyed stability, etc. Just like God is hidden, so too are the inner secrets of the creation, which can be revealed to a certain extent by decoding the symbols. It is like explaining the formless through forms. Sacred geometrical shapes like triangle, square, hexagons, octagons, and circles are profusely used in a *maṇḍala* radiating out from the centre to give form to the intangible. Sacred geometry is an art and science, which reveals the nature of our relationship to the cosmos. A study of the sacred geometry and mathematical ratios unfolds the nature of patterns, giving an insight into the mysteries and the laws of the universe, its harmonics and proportions. The value of these aspects is widespread and foundational to the sacred structures as a temple, mosque, monuments, churches, etc. The spiritual significance of geometry from ancient early Egyptians to Vedas in ancient India was studied by Pythagoras, a mathematician who lived in 580 BCE. According to him, the rhythm of harmony and the mathematical law was the bridge to infinity.

Other designs like *svastika* (refer section 2.1, for details), lotus with layers of petals and lotus buds, scrollwork are ideograms representing cosmic dynamism, creative energy and also symbolic of Hindu philosophical thoughts, providing clues to decode the information of a *maṇḍala*. Some images, for example, the *svastika,* or the lotus flower are universal, but some are unique to a religion, like the symbol of *oṁ* or the Cross. Some symbols like the weapons or accessories held by the multiple hands of Hindu gods are categorised under the religious symbolism.

Kīrtimukhas, like the face of a lion can be seen on all the four cardinal directions or the four intermediary directions of the *maṇḍala* as well as in the *vimāna* of the temple. These faces are the dramatic means of projecting symbolism in religion, representing the supernatural force of protection, and frightening the enemies or demons, providing a focus for worship. Animal face was also used to symbolise the baleful twin brother of the creator God. In Indian tradition, it is also symbolic of *māyā* and the mask of God.

The *nāgasūtra*, a labyrinth of laced scrollwork filling the space between the square boundary and the octagonal frame of the *maṇḍala* or on either side of a *kīrtimukha* is a symbol used in ancient temples as the sacred initiation routes imitating the weaving paths of the Sun or the planets. Such intricate designs also represent the protective symbols of frustrating the evil sprits with blockages.

Spiral designs of scrollwork in continuous mode is indicative of the pulsating cycles of energy, the continuous and ongoing progressive movement of life force, and manifestation can be seen in many *maṇḍala*s as decorative designs of rectangular conduits or on the body of the *maṇḍala*. The labyrinth designs of intricate passage with decorative loose knots represent infinity and longevity and are also symbolic of initiation routes.

Fractals — the self-repeating motifs are another type of symbolic representation that is used in *maṇḍalas*. *Maṇḍala*s appear mostly symmetrical and orderly in the repeating order of the design with a careful balancing of visual elements creating harmony and rhythms of life. All *maṇḍala*s have a central point (*bindu*) as it is called, which is the unmanifested state of the deity and focus on a progression towards this spiritual centre.

GEOMETRIC PATTERNS

The prefix of "sacred" was used with geometry because it was seen as inherent in nature, a perfect combination of logic and beauty and hence was elevated as the revelation of God.

POINT

The point (*bindu*) is the centre of the inner circle, may be visible or remain invisible, or may be transformed into an anthropomorphic form of a specific God. It is interpreted as the principal form, from which all forms and creations radiate. It is in the nature of light, the light of consciousness and the indivisible centre. The Vedānta system calls this consciousness as *Brahman* and recognises its mysterious presence as *ātman* (the secret self in all beings). The Śaiva school call it as "Śiva" — the supreme cognition that is existing in all that exists. The point also represents the void of space or the element ether — a symbol of purity where all polarities are harmoniously united. Point in a *maṇḍala* is the source of positive energy, residence of the deity, and perpetual bliss that is also interpreted at microcosmic level as the positive energy that resides within all of us that continues to expand, enrich and unfold its radiance to ultimately merge into the enveloping cosmic force. The technical term *caitanya* used to denote the universal intelligence or spirit, the changeless and boundless central core point — that is without parts (*niṣkala*), and that which is unproduced and hence indestructible — is all symbolised in the dot. Hence it does not come under the subject of knowledge. It is a principle of pure experience, realised only by the ecstasy of spiritual illumination.

A point is the symbol apparently free of dimensions. It is the ancient symbol of gathering centre in which the outside energies are drawn, making it a symbol of infinitely compressed energy.

The point is encircled by concentric circles, constituting the body of the *maṇḍala*, suggesting the concept of the expansion of the positive energy.

CIRCLE

Circle is the most common and universal space imitating design seen often in the *maṇḍala*. It is the most appealing and a wonderful geometric shape, most symmetric of all shapes in two dimensions, without any intersection and alike in all points on its circumference. God is perceived to be perfect in all aspects and hence the circle is often used to symbolise godly power. Circle is a symbol of absolute intelligence, symbol of sun and limitless or boundless aspects of the cosmos. It signifies a mystical thought of completeness without a beginning or end and hence compared with eternity and the soul. It is also a figurative and symbolic interpretation of the relationships of substance like energy, mass, form, time, space, and movement. The circle provides the general or the universal roadmap for how things are organised, and how the energy is conserved in the universe. The circles of the *maṇḍala* with a centre can be compared to the pattern of power in the likeness of a human body or the *garbhagṛha*, the deity dwelling at the centre of the *maṇḍala*. In iconography, dynamism is added to a circle by the addition of rays, spokes of different shapes and number of petals attached to it.

*Maṇḍala*s in temples played a role to satisfy the *jijñāsus*. Further, knowledge, like the rays of rising sun, melts the block of ice (can be compared to ignorance) and then, one does not feel God as a person, nor do one see God's forms but sees it as a force. Certain symbols are used in *maṇḍala*s, which help to convey the knowledge contained in texts in a precise and concise form, which would otherwise take ages to understand them. Symbols thus give form to the intangible.

TRIANGLES AND HEXAGRAM

Triangle is a very versatile geometric symbol — a sign for God in several religions. It can be viewed from the external — the formal and internal — the vital considerations. Formally triangle is the smallest design indicative of space, and vitally it is the fundamental component of *cakra*s — the symbolic representation of body temple. Geometrical abstractions can be traced back to the Vedic times (second millennium BCE) as the rituals of Vedic religion were of non-anthropomorphic nature and elements of nature were worshipped. Fire (*agni*) was worshipped as cosmic *puruṣa* with a graphic symbol of an equilateral triangle sitting on its base, and the altar was given the fundamental square shape combined with other geometrical figures. Fire was conceived as the centre the *axis mundi* (the axial symbol), and the eternal upward direction of fire was conceived to unite heaven and earth. The association of triangle with the point upward is the symbolic shape of the static ultimate truth, the element fire, or "Śiva" triangle. The inverted triangle is symbolic of *prakṛti* the dynamic as it resembles the female pubic triangle, the place in which everything originates. When both types of triangles are intertwined, it means the sacred union of *puruṣa* or "Śiva" and *prakṛti* or Śakti, and the resulting hexagram is considered a sacred geometric form, which is also represented as a six-petalled lotus (*ṣaṭkoṇavalaya*), where deities as forces are invoked in the corners of the resulting triangles. A hexagram is also symbolic of the element wind — as per the *maṇḍala*s of the five elements (for details refer section 1.12, iconographic representations of the five elements). Explaining this, the common area of intersection of male and female forces is the hexagram, which represents continuity of human race, a progression of movement. This is analogous to the movement of wind. The numerical value of triangle is three and a hexagon is six — which has various explanations in philosophy.

SQUARE AND OCTAGON

In ancient symbol system of India and China, element earth was represented as a square. Square is called a fundamental figure, as it sets the boundaries, in the four directions of north, east, west and south. All matter is confined to a space, which can be defined as having boundaries. Hence element earth, the container of matter, is represented as a square, even though earth is round in shape. The symbolism of square is connected to numerical value of four and the four cardinal directions. A square stands for permanence, balance, security and rational organisation of space. It refers to the universe as conceived and projected by man, while the circle refers to the process of nature or cosmos as a whole. Square is related to the conscious and the rational aspect, and hence considered as masculine while a circle represents both the sub-conscious and superconscious aspects of nature and feminine. In their integration, both the circle and the square represent the holistic world view.

When two squares are intersected it results in the eight corners or an octagon. Octagon is the nearest skeletal frame to a circle and hence octagonal frame is used to transcribe a circular shape in architecture. The eight corners according to the Hindu philosophy represent the four cardinal directions and four mid-directions, associating it with the eight divine gaurdians of directions by the name *aṣṭa dikpālaka*s. The symbolism of an octagon is also given as an eight-petalled lotus (*aṣṭa-dala padma*), meaning the totality of space and a symbol of infinity. The circle of a *maṇḍala* is enclosed in a square boundary called *bhūpura,* which is the substratum, the receptacle that manifests the world. This square boundary, in a *yantra,* or in the temple platform, at its periphery of four cardinal directions, has T-shaped doors called the cosmic doors that represent the earthly passage between the external — material, and the internal — the sacred space of a *maṇḍala*. The gates are guarded by the deities of spheres, the *lokapāla*s, presiding over the T-shaped gates, whose function is to protect the sacred precinct from the negative or disintegrating forces.

Regarding the geometric plan, it is essential to identify certain ideas in Hindu outlook. Since circle is found everywhere in nature, it is considered the most natural and most favoured geometric design observed in Hindu sacred architecture. But square is a consciously artificed shape. Temple plan is based on a square because it is conceptualised as a perfect architectural form. The circle and curve represent life in its growth and movement. Square is the mark of order of finality to the expanding life and its forms. A circle involves motion, while the square stands for balance of dualities. Circle symbolises the spiritual plane, while square, the material and physical plane. The square with its four corners — like the corners of a house — represents earthly things, while a circle — perfect, endless and infinite — has been taken to represent the divine or godly. In most of the *maṇḍala*s the circle is inscribed in a square, so as to be tangent to all sides. Squaring the circle is a unique symbol of bringing the earthly and mundane into a proper relationship with the divine. *Maṇḍala*s in Hindu temples are a synthesis of many symbols. By their superimposition, repetition, proliferation and amalgamation, its total meaning formed ever new.

CONCENTRIC CIRCLES

The ritual of going round a sacred space, a pole or altar signifies paying homage to the centre, and a gradual progression towards the centre as enlightenment.

*Maṇḍala*s come with centre and concentric circles around it. It is interesting to know how the circles or curves operate at the individual as well as global and larger level. The overall form consists of these circles, concentrically arranged. The innermost circle is the domain of core consciousness. It is the most basic, vital area in which the primordial evolutionary impulses are contained. It is least accessible to voluntary control and corresponds to the deepest cortical portions of the brain. The core zone recapitulates the earliest evolutionary phases of life. From this level emanate the most fundamental animistic vision and hallucination. This is compared to the *suṣupti avasthā* of *jīva.* Every soul exists in anyone of the states of awareness called *jāgrat* (wakeful), *svapna* (dream state) and *suṣupti* (deep sleep) *avasthā*s or states of existence. The second circle represents the intermediate or the state of consciousness, otherwise called *svapna avasthā*. The zone in a *maṇḍala* is repository of ideas, dreams, myths and symbols, immediately accessible for human implementation. The manifestations are accessible through the effort of will, to realise the contents of this zone. The third and outermost circle is the circle of consciousness. This is the realm of everyday, what is called the waking or *jāgrat avasthā* of consciousness. This zone is mostly controlled by the ego consciousness. When viewed from inner core to the outer circles it is the unfolding of divine energies, association with progressions, development and expanding qualities. This process is compared to evolution and the converse is involution.

The innermost circle and dot where the deity resides is compared to the *turīya avasthā* of a soul — the zone of absolute Bliss. The goal of every *jīva* or Soul is enjoying a blissful state and for this it has to cross the outer layers of *jāgrat, svapna* and *suṣupti avasthā*s. Every *maṇḍala,* whether it is the central one or one of the five or nine *maṇḍala* representations, has three or five concentric circles. When the concentric circles are five in number, it represents the *pañcakośa*s.

1.5. Lotus Bud and the Kośas : The Sheaths, Enveloping the Soul

Lotus bud signifies purity, a thing that does not get affected by the environment, and spiritual unfolding. God is the highest product of our highest intelligence. The symbol of lotus is specifically used to denote the unfolding of spirituality, and the bud to the concept of God that is hidden in the core of the unblossomed state of creation. It is intentionally pictured like a bud covered with sheaths to indicate that one has to uncover the sheaths of *māyā* to experience or visualise the core. The lotus bud in three-dimensional form is designed in the topmost part of the temple, and in the central design of the *maṇḍala* in the *bhuvaneśvarī*. The structure of the *maṇḍala*s has three distinctive zones:

1. The outermost square boundary or the courtyard called the *bhūpura*.
2. The inner zone of concentric circles called the *valaya*s.
3. The innermost point — the *bindu* located in the lotus bud.

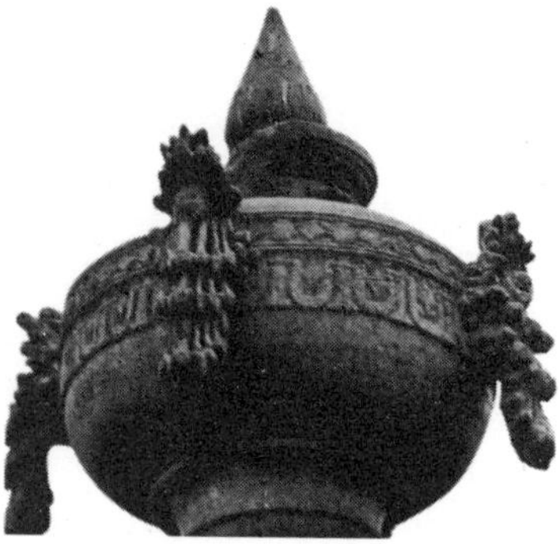
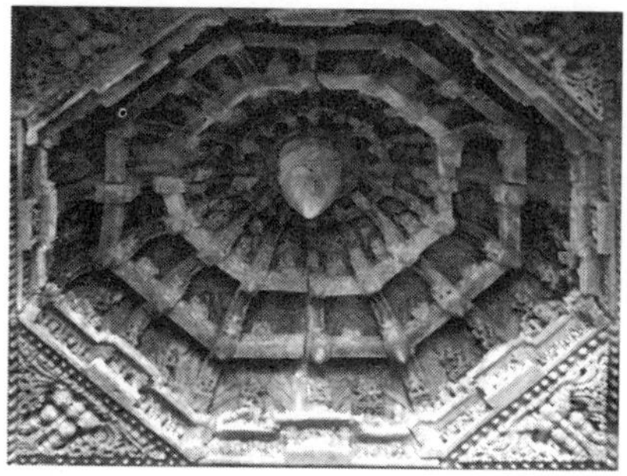

Pl. 5: A comparative picture of the lotus bud in the *stūpikā* and the *maṇḍala* of the *bhuvaneśvarī*.

Kośa means a closed flower bud. In Vedāntic philosophy, it is the term for the five vestures or layers, which successively make the body enshrining the soul; much like the pericarp of the lotus is covered by the successive layers of petals. In an unawakened state of consciousness, the body erroneously identifies with these layers successively, assuming the soul to be each of these layers. The true nature of *ātman* remains hidden under the spell and imposition of these layers called *māyā*, till it is cleared by gnosis. The illusory appearances or the manifestations of these sheaths vanish like magic on realisation, revealing the true nature of "*ātman* — equated to *Brahman*."

These five layers of the *kośa*, according to the *Taittirīya Upaniṣad*, are doctrines of psychological interest. They are:

1. *Annamaya kośa* : The sheath of physical matter and the earthly body of food and nourishment. (But the body itself is unstable and hence cannot consequently be the *ātman* which is stable).

2. *Prāṇamaya kośa* : The sheath of vital air and life. The five manipulations of vital breath which accompany the body when alive leaves the body after death (but *ātman* is indestructible).

3. *Manomaya kośa* : The sheath of conscious activity or the sensorial vesture — the mind. The fluctuating overflow of passion is for ever in movement (hence cannot be the soul which remains undisturbed by any kind of emotion).

4. *Vijñānamaya kośa* : The sheath of intelligence (*buddhi*) or the cognitional vesture. *Buddhi* — the foundation of psyche can reveal only the nature of *ātman* as matter. Intelligence still manifests as ego which obscures the nature of *ātman*.

5. *Ānandamaya kośa* : The sheath of bliss and beatitude. Bliss is the true nature of *ātman*, that is experienced after knowing its nature. This experience is, however compared to the state of deep sleep called *suṣupti*, undisturbed by the manifestations of emotions or the memory of ego. But this is not eternal (*ātman* is eternal).

The true nature of *ātman* (at microcosmic level) or the *Brahman* (at macrocosmic level) is beyond the fifth plane — outside the sheaths.

These are the five layers of reality that have to be transcended in order to realise the *ātman*, as *ātman* is enveloped by these layers. In a *maṇḍala* with lotus design, if the concentric circles of the *valaya* are five in number, it may mean that the *maṇḍala* suggests about the opening out of the five layers of realities that are to be unveiled, before reaching the centre or the *guru maṇḍala*. *Brahman* and *ātman* are the objective and subjective psychical principles that are looked alike. "He who is in this *Brahman* in man and who is that in Sun are one."

These five layers in an individual are categorised into three kinds of bodies like:

1. *Sthula śarīra* — the gross body,
2. *Sūkṣma śarīra* — also called as the *liṅga śarīra*, the subtle body, and
3. *Kāraṇa śarīra* — the causal body.

The *sthūla śarīra*, the gross physical body that every individual has is compared to *annamaya kośa*, which is full of matter and composed of the gross elements. The *sūkṣma śarīra*, the subtle body of mental functions is made up of subtle elements and corresponds to the three layers — the *prāṇamaya*, *manomaya* and *vijñānamaya kośas*. The *kāraṇa śarīra* corresponds to *ānandamaya kośa*, the dwelling place of *ātman* or *Brahman*, which is disassociated from the bodily and mental functions and assumes the form of bliss.

When the *maṇḍala* on the whole is viewed as a lotus flower, the three parts of the *maṇḍala*, the outer square boundary of physical layer is the *sthūla śarīra* of the *maṇḍala*, the inner three or five concentric layers make the *sūkṣma śarīra* (the contents of which vary according to the theme of the *maṇḍala*. The most common representation is concentric layers of lotus petals) and the innermost point corresponds to *kāraṇa śarīra*, the dwelling place of *Brahman*.

These categories, according to the Hindu philosophy, are seen at both microcosmic and macrocosmic levels. If an individual is the microcosmic, *maṇḍala* becomes the macrocosmic, as *maṇḍala* is the representation of the universe. The point of *bindu* encircled by three concentric circles suggests the concept of the expansion, enrichment and unfolding of the radiance of positive energies, to ultimately merge in the enveloping cosmic force.

1.6. Lotus Designs

Lotus flower (*padma* or *kamala*) has the most ancient and prolific symbolism in Hindu tradition, appearing commonly in Indian art and iconography. It is sacred not only because it transcends the darkness of water and mud, where the roots are, but also because of its perfectly symmetrical petals which resemble a *maṇḍala*. According to the iconographic representations, it is also to symbolise the element water as lotus is a water-born plant. The unique beauty of lotus is expressed as a decorative flower, with radiating petals — as a synonym for perfection, appearing as a single or multilayered lotus. In Hindu mythology, the sacred lotus is depicted to grow from the navel of Lord Nārāyaṇa, on which lord Brahmā, the creator is seated. In Indian religious art we see the representation of gods of various ranks seated on lotus pedestals, to symbolise the aspects of divinity, purity, immortality and realisation of the inner potentials. Lotus petals, also symbolic of spiritual unfolding are depicted as the lotus unfolding its immaculate petals to the Sun (Knowledge), suggesting the human spiritual growth from the folded bud of heart and the soul's potential to attain the divine perfection. Even in the Buddhist tradition, lotus is compared to the psychological state of purity of thought. As said by Buddha in the *Dhammapada*, "we are shaped by our thoughts. We become what we think. When the mind is pure, joy follows like a shadow that never leaves." The multiple layers of petals in a lotus *maṇḍala* is symbolic of the radiating or expanding joy, an outcome of the purity of thought.

Regarding the structure of the lotus flower in *maṇḍala*s, the flower is divided into four parts — the pericarp (*karaṇika*), the stamens (*kesarī*) arising from the base, the petals (*patra* or *dala*) which is the knitted part of the flower, and the tips of the petals (*dalāgra*) that are not knitted. The number, shape and the form vary according to the goal in view. The lotus is positioned in the square boundary, whose corners are specially decorated with *kīrtimukhas*, which form the four legs of the lotus throne (*siṁhāsana*), on which the god is invoked. Some *maṇḍalas* have a zone decorated with scrollwork in between the lotus and the square boundary, called the street, lane (*vīthi*), that is compared to the inside space of movement within the *garbhagṛha*. The whole structure is placed in a square boundary which has the design of "weapons" (*vajra*), in a miniature form in the extreme corners. The lotus *maṇḍala* grows bigger and complicated with more number or *vīthis*. The small lotus designs are considered as the house of gods and the bigger multi lotus designs are the citadel or towns of God.

In *maṇḍalas*, the lotus design can be in the form of:

1. Single-layered lotus
2. Multilayered lotus
3. Multilayered multiple lotuses.

SINGLE-LAYERED LOTUS

The levels of awareness are represented as a wheel, in combination of lotus design. In the Hindu philosophy the *kuṇḍalinī cakras*, channelising the latent psychic energy along the physical body, are represented in the form of single-layered wheel with specific number of lotus petals. The seven *cakras* are associated with the elements of nature with specific symbolic design, specific number of petals and with the psychological attributes in its unfolding. They are:

1. *Mūlādhāra cakra* : Earth, square, 4 petals, solidarity, self-reference and ego.
2. *Svādhiṣṭhāna cakra* : Water, crescent moon or circle, 6 petals, power, emotive, ego.

3. *Maṇipūra cakra* : Fire, triangle, 10 petals, energy, passion and motivation.
4. *Anāhata cakra* : Air, hexagon, 12 petals, empathy, compassion and love for another soul.
5. *Viśuddha cakra* : Sky, oval or round, 16 petals, communicative, purity in thoughts, and inspiration.
6. *Ājñā cakra* : *Manas* (region of mind), round, 2 petals on side, universal love, devoted service, and a visionary.
7. *Sahasrāra cakra* : Pure consciousness, thousand petals, ultimate realisation, liberated soul, blissful.

MULTILAYERED LOTUS

A *maṇḍala* with multilayered lotus design is viewed as a cosmic configuration, in which an image or a symbolic substitute of a

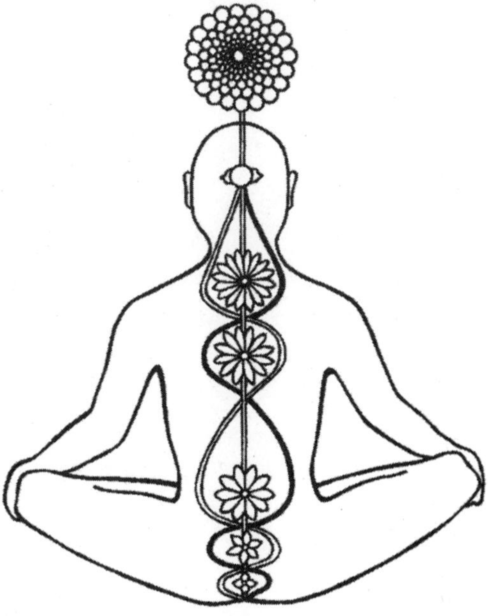

Pl. 6: Figure of the levels of awareness in *cakra* representation of single-layered lotus.

prominent God is positioned in the centre or in the pericarp of the lotus, surrounded by a specific number of subordinate deities

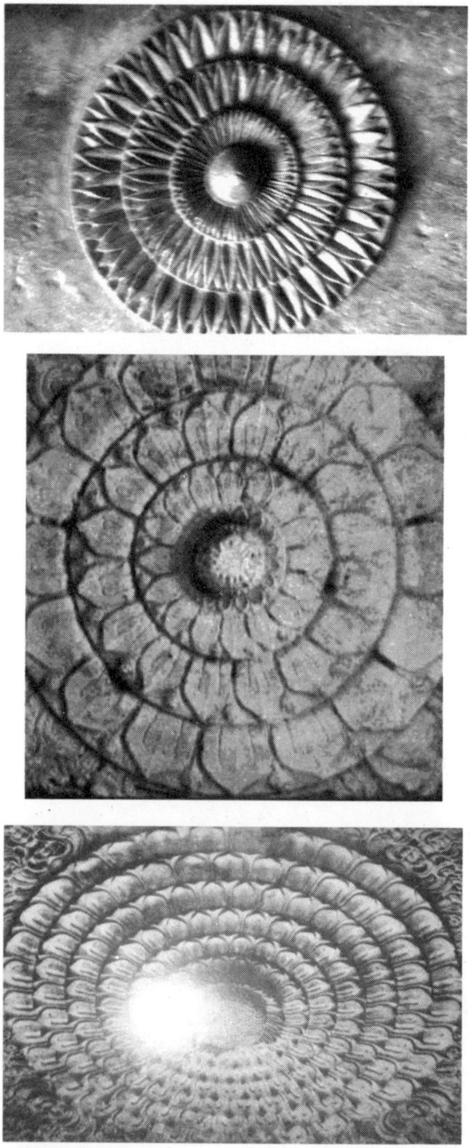

Pl. 7: Figure of three, five and seven-layered lotus.

of lower rank, or the epithets of a deity that are ordered hierarchically in the petals, with varying number of rings. According to the theme of the *maṇḍala* and the central deity, the layers or the rings vary from three to five or seven. The lotus in full bloom is also symbolic of the concept of purity of heart and expansion of joy. The central point of the lotus *maṇḍala* or the pericarp of the lotus is visualised as the dwelling place of the deity that is in total bliss (*ānanda*). The *ānanda* is visualised to expand to infinity through the radiating petals that are attached to the centre observing the wave pattern. The eight-petalled lotus means the spread of bliss in all the eight directions. Twelve was associated with Sun God, sixteen to the parts of *puruṣa* and so on. The psychic attributes are read according to the *cakra*s.

The three tiers of the lotus design are viewed as the cosmic power present in the beginning, midway and the end part, the all-pervading, or as being present in the three qualities of *sattva, rajas* and *tamas*. It also signifies the progress of the human existence which is threefold — physical, intellectual and spiritual. The movement and progress is viewed from the outer circle that is physical and the inner one that is near the *bindu* to be the spiritual plane. For the spiritual progress, physical and intellectual base has to be progressive, meaning to reach the spiritual plane one has to protect themselves from the reactive moments in the physical and intellectual spheres.

A five-layered lotus may signify the five manifestations of the elements like earth, water, fire, air, and ether of which the universe is made of at both macrocosmic and microcosmic levels, the central deity being present in all.

A seven-tiered lotus signifies the seven levels of awareness at microcosmic level or the seven worlds in ascending order like the *bhū, bhuvar, svar, mahar, jano, tapo* and *satya loka*s.

The psychological attributes of the *kuṇḍalinī cakras*, number of petals, shape of petals, and the significance of the sacred numerology are all considered while designing the structure and theme of the *maṇḍala*. Even in a multilayered lotus, 16 petals may stand to highlight the aspect of purity of thought, a thousand-petalled one may be an expression of a liberated soul or total surrender and the 12-petalled one as a sign of meditation.

In all forms the centre is the infinitely compressed point of bliss and the concentric layers mean the liberation of energy.

MULTILAYERED MULTIPLE LOTUSES

Another depiction of lotus prop is seen where the whole lotus flower motif is repeated at five or nine places. When it is repeated at five places, it is considered as a *pañcāyatana* representation. A nine time repetition of lotus is seen in the *maṇḍala*, depicting the *aṣṭa dikpālakas* (the protectors of cardinal directions) with the main deity in the centre or in the depiction of *navagrahas* — the nine planets in nine square grids. *Tattvābhimānī devatās* (the sub-ordinate deities of the main principle or the epithets of a deity) are also presented in the circles of a *maṇḍala* as full bloom lotus but in miniature form.

When the lotus motifs are repeated in circular patterns with the central deity in the central lotus, it is read as a *bhadramaṇḍala* that is auspicious and protected from all sides.

1.7. Shape of Lotus Petals

The shape of each petal also varies in its symbolic meaning and it varies according to the purpose of installing a *maṇḍala* and the deities who are installed. They give form and expression to the inner thoughts. They may be curved along the edges or absolutely round in shape or may be with pointed tips and so forth (refer *Pls.* 7, 8, 19 and 20, to see the different shapes of petals).

1. For the meditations on gods bestowing good fortune, like Kāmeśvara (the *śakti* or power of Śiva) and other deities, the petals are designed with pointed tips.
2. The installation of *lokapālas*, the *grahas* or *gaṇas* — the troupe of deities are indicated with broad petals and either round or curved at the edges.
3. The worship of Vidyeśvaras (the eight pacific aspects of Lord Śiva, who reside in the pure regions) is indicated by lotus petals which have the shape of cow's ears.
4. Goddess of speech (*vāk*) or Gaurī and the Rudras are represented on lotus petals, which look like the leaves of *aśvattha* tree (the holy fig tree).
5. For supernatural powers in general, the lotus petals are with curled-up tips.
6. When petals shape is even, both at the base and tip, called *aṇimno natagram samam*, (See, *Pl.* 20) minute and small like the point of a needle, it indicates liberation (*mukti*) and the superhuman power becoming as small as an atom.

1.8. Pañcāyatana and Bhadra Maṇḍalas

PAÑCĀYATANA

Cult deities like Viṣṇu, Śiva, Sūrya, Gaṇapati and Durgā were also represented in aniconic stone symbols in the *pañcāyatana* worship, where *guṇas* were conceived as present in an undifferentiated form. Most of the *maṇḍalas* in temples are represented with the central deity, surrounded by other four deities either in cardinal directions or in the corners, in aniconic form representation of lotus patterns. The five deities are: Gaṇeśa — Gaṇapati (symbolising enthusiasm), Sūrya — the Vedic sun god (symbolising illumination), Viṣṇu or Bālakṛṣṇa — symbolising aspect of meditation, Durgā or Goddess —

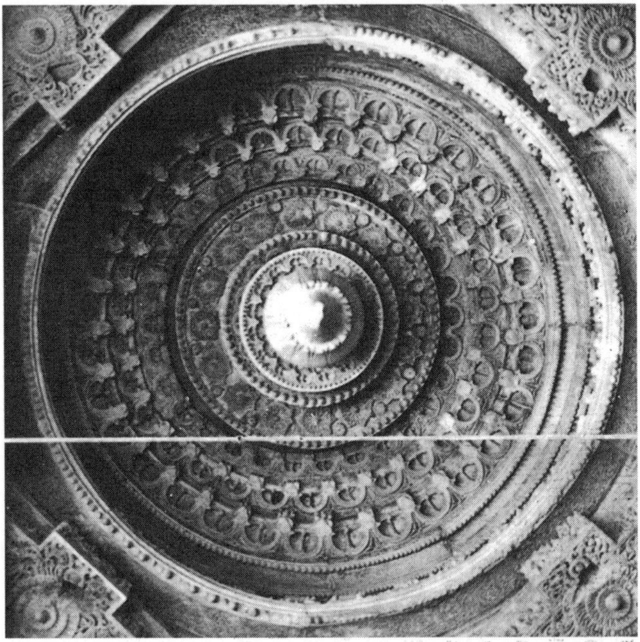

Pl. 8: Figure of five lotus design of *pañcāyatana*, where the central lotus is bigger than the ones in the four corners.

symbolising consolidation, Śiva — symbolising renunciation — the bestowal of grace. Among these fivefold functions of creation, the last is the culmination of all other functions. When the lotuses are five in number and placed on the four directions of the central grid, it is called *pañcāyatana* and the name goes by the deity that is invoked in the centre. Even in the temple complex, we see the smaller shrines of the four deities in the four directions with the main deity's shrine in the centre.

Pañcāyatana is also called the *pañcopāsane* (fivefold worship), as reflected in temple architecture. They are the principal deities of the five approved Brāhmanical cults, called Gāṇapatya, Saura, Vaiṣṇava, Śākta and Śaiva. The chief cult object in it is aniconic in form, which contained emblems or particular stones of the respective cult deities. A definite date to prove when *pañcāyatana* came to be in vogue is yet to be proved; however, archaeological evidence says that they were introduced long before the medieval period. It should be noted that any deity can be placed in the centre and the other four deities on the four directions of the square, to indicate the cult affiliations, and the *maṇḍala* is called after the deity — like when Śiva is invoked in the centre, it is Śiva *pañcāyatana*, when Durgā is in the centre, it is Durgā *pañcāyatana* and so on. The *pañcāyatana* worship established a harmony between the various cult followers and achieved religious tolerance.

Philosophical perspective of *pañcāyatana* suggests that every devotee has to pass through five phases in life — to be eligible for liberation. They are Gaṇeśa — enthusiasm (to know about realisation), Sun — illumination — knowing the form of God, meditation — Viṣṇu — to meditate on spirituality, Durgā — consolidation of knowledge gained, and finally Śiva — the capacity to renounce all that is gained through *vairāgya*. The entire five cult gods enjoy equal status and all five phases philosophically are equally important. *Pañcāyatana* is usually represented as five lotuses, either in same size or the central one slightly bigger in size.

BHADRAMAṆḌALAS

Bhadra means auspicious or prosperous in Sanskrit. Structurally when a *maṇḍala* represents a combination of square grids, or when the square-shaped *maṇḍala*s are divided further into a grid of squares, it is called a *bhadramaṇḍala*. Mostly lotus designs or the iconic representations in rare cases are incorporated inside the square grids. It is always the *tattvābhimānī devatā*s in a *bhadramaṇḍala* and gods of different cults in a *pañcāyatana*. A five-square grid *maṇḍala* has to be analysed considering these aspects. *Bhadra*s are designed by drawing a specific number of vertical and horizontal lines that form square grids — called *pāda*s or *koṣṭa*.

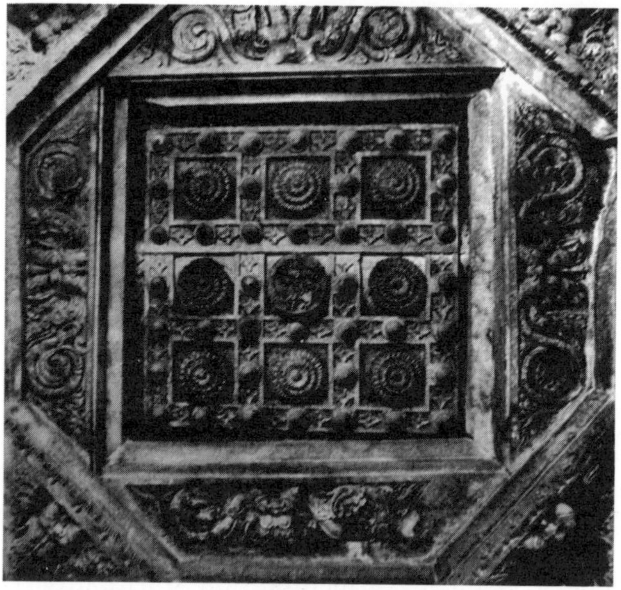

Pl. 9: Figure of nine square grids with three-layered lotuses with the *kīrtimukha* and *nāgasūtra* on the four sides.

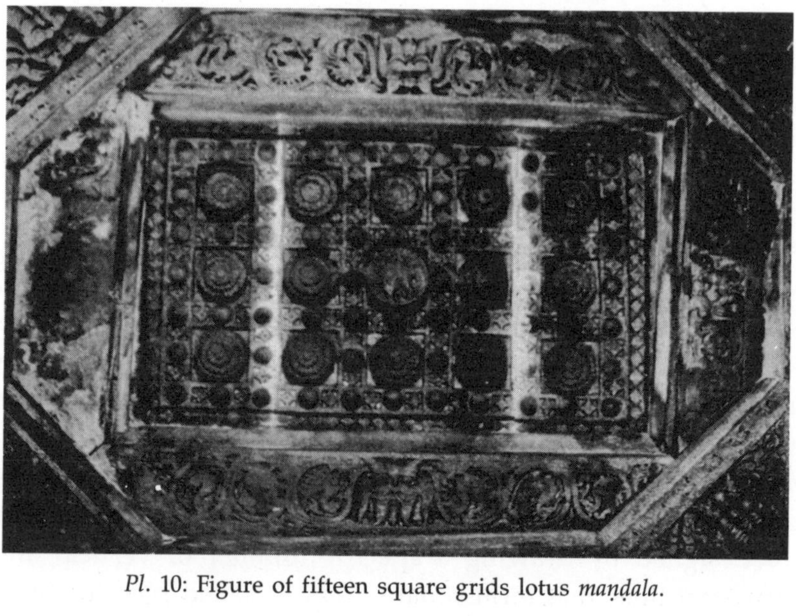

Pl. 10: Figure of fifteen square grids lotus *maṇḍala*.

The number of grids may be 5, 9, 15, 64 or 108 square grids in one *maṇḍala*, depending on the theme and purpose, and they are called by different names also. *Sarvatobhadra* is the term for a *maṇḍala* where the central deity is conceived in the central block, surrounded on all sides by either smaller or similar size square grids, in a nine-block structure. It may also represent nine *padmas* or lotus design enclosed in nine square grids of three in each row, which is called *navapadma-bhadramaṇḍala* that is auspicious from all directions. *Sarvatobhadra maṇḍalas* are like completely closed circuits, each of the outer square grids (*pāda*) is presided over by a guardian divinity, sometimes represented by emblems or fractals of self-repeating motifs. In all types of *bhadramaṇḍalas*, the basic function of these divinities is to protect the cosmic energy of the deity invoked in the centre — the sacred precinct, from the disintegrating and negative forces. In some temples the themes of *pañcāyatana* and *navapadma maṇḍala* are combined in one *maṇḍala* where the central and the *padmas* on the four directions are alike suggesting the *pañcāyatana* order and the other four are with different type of petals.

In the *pañcadaśapadma maṇḍala* (15 grids) of Marale Cennakeśava temple, the three *padmas* on either side go in the name of the two consorts of Keśava — Śrīdevī and Bhūdevī. (See *Pl.* 10)

The *bhadramaṇḍalas* are employed in temples as the concluding ceremonies of religious observances, as the belief goes with the *bhadra* (the fruitful support), for a positive result. When a phallic symbol of Śiva as the *liṅga* or the iconic representation of forms of Lord Śiva is incorporated in a *bhadra-maṇḍala,* it becomes *liṅgatobhadra* — which is employed in Śaiva temples or rituals. Similarly with the *mantra* of Rāma or pictorial representation of Rāma, the *maṇḍala* is called *rāmatobhadra*, and with Gaṇeśa, it becomes *gaṇeśa-bhadra. Cakrābja maṇḍala* is another type of *sarvatobhadra maṇdala* that is circular in structure, but comes with a conch-shell in each of the corners. Specific shapes like an enclosure (*paridhi*), well (*vāpi*), creeper (*vallī*), chain (*śṛṅkhalā*) or crescent moon (*khaṇḍendu*) are also traced within the framework of a *bhadramaṇḍala*.

The tradition of constructing *bhadramaṇḍala* is used in invoking any deity and is still alive in Hindu religious rituals, by drawing the lines with thread, filling the squares with coloured powder or grains of different colours, but of late the tedious procedure is getting replaced by easily made commercially produced charts.

1.9. Kīrtimukha: The Face of Glory

Kīrtimukha (see *Pls*. 9 and 10), the face of glory, also meaning an expansion and extension in Sanskrit — is an artistic and essential symbol used in the walls and *vimāna*s of temples, divine sculptures, and in the corners of the outer square boundary of temple *maṇḍala*s. They also appear on the apex of the arch, or in the centre, or on the frame of the divine sculptures, to ward off the evil spirits. They are repeated profusely in temples as fractal representation. It is the face of the lion and human face in fusion, for which reason it is also called *siṁhamukha* also. It looks like a hostile mask, of mixing the animal and man's countenance, that looks powerful and inflated with breath. The nose looks prominent with vibrant nostrils. Eye sockets are bulging and protruding. Sometimes they have horns of animal on their forehead. The face of glory is an incomplete face as the lower jaw and chin are absent. The upper jaw has a row of sharp animalish teeth.

They come with variations, in combination with serpent, ram's horn, fish, bird, and crocodile.

The face of glory is known as *grāsamukha* in western India, *rāhumukha* in eastern India, and *kālamukha* (time) also. *Grāsa* and Rāhu are synonymous, meaning to devour — the devourer of time, maybe with the intention that he takes away death or destruction of the core structure and make the divine images to be permanent in their body and soul aspect. It may be because of this they are seen as architectural motifs in all the cardinal directions on the *vimāna* of the temple. The inflated breath on its face is indicative of death, the darkness and *tāmasika* quality. Rāhu is the son of lioness (a solar symbol). Purāṇic stories tell that Rāhu had tasted few drops of nectar (*amṛta*) and Lord Viṣṇu chopped off his head on knowing this. The body died but the head remained immortal and it tries to swallow the sun and moon on eclipse time even to this day. Hence *kīrtimukha* is also indicative of the permanence of *tamas*. He is depicted in the diminished face. Hindu philosophy believes that all beings exist in any one of the three (*tāmasika, rājasika* or *sāttvika*) states of mind. In temples and divine sculptures the *sāttvika* and *rājasika* states find an expression in the face and body, but the *tāmasika* aspect is symbolised only in the *kīrtimukha* above the head in the outer frame. Prior to the manifestation of light, everything was in darkness, in *tāmasika* state. If the Image of divinity is viewed as light of consciousness, its previous phase of nothingness is seen in the face of *kīrtimukha* in the outer structure. With a psychological perspective, it is also believed as a symbol that wards off or devours evil sights and spirits.

The motif became almost an essential feature in temple architecture from the tenth century onwards. The *maṇḍala*s of Bādāmi cave temples do not have much of its representation, which is prior to fifth century (refer *Pls.* 12 or 13 in ch. 2).

In the *bhadramaṇḍala*s (refer *Pl.* 10) the face of glory is combined with serpent shape in one and birds in tendril motif in the other.

1.10. Number Symbolism

The *maṇḍala*s in Hindu temples are mostly symmetrical in design. They are studied by the geometrical divisions within, the number of spokes of a wheel, the shape and number of petals of lotus design and the fractal representations of the lotus bud motifs. *Maṇḍala*s of circular design often are seen with petals or divisions in even numbers and the square *maṇḍala*s were mostly with odd number of divisions. The ancient Greeks considered odd numbers to be active, masculine and even numbers to be passive and feminine. Ancient Chinese called odd numbers as *yang* (celestial and auspicious), while even numbers were *yin* (terrestrial, and less auspicious). According to ancient Hinduism, numbers were considered as living vibrations. Life of communication was based on a sea of numbers, and numbers were also translated into art. Each fundamental number denoted either a god, the quality, or the direction and the other numbers signified gods of different ranks, or a concept as gods were correlated with numbers and significance to regulate the order of the world. The principles of creation or the law of time and space was understood by the interplay of even and odd numbers and through specific geometrical shapes. The numbers thus decoded the deeper meanings of its significance, and the development of a scientific thought, religion and art. In almost all religions, numbers symbolised divine order and the cryptic keys to cosmic harmony.

Lotus design appears almost in all *maṇḍala*s, as it was considered a symbol of the East to signify a sign of purity, transcendence and the sphere of the absolute. A lotus design may have one ring or many concentric rings of petals, and the number and shape of petals also varied according to the theme. Some *maṇḍala*s have the replica of the central lotus bud repeated in varying numbers and miniature sizes.

The numbers of petals in each circle of the body of the *maṇḍala* are mostly even, based on the symbolic meaning of the sacred numerology or the *cakra* representations, with the numbers, 4, 6, 8, 12, 16, 24, 32, 64, 108, etc.

EVEN NUMBERS

***No. 2*:** Number 2 is the representation of binary principle. Psychologically it represents attraction, repulsion, equilibrium or paired strength. The two halves of a unit are associated with the division of primordial unity. The two petals on either side of an egg shape — a symbol of *ājñā cakra* is hardly seen in the *maṇḍala*s of temples.

***No. 4*:** Symbolic of the four directions of space, and psychologically it stands for enthusiasm of *mūlādhāra cakra*. The traditional symbol of *svastika* comes as a four-armed cross which is the most common emblem of totality and the four directions. The four arms or petals may also symbolise the four purposes of the tree of life, viz., *dharma, artha, kāma* and *mokṣa*. The four heads of Lord Brahmā symbolise the ruler of all elements. Four is a "rational" number symbolising intellect.

***No. 6*:** Six is symbolic of equilibrium. A cube with surfaces represents stability and truth. It is graphically represented as a hexagon, resulting from the interpenetration of two triangles with their apex in opposite directions. The upward triangle is the male — the static, and the downward triangle — the female or the kinetic forces in a perfect state of union and a state of equilibrium. The numerical equivalent of this is six — which may be represented as a six-petalled lotus. A hexagram is also indicative of the element wind and its movement.

***No. 8*:** Number 8 is symbolic of "complete," symbolic of the four cardinals and intermediate directions, symbol of infinity in space and time. Number 8 when rotated by 90° also indicates the symbol of infinity. The deities of directions are installed in the eight petals of a lotus while the central deity or cosmic power is in the centre. The eight petals are explained in *Bhagavad-Gītā* (1.4), to be indicative of the eight different forms of *prakṛti* like the earth, water, fire, air, ether, mind, intellect and ego. It is called as *aṣṭakoṇa* or *aṣṭadala padma*, as an octagon results from the superimposition of square on square. Eight-petalled lotus is symbolic of *anāhata cakra*, an emblem of cosmic equilibrium.

In some specific *maṇḍala*s or *yantra*s, eight petals signify the 8-syllabled G*āyatrī*.

***No. 10*:** Number 10 is symbolic of perfection — the mythical number of completion and unity. The *Daśāvatāra*, 10 incarnations of Lord Viṣṇu is a symbol of whole creation. Ten is the number of completeness even in the simplest level of the 10 digits in the hands and feet of humans.

***No. 12*:** Twelve is symbolic of cosmic organisation. According to the sacred numerology, it stands for Sun (*āditya*s), the 12 images of the sun, or the 12 months of the year, 12 zodiacal signs and so on. Number 12 is the base number of space and time like the 12 hours of day and night, and solar astrology was based on the movement of the sun through the 12 zodiacal signs. In some specific *maṇḍala*s, 12 petals are symbolic of the 12 vowels and the consecutive layers of 16 petals indicate the consonants.

***No. 16*:** Number 16 is a sacred number, has many references according to Hindu philosophy. Number 16 corresponds to the *viśuddha cakra* of *ṣaṭacakra bhedha*, relating to the intensity of the energy working at physical and psychological levels of realisation. *Viśuddha* means a zone of purity, associated with the element ether, the sky, and hence 16-petalled lotus signifies purity of thought. According to the psychological attributes of *kuṇḍalinī cakra*s, *viśuddha* stands for communication and inspiration and the faculty of sound (*śabda*) is activated at this level of consciousness. *Viśuddha cakra* is supposed to open the gateway of *jñānaloka*, connecting the body to the spiritual world. The mysterious power of sound and the activity of communication make it a dwelling place of Goddess of knowledge. The concept of purity may be represented as 16 rays also in the ceilings of temples.

According to *Bṛhadāraṇyaka Upaniṣad,* the creator is 16-fold in power — *ṣoḍaśa kalā prajāpati.* He has 16 forces as 16 aspects of energy and digits of expression. These 16 digits are compared to the 16 digits of moon with the waxes and wanes. Moon is compared with the mind, which explains the psychological traverses of the mind that is 16-fold, the *16 kalā*s or the powers of mind. Of the 16 parts, 15 are temporal and one is transcendent.

16 petals also refer to the 16 parts or *kalā*s of *puruṣa* — the static consciousness, 16 vowels or in some *maṇḍala*s it may represent the 16 *nitya śakti*s of lunar cycle. Sixteen is also with reference to the 16 attractions that veil our existence, that blind our spiritual sight, keep us away from knowledge and changing one to the ceaseless cycle of life. Each petal of the *maṇḍala* of *Śrī-Yantra* symbolises a deity of attraction, who stimulates the self-consciousness. The explanation for 16 depends on the theme of the *maṇḍala* that is depicted. Sixteen petals, in some *maṇḍala*s, is multiplied in the next two circles, making it a 32 and 64-petalled lotus, which means an expansion of the basic concept.

Likewise a 24-petalled lotus symbolises the 24 epithets of Lord Viṣṇu.

***No. 32*:** Thirty-two is doubling of the concept of 16 or it may indicate the 32 placements of numbers — rising from zero to infinity. Thirty-two is also indicative of the 32 types of weapons held by the various Gods.

***No. 64*:** Sixty-four may indicate the 64 types of knowledge and each petal indicating the corresponding goddess installed, or, may just mean the expansion of number 16 — depending upon the theme of the *maṇḍala.*

No. 88: Eighty-eight indicates the officially recognised constellations, named after animals (like Leo) or mythological characters like Orion — the hunter.

No. 1000: A thousand-petalled lotus symbolises the *sahasra-dala padma* — symbolic of uniting with the ultimate truth, and the cosmic blessings showered. Thousand is symbolic of relating to void, eternity and totality.

ODD NUMBERS

No. 1: One is the symbol of God and primordial unity. It is equated with Sūrya (the sun) and the origin of life. Of the heavenly bodies, Sun is always positioned in the centre of the *maṇḍala* — the indivisible and the mystic centre from which everything radiated.

No. 3: Three is the most positive number in the religious thoughts. The three-headed God *trimūrti* of Hindu tradition symbolises the trinity of Gods — the Brahmā, Viṣṇu and Maheśvara, the creator, sustainer and the destroyer. The soul is seen to exist in the three divisions — the body, mind and the spirit. The rhythm of cosmos and divinity is represented in the three letters of the mystic chant *AUṀ*. Number 3, graphically represented as a triangle, is the primary and first symbolic form to emerge, as anything lesser than three lines cannot indicate the enclosure of space. It is the sign of sacred and cosmic womb, the primal symbol of cosmic location and creation. The female emblem of power — *śakti* principle (*yoni maṇḍala*) is associated with the inverted triangle, while the triangle with the apex upward denotes the male principle -— the emblem of Śiva, the numerical equivalent being number 3.

The three lines are also interpreted in metaphysical concepts, for the *śakti* — the power of *icchā* (will), *jñāna* (knowledge, cognition), and *kriyā* (activity).

No. 5: Five is represented as a star pentagon or a five-petalled lotus, indicating the five elements (*pañcabhūta*s — earth, water, fire, air and ether). It illustrates the organisation of space into the numerical order of 5. It also bears specific reference of Lord Śiva in his fivefold aspect or *kalā*s as they are called, representing the Śaiva universe, in his creative and destructive powers. It also represents the five letters — *pañcākṣara* of *na-maḥ-śi-vā-ya*, the five elements of nature or the five senses. When represented as five lotuses, it indicates the *pañcāyatana* — fivefold worship of the cult deities. It may also represent the *bhadramaṇḍala* of a specific deity like the Gaṇeśa *bhadramaṇḍala*.

No. 7: Seven is a mystical and sacred number to Hindus as it signifies the completion of natural cycle of time as seven days of a week. Its significance in astronomy refers to the group of seven stars — the Big Dipper, the celestial bodies identified with the seven days of a week. The rays of sun are represented as seven rays. Big Dipper (*saptarṣi maṇḍala*) has two pointive stars "Dhube and Mark." From amongst the total seven, which point at the North star polaris that is a bright star at the north celestial pole, is found to be very important for navigation.

The rays of the Sun are represented as seven linking it with the seven colours of the rainbow. Number seven is also connected with the seven sacred rivers of India like the Gaṅgā, Yamunā Godāvarī, Sarasvatī, Narmadā, Sindhu and Kāverī which are recited in the everyday prayers even to this day. A seven-layered wheel of lotus petals indicate the 7 ascending levels of consciousness.

No. 9: Nine is a powerful number of Hindu traditions, corresponding to the nine planets. In a nine grid square *maṇḍala*, depending on the central deity, the *maṇḍala* may be explained to be either *navagraha maṇḍala*, or *aṣṭa dikpālaka*s with the representation of Lord Śiva in the centre. No. 9 is represented as the mysticism of the triple synthesis of body, mind and spirit of the three worlds — the underworld, earth and heaven.

The numbers 11, 13 and 17 are usually rare in a *maṇḍala* graphic representation and hence not discussed.

No. 27: Twenty-seven is indicative of the heavenly bodies — the stars.

1.11. Fractals: An Interpretation and Representation

All *maṇḍalas* in temples come with self-repeating designs called fractals. Fractal, a latin word, means "fragmented or irregular." The basic concept of fractals is that they contain a large degree of self-similarity. Self-similarity means each small portion, when magnified, can reproduce exactly the large portion. It exhibits the same degree of complexity regardless of the scale at which the structures are observed. This means they contain little copies of them buried deep, within the original and also have identical details, they are the repeated identical motifs associated with the original structure. Fractals exist in nature like each of the leaflets of a fern plant, or the leaflet of *gulmohur* tree resembles one leaf in structure, which is further identical in shape as the compound leaf. Similarly, the structure and construction of the Koch snowflake is another best example of the aspect of fractals existing in nature.

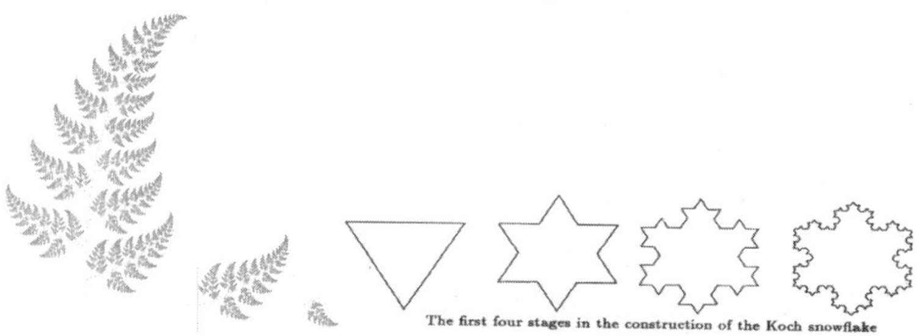

Pl. 11: Fractals in the leaf of the fern plant and in the structure of snowflakes.

Ancient Indian temple architectural traditions have adopted the fractal representations of cosmos in a symbolic form to reinforce the idea how nature propagates its essence regardless of the magnitude of its expression. The temple tower is surrounded by smaller towers, further surrounded by still smaller towers, for eight or more levels. It suggests housing the sacred deep within. Fractal aspects of Hindu architecture reflect the fractal nature of Hindu cosmology. Through these identical structures, realisation of oneness with the supreme is established by dissolving the boundaries between man and divine. For this purpose, certain notions and motifs are associated with the form of the building, just as a temple is seen as a miniature form of Mount Meru. The residence of gods was described to be on Mount Meru. The Purāṇas have given greatest importance to Mount Meru, describing it as the axis of the world. Mounts Mandāra and Kailāsa are the peaks of Meru. These mountains have given the grandest models to the architectural genesis of their shape. Mountains figuratively were envisaged as layered representation of progressive stages of spiritual ascent. Temples are shaped as mountains, which were conceived as the meeting place of heaven and earth, a symbol of transcendence to eternity, with a belief that deities inhabited mountains. The structure of a temple tower with the smaller towers at various levels is thus the fractal representation of mountains — conceived to be the abode of gods. The fractals of the Koch snowflake is also an inspiration to draw the basic plan of *vimāna*s of many Hindu temples.

The Jain and Hindu cosmologies provide imaginative solutions by connecting the micro or the inner and the macro, the outer worlds by the *piṇḍa-brahmāṇḍa* theory. Every single body is the *piṇḍa* while the universe is the *brahmāṇḍa,* and *piṇḍa* is the replica of the *brahmāṇḍa* at microcosmic level.

*Maṇḍala*s have a centre that is shaped like a lotus bud which is conceived as the supreme power. The body of the *maṇḍala* has the miniature replicas of this central motif repeated in three-dimensional forms in all the concentric circles in large numbers. The Vedic literature presents the concept that there are two fundamental types of conscious entity: the beings of limited individualised like us called *jīvātmā*s pertaining to material energy, and the supreme superconsciousness called the *paramātma* — the overseer of the material energy. In the diagram of a *maṇḍala*, the fractal motif of lotus buds in different sizes is compared to the *jīvātma* and *paramātma*, in their respective places. It is a structure that reintegrates the part to a whole, like a devotee seeks to experience the infinite in a temple. The concept of Advaita philosophy can be understood better when the nature of fractals is analysed. The concept of fractals has been used to analyse and demonstrate the similarities in macro and microcosmic units, giving a profound sense of understanding that we are born from the cosmos and a part of it. They are visually satisfying with universal appeal, because they are able to provide the viewers a sense of scale at different levels and a distance of viewing. Hindu temples have the concept of fractals, where part and whole have the same character. Fractals reinforce the thought that all living things are interconnected and part and parcel of the same divine reality. Hindu temple is a symbolic structure that represents certain fundamental concepts of Hindu philosophy about the nature of cosmos.

SIGNIFICANCE OF FRACTALS IN MAṆḌALAS

The conception of Godhead can be seen in various forms and sentiments. During the early stages of spiritual life, a devotee cannot help but seeing God as outside of himself and worships him as an outside object. In the second stage, he realises him as the indwelling spirit, the ear of ear, sight of the eye or life of the body. Next he realises him to be the one who is in fire, water, earth, in the whole universe. God is seen in any form as man or woman, youth or a baby — born in manifold forms, as the principle, immanent in all beings and things. Proceeding further, the devotee realises him to be beyond speech or thought (*Taittirīya Upaniṣad,* II.9), invisible, devoid of all connotations, indefinable, unthinkable and essentially of the nature of consciousness. God is experienced as an indwelling spirit behind each and every natural phenomenon. The concept of the omnipotence, omniscience and omnipresence was probably the concept of fractals in *maṇḍala.* God was seen in the centre of the *maṇḍala* in a symbolic form which was depicted in the different levels or concentric circles of the *maṇḍala* with innumerable fractal representations of God, as conceived in the centre of the *maṇḍala* in the symbol form.

Fractals are a major component of all *maṇḍala*s.

The Upaniṣads, the last text of Vedic or Vedānta, develop the idea that all life proceedes from *Brahman,* defined as the invisible one — *ekam advitīyam. Brahman* is not only transcendent but also immanent in all. The individual soul cannot be differentiated in itself from the absolute. Man is the part of God, light of God, and he is thereby cannot be distinguished as a separate entity. This is the famous "Thou art that." Divine can be grasped in multiplicity of forms, which is expressed as fractals. (It can be compared to a drop of water from the sea which has all the qualities of the ocean water, but it is not the sea.) Hindu philosophy views cosmos to be holonomic and self-similar in nature. Hindu temples are models of cosmos and their forms represent cosmos symbolically. Even the temple *vimāna* has several, smaller, self-repeating peaks at various points that appear identical to the structure of the main *vimāna* of the temple. The fractal structures represent the quest for *mokṣa* (the ultimate spiritual liberation). The realisation of oneness by setting out to dissolve the boundaries between man and divine is seen as expressions of fractals at macrocosmic and microcosmic levels.

1.12. Iconographic Representation of Pañcabhūtas (The Five Elements)

The conception of the *pañcabhūta*s or *pañca tattva*s, the knowledge of what are they and how they are represented in iconography, is very desirable for a proper appreciation of various factors in both *maṇḍala*s and *vigraha*s. The five elements — the *pṛthvī, āpaḥ, tejas, vāyu* and *ākāśa*, the concept that all matter is formed basically of these elements both at microcosmic and macrocosmic levels are represented in *maṇḍala*s, and hence they are revered. *Bhūta* means a state of existence; the root word is a derivative of *bhū* — meaning "to be." *Tattva* means an element, the primary substance. On the psychological side of the elements, fire and air are considered to be extroverts while earth and water are considered as introverts.

A careful study of Vaiśeṣika Darśana shows that the five states of existence or the *pañcabhūta*s are the *pṛthvī, āpaḥ, tejas, vāyu* and *ākāśa* that stand for solidity, liquidity, radiation, gaseousness and ethereality. The *śloka* reads as:

> *yat kaṭhinam sa pṛthvī, yad dravam tat āpaḥ,*
> *yad uṣṇam tat tejaḥ, yat sañcarati sa vāyuḥ,*
> *yat suśiram tad ākāśam.*

In iconography,

> *Pṛthvī* or solidity is represented by a square in a single plane or a cube in a three-dimensional space.
>
> *Āpaḥ* or liquidity by a circle, waterpot, or water-born plants and animals.
>
> *Tejas* or radiation by light, stellate figures, as a triangle, or interlacing triangles, or bright objects.

> *Vāyu* or gaseousness by smoke, smoke colour or flying bodies, and as a hexagram in design.
>
> *Ākāśa* or ether by emptiness (*śūnya*), round shape (infinity), heavenly bodies as the sun, moon and stars.

The term *pṛthvī* means earth in Sanskrit. As a fixed principle, the graphic symbol or the design attributed was a square or a cube, even though it was well established that earth was round. *Pṛthvī* was depicted as a cube with a vision that all that is *kaṭhinam* (solid) had a definite shape, occupied definite shape and volume. A cube was the easy geometric design giving the height, breadth and depth. Even the muscles and bones of the physical body were considered as the *pṛthvī* and denoted by a cube archaeologically. Hence, *pṛthvī* goes by the concept rather than by etymology. Although earth is associated with passivity and darkness, it is usually separated in symbolism from the underworld, as a source of life, a symbol of fruitfulness and the eternal ability to produce, rather than an abode of the dead.

Similarly the element water denoted all that is free-flowing, and needs a container to hold it, and takes the shape of the container. Hence it was represented in art forms as a pot, or a lower part of the pot, where water took the shape of half moon. Half moon or full circle is also the symbol of element water (*āpaḥ*). Alternatively water was also indicated by the representation of water-born plants, flowers or animals like fish. River was also represented in an anthropomorphic form, like river Gaṅgā is represented on the head of Lord Śiva, and rivers Gaṅgā and Yamunā also had specific representations of animals. Water is revered as the symbol of formless potentiality, an emblem of cleansing, fluidity, mingling, cohesion, birth and regeneration. The *Ṛgveda* has verses in praise of water as the bringer of all things.

The element fire, conceived as an actual God formerly and later as a divine power was a symbolic element in the practice of cremation (the end of life). Smoke and fire were symbols of ascension, always moved upwards, whichever direction it was held and were the means of communication on a cosmic and the mundane levels. It is a masculine and active element, symbolising as both creative for its regenerating quality and destructive for its consuming force of natural energy. It is considered as a living element, growing by what it is fed on, dying and re-appearing. The concept that illumination and radiation made the shape or form of things visible, was a symbol of revelation and illumination, as a force that drove away ignorance. It was used as a metaphor for wisdom and a terrestrial representative of Sun, with which much of the symbolism is shared like that of purification, transformation and regeneration. It was on the basic design of the fire in natural form with its apex always pointing upwards that a triangular shape was assigned. Philosophically, even knowledge that drives away ignorance is depicted in a triangular shape, so also the human navel region, which is the seat of heat in the body — the other aspect of light.

Air (*vāyu*), the concept of unseen element, but whose presence was just felt was the primal element that was equated with the soul. As wind, it was also personified with wind gods who were violent and unpredictable sometimes. Air shares much of the symbolisn with breath and wind, associated with freedom, and purity of spiritual life. In Indian art, it was depicted by the flying objects like flying robes and *gandharva*s whose abode was sky. In concrete forms, it was indicated as a percussion instrument, the medium in which sound waves travelled. The geometric design was a hexagram, which was a result of two intersecting triangles representing the *puruṣa* and *prakṛti*, and the resultant change in the movement of life force.

The ethereal zone was often represented by the pictures of sun, moon and the stars. Moon was an ancient symbol of cosmic power, beauty and serenity. The use of crescent moon as an emblem was conceived as the boat of moon God in which he navigated the vast reaches of space. Hindu gods and goddesses are often represented with the crescent moon on their hair denoting chastity and divine status. They also denoted royalty, governance and spiritual ascension.

Yat suśīram — has two meanings, firstly that which is hollow, secondly cold and pleasant, and heavenly. *Ākāśa* the sky was represented as an empty space. The infinite aspect of space was represented in the *maṇḍala*s as a circular design, space around the point, where point was conceived as God, and the empty space — his abode.

The five states of existence were philosophically viewed as the stages of awareness. In humans, the psychological behaviour patterns related to ego were also viewed to change from solidity, liquidity, to radiation, gaseousness and ethereality, with the advancement and evolution of awareness levels.

Theory of the five elements was discussed in the Sāṁkhya-Pātañjala system of philosophy and the *Yoga-Bhāṣya* of Vyāsa, where the origin of the five elements (*bhūta*s) — earth, water, fire, air and space — was understood to be the basis of the material universe, and these elementary substances consisted of ultimate units called *aṇus* (atoms) and *tanmātra*s — the infra-atomic particles. The properties of each of the *pañcabhūta*s vary with the grouping of *tanmātra*s in the atoms of each. Kaṇāda — the founder of Vaiśeṣika system of philosophy — described the concepts of atoms and molecules of the five elements, and their characteristic properties. Based on these explanations, Vaiśeṣika Darśana gave the distinctive iconographic traits to the five great elements, relating them to the philosophy of *cakra*s (the nerve plexus), sense organs, specific geometric designs, and the associated numerological numbers. The five elements of earth, water, fire, air and ether are bound by the eternal laws governing nature. And the symbolic designs are given based on these laws — like water always takes the shape of the container, and fire goes always upwards, air is always moving, etc.

The various shapes and forms of *maṇḍala*s and *vigraha*s (diagrammatic representation and iconic forms) are determined by conventions of the type noted above. The representation of the *pañcabhūta*s can be seen in the icon of dancing Śiva (the Naṭarāja), as standing on a rectangular pedestal, and his physical form, representing *pṛthvī, āpaḥ* in the personification of river Gaṅgā on his head or as a fountain of water from his locks of hair, *tejas* as the lord holding fire in his left hand, *vāyu* indicated as the flying robes and the sound of his *ḍamaru* (the small percussion instrument), *ākāśa* as the heavenly body — the moon as a decoration on his crown. The conventional representations hint the theme that Lord Śiva is present in *pañcabhūta*s and these are present in him also. He is the vigorous dancer and the creator of the art of dance and rhythm in all its aspects, which means the amalgamation of the creator and his creation.

Though the *maṇḍala* is a universal constant, it is also an act of faith and an integral part of a personal vision quest.

2

The Structure, Philosophical and Scientific Perspectives of Maṇḍalas in Temples

Caves of Bādāmi: A Historical Background

BĀDĀMI, a *pañcāyat* town in Bagalkot district of Karnataka state in south India, picturesquely situated between two rocky hills, is famous for cave temples of sandstone on the precipice of a hill. Bādāmi is 46 km away from another ancient town Aihoḷe. The place, formerly called as Vātāpi, was the regal capital of the early Cāḷukyas, who ruled much of Karnataka and Andhra Pradesh between sixth-eighth century CE. Bādāmi was founded by the early Cāḷukyan ruler Pulakeśin-I, in CE 535-66. His sons Kīrtivarman (CE 567-98) and Mangaleśa (CE 598-610) constructed the complex of four cave temples — three of them are man-made caves and the one a natural cave, all in close proximity to each other and situated right next to the town of Bādāmi. The credit of scooping and completing the cave temples goes to the Cāḷukyan king Maṅgaleśa.

The caves in Bādāmi are carved out of the soft sandstone on a cliff in the late sixth century. The caves consists of a simple veranda with stone columns and brackets, leading to a columned *maṇḍapa* and then to a shrine cut deep into the cave. All the caves bear exquisite carvings, sculptures and beautiful murals. Out of the four caves, three are dedicated to Hindu deities and the fourth one is associated with Jainism.

Cave No. 1 is dedicated to Lord Śiva, Cave No. 2 to Lord Viṣṇu, Cave No. 3, which is the largest and the best, has carvings depicting both Śaivite and Vaiṣṇavite themes and Cave No. 4 is dedicated to the Jain *tīrthaṁkaras*. These cave temples represent the secular nature of the rulers with religious tolerance following the inclines towards Hinduism, Jainism and Buddhism. From archaeological and architectural perspective, they provide critical evidence of the early styles and stages of south Indian architecture.

The *maṇḍalas* of Bādāmi caves analysed here belong to Cave No. 2, which has beautiful figures of the different forms of Lord Viṣṇu. The two *maṇḍalas* — the *svastika maṇḍala* and the *maṇḍala* with lotus and a school of fish designed radially to the central hub are very symmetrical and interesting.

2.1. Laws of Motion in the Svastika Maṇḍala of Bādāmi Cave (*Pl.* 12)

STRUCTURE OF THE MAṆḌALA

On one of the ceilings of Bādāmi cave temple no. 2, is a *maṇḍala* with four *svastika* designs in a square framework. The *maṇḍala* is basically square in shape and further divided into a grid of 9 squares called *pāda* or *koṣṭa*, and assembled in a specific pattern of *svastika* and Marut gods in alternating squares. It can be classified under *bhadramaṇḍala* — meaning auspicious from all sides.

The *maṇḍala* at the Bādāmi cave ceiling is a *svastika bhadramaṇḍala* as there are four *svastikas* in all the four sides of the central deity. The central square block has the design of an 8-petalled full bloom lotus with the circular pericarp in the centre. On all the four sides of the square, are the *svastika* designs, with four-petalled lotus in its centre. The four *svastikas* and the inner square boundary are interconnected, even though they have different

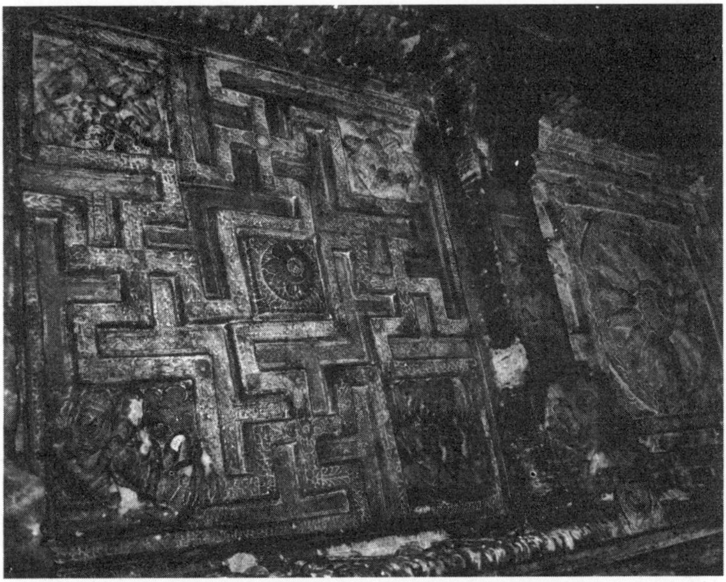

Pl. 12: *Maṇḍala* at the Bādāmi cave temple.

configuration of the top and bottom *svastika*s with left arms and the horizontal ones with right arms. Intricate design of scrollwork is carved on the inner square boundary as well as the arms of *svastika*s. On all the four corners of the square framework and alternating with the *svastika* designs are the flying Marut gods as couples in square grids.

PHILOSOPHICAL PERSPECTIVE

The centre of the *svastika maṇḍala* is the design of a full bloom lotus with the circular pericarp in the middle. The shape of the petals is broad at the base and rounded tips, which hints that a troop of demi-gods or the *tattvābhimānī devatā*s are installed in the petals. The eight petals pointing to the circumference of the circle also illustrate the unfolding of the divine power in the eight directions. Number 8 is also a symbol of infinity in ancient Indian cosmology. Since the symbol of *svastika* signifies the solar symbol, the lotus in the centre is the seat of sun god.

In iconography, sun, the dominant symbol of creative energy, has a vast range of emblems like the ring of wheel, the *svastika*s or the turning cross form.

Svastika is an auspicious and traditional symbol that appears in all cultures bearing an elemental power and significance. *Svastika* as a mystic symbol can be traced back to early Indian history. It is derived from the amalgam of two Sanskrit words — *su* meaning "good or well," a positive way and *asti* meaning "to be" (a verbal aspect). *Ka* is a suffix to intensify the verbal meaning. *Svastika* is "that which is associated with well being" and a symbol of peace, good fortune, good luck, prosperity, welfare and victory. It stands second to sacred symbol of *OṀ* in its significance. The symbol is extensively used in Hinduism to drive away evil even though it was used as a Nazi symbol.

On the four corners of the *maṇḍala* are the figures of Marut gods — the cloud bearing gods of storm or tempest. They are represented as couple in a flying posture. Marut gods are the divine spirits, personified as gods of war and the iconographic representation of them holding weapons like sword, spear or battleaxe, hammer, resting upon their shoulders or holding knife in their hand proves this. In one of the corner figures, they are depicted as drinking the *soma-rasa* — the favourite drink of them according to the *Ṛgveda*. Since *svastika* is a solar symbol and hinting about the cyclical movements associated with it, and the association of Marut gods with *svastika* in the *maṇḍala*, it can be read as the cyclical order of the storm, rain, drought patterns, as the activities of Marut gods that go by rotation. The figure where Marut gods are drinking *soma-rasa* may be indicative of the mysterious power of transformation, natural fecundity, change, or the time of productivity and regeneration after the rains. The Marut gods holding sword and knife, according to symbolism of weapons is indicative of authority, knowledge, justice, and divine wisdom that can be linked to the balance in the weather. Marut gods holding hammer or the axe hammer is indicative of the destructiveness of thunder and lightning. Marut gods holding battleaxe is a near universal symbol of decisive and uncertainty power, linked with sun and storm iconographically. The flashing of this weapon is symbolically associated with fire or devastating fire hazards of nature. Alternatively the dual half moon curve axe is indicative of lunar symbol or the reconciliation of opposites. The *svastika maṇḍala* may be a pattern to predict the pattern of nature, when the rotation pattern of *svastika* is considered.

The seemingly unpredictable and many times the destructive power of natural forces implied as a continuous struggle for human existence. The control was sought by the co-operation between the human beings and the divine spirits which appeared to be crucial for the survival. Prominent among the gods of *R̥gveda* (VII.7.4, and I.168.8) are the Maruts the storm gods, who are youthful warriors armed with spears, sword and battleaxe. They wear headgears and decked with golden ornaments like anklets, armlets, etc. Maruts are fierce and terrible, shattering the clouds with their sword and shed rain. Maruts are powerful and destructive usually but benefiting also. They are comrades of Lord Indra. They are said to be pleased by flattery.

Marut gods became a part of the *maṇḍala* so that they are pleased with the reverence shown and do not cause destructive storm that causes damages.

Among the artefacts excavated in the remains of Haṛappan Culture (3000 BCE) a number of seals depict *svastika* symbol. It is basically an equal armed cross, another universal symbol. The vertical axis — the great pole has the ascensional meaning of cosmic energy at macrocosmic level and symbolic of the human spine at microcosmic level. The horizontal axis represents the path from birth to death, the beginning to end of earthly life. Cross is indicative of the four cardinal directions — north, south, east and west — and its relation to the centre. It also suggests uniting the horizontal and vertical directions — a pair of opposites and representing the totality of space with four cardinal directions and stability. Some temporal events in nature are periodic and eternal like the span of the day, month, year, the seasons, etc. In a *svastika*, the four arms of cross have extensions, turned at right angles, which hint a direction of rotating movement or whirling momentum in cyclic order. These may represent the cyclical rotation of time, the seasons, the *yuga*s or the planetary movements which are linked with the central deity or maybe the sun as the supreme power, who is the creator and controller of all the movements. Regularity in the changes and events of nature sets a pattern and life could be systematised based on time. Periodicity gives rise to regularity. *Svastika* is thus used as a sun symbol also which is extremely holy and auspicious, one of the 108 symbols of Lord Viṣṇu, and representing the sun's rays, without which there would be no life.

In the *maṇḍala* of Bādāmi cave, each cyclical movement of one *svastika* is connected to the next one, ultimately tracing the total cyclical movement of life or the creative force and the aspect of generation of cycles that is associated with the solar power in the cosmos.

The *svastika*s can rotate in either direction. The two symbols of the arms of *svastika* are: the right-facing arm is the evolution and the left-facing arm is involution. The other significance is regarding the solar and lunar power, male and female forces. Even according to Buddhist symbols the arm of *svastika* when turned to left signifies the male energy and when the arm is to the right, it is the female generative power. A *bhadramaṇḍala* is usually employed in the concluding ceremonies of a religious observance, which assures fruitfulness when installed, giving excellent results in the attainment of specific goals.

A SCIENTIFIC PERSPECTIVE

According to the iconographic representations of *pañcatattvas*, *vāyu* is indicated by flying objects and bodies. The representation of flying Marut gods on the four corners of the *maṇḍala* clearly indicates that the theme is related to *vāyu* and its quality of the movement. The concept of several types of movements was expressed in ancient architecture in an abstract way. A pictorial representation of *svastika* suggests the solar wheel, and its appearance in many cults was linked with sun or sky gods. The significance of the symbol *svastika* is also related to the eternal cyclical movement of aspects like solar energy, cosmic regeneration, time, seasons, rotative force, or planetary bodies. Another notable graphic feature of the *svastika* in the Bādāmi cave *maṇḍala* is that its four arms divide the space into four squares, showing the association with wind gods to the four seasons or cardinal points.

The cosmic power in the centre is presented in a lotus enclosed in a square boundary, hinting that it is static, or is inertial, and resistant to acceleration as square boundary is indicative of stability. The cyclical rotations of cosmology (like the four seasons, the *yuga*s or cosmic years or planets in succession) are the eternal movements around the cosmic power of sun, drawing energy eternally from the governing body (as they are connected to the square). The *svastika*s indicating individual cyclical movement and interconnecting cyclical movement of four *svastika*s, with a non-moving power at the centre indicate the laws of motion.

When analysed why the four *svastika*s are interconnected with a static body in the centre, a parallel to Newton's laws of gravitation can be drawn. Of Newton's numerous profound insights into the working of the universe, the theory of gravity can be applied here. The invisible force of gravity pervades every object in everyday life, regardless of the physical composition. The force of gravity dictates the cosmic movements that are tirelessly and meticulously executed by billions of cosmic inhabitants, which is indicated in the *maṇḍala* by the interconnectivity of the square boundary to the *svastikas*. The single force of gravity that is a fundamental force of nature is held responsible for the wealth of terrestrial and extra-terrestrial happenings like the planets revolving around the sun.

Since the theme of the *maṇḍala* is related to movement, it can be viewed from the scientific perspective of physics, dealing with the laws of motion.

1. According to Newton's law of motion, objects at rest continue to be at rest and objects in movement, continue to be in movement, until an external force acts on them to stop. Sun was conceived to be static, in relation to the world, and not moving. But the planets moved in their orbit endlessly around the sun.

   On all the four corners are the celestial supernatural couple, the cloud bearing Marut gods in flying movement. But in classic physics, there is mechanics of certainty (like the movement of planets) and mechanics of uncertainty, for example, the natural calamities like flood, drought, volcanic eruptions, tsunami, etc. The four *svastikas* and its cyclical movements are the depiction of mechanics of certainty and the flying Marut gods — mechanics of uncertainty as Maruts are believed to be the gods of storm residing in the upper strata above the surface of earth. According to physics, mechanics of uncertainty may act as unseen objects that create local and unpredictable disturbances but the cyclic rhythm of cosmos continues to be undisturbed.

2. Further, the four *svastikas* show different configuration of movement as two horizontal ones are in clockwise movement and the two in vertical line are in anticlockwise movement. Classical physics produces a conceptual lead that motion could involve a range of configurations. A system displays continuous motion, even when the configurations of movements inside it are not in a definite pattern. This phenomenon is explained by the astrophysicist, Stephen Hawking, in comparing it to the movement of a train. In a moving train, some people may be running in one particular direction and some others may be running in an opposite direction. But the total movement of the train remains unchanged by the internal movements. Similarly the configuration of movement in *svastikas* is different, but the total movement of cosmic cycles remains uniform and undisturbed. In other words, things that change forever, to the tune of time and space, can continue to do so on a changeless substratum.

   The chaos of vast scale in ancient days was conceived through the existence of supernatural beings and the order in cosmos was maintained by the existence of relevant gods. The centre of *svastika* probably was conceived to be active with the relevant god and the supernatural beings were represented in the outer corners of the design.

3. Through the clockwise and anticlockwise movement of *svastikas*, around the circumference of a lotus, it may represent opposites like day and night, which is a cyclical and periodic phenomenon, caused by the presence of sun.

4. Rectangular conduits of the arms of *svastika* may also represent the wave guides, which are used as the most effective and efficient way of energy propagation.

5. The theam of *svastika maṇḍala* can be viewed with the perspective of the movement of electrons and protons of an atom that are in continuous movement around the static central core, but the atom remains still at sub-atomic level, in the matter consisting of millions of atoms.

This *maṇḍala* when viewed from a scientific perspective is a beautiful picture, explaining physics through sacred symbols. Ancient Indians expressed their observation of nature such as laws of motion or the mysterious ways of the working of cosmos, through *maṇḍala*s as art forms in the medium of stone. These were like Montessori pictures, expressing the thoughts in an open and spontaneous way to enlighten the public about the congruence of science and spirituality. It is also a clear statement of science as understood in that period.

2.2. The Dissolution of the Universe — The "Crunch" in the Matsya Maṇḍala of Bādāmi Cave. No. 2 (*Pl.* 13)

A HISTORICAL BACKGROUND
(Refer Historical Background of *Pl.* 12)

Structure of the Maṇḍala

Adjoining the *svastika maṇḍala* in Bādāmi Cave No. 2 can be seen the other *maṇḍala*, which has a striking design of squaring the circle. The *maṇḍala* has a unique representation of fish arranged as the spokes of a wheel, radiating out from the central circle. Both the *maṇḍala*s seem to have a theam in continuation.

The central part of the *maṇḍala* has a lotus. The pericarp is in a circle from which the first circle of radiating petals with pointed tips emerges. Encircling this is a layer of lotus petals that are broader at the base and are nine in number. The body of the *maṇḍala* comprises 16 fish arranged as the radiating spokes of the hub and encircled by a bigger circle decorated by scrollwork of tendrils and water-born flowers. This circular design runs tangent to a square on the four sides, which has the design of laced triangles. This is further enclosed within a bigger square boundary. Small human figures are positioned in between the two squares in such a way as to indicate that they are going round the inner structure representing continnum. The diagram looks beautiful on the ceiling of the cave.

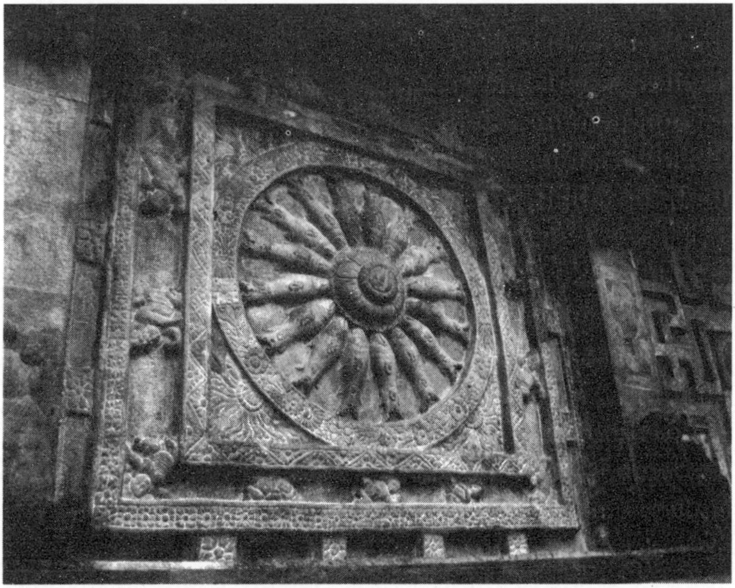

Pl. 13: *Matsya Maṇḍala* at the cave temple of Bādāmi.

PHILOSOPHICAL PERSPECTIVE

Since the Cave No. 2 of Bādāmi is dedicated to Lord Viṣṇu, the central deity of the *maṇḍala* can be considered to be Lord Viṣṇu. The theme of the *maṇḍala* is probably related to the episode of *Matsya Purāṇa*, and the incarnation of Viṣṇu as a fish.

According to this, when the earth faced the deluge, Lord Viṣṇu incarnated as a fish, for in the streamlined body of a fish, he could easily sail through the turbulence, and thus saved the Vaivasvata Manu (the seventh Manu, regarded as the progenitor of the present race of living beings) from the anticipated floods.

Manu is believed to be the forefather of humanity — the father of human race. When the turn of a *manvantara* approached and the *pralaya* (the deluge) was anticipated, Viṣṇu came in the form of a big fish because in the form of fish he could survive the devastating floods and carried all varieties of human race and nature in seed form. At the beginning of the new era he brought back the seeds to life and the race of Manu to life. Fish is hence a sacred symbol of a saviour for Hindus.

In the *maṇḍala*, the lotus with nine petals may symbolise the nine planets and the 16 fish all of which look similar in size and shape according to the sacred numerology represent the 16 parts of *puruṣa* — the expression of *ṣoḍaśa kalā prajāpati* as it is called, which means the 16 forces or the aspects of energy. Viṣṇu's incarnation encompassing all the 16 forms of energy is probably depicted in the *maṇḍala* as 16 fish that absorbed the power of life. The miniature human figures floating in all directions may represent the scattering of human race in the course of the devastating floods.

The sayings of the *Matsya Purāṇa* that Viṣṇu saved the seeds of the race of Vaivasvata Manu leads to a question of what is the meaning of seeds of human race. Swamy Chinmayananda has explained about the meaning of the seed and its relevance in the cosmos in his commentary on *Bhagavad-Gītā* (X. 39). The analogy of seed is an inexhaustible theme for the meditators to contemplate upon. Seed state is compared to a dormant state of life, the content of which manifests itself to a full form under favourable conditions. The grown-up tree with inconceivable heights thereafter bears no relationship to the seed from which it sprang up. The "seed condition of the universe" is equivalent to the dormant condition of the tree, as a seed before its manifestation is called the state of *pralaya* as conceived and accepted in our Upaniṣads. The cosmic dissolution of *pralaya* becomes more intelligible when it is compared at a microcosmic level of human life. In the state of deep sleep, called the *suṣupti avasthā*, the individuality of temperament, character, capability, status, education and such qualities are in a state of dormancy. It means the personality peculiarities remain in a seed condition. After the restful period when the mind comes to wakeful state, the dormant qualities manifest fully. *Pralaya* — according to the Purāṇic theory is *naimittika* (time bound) — as it is occasioned by the night of Brahmā and hence considered *prākṛtika pralaya* (a natural process of dissolution).

The period of deep sleep, when at both microcosmic and macrocosmic level the universe merges to the seed state, is called *pralaya*. At every phase of total dissolution (*pralaya*), all the living creatures and all other aspects of previous active phase of material existence are said to recede into a dormant state in a subtle form, just as all our feelings, thoughts and knowledge lie dormant in our individual consciousness during deep sleep and they re-emerge into manifestation on getting into wakeful state.

According to the Hindu philosophy, the cosmos itself undergoes immense and infinite number of births, deaths and rebirths. At the period of dissolution Lord Viṣṇu incarnates in different forms (the *Daśāvatāra*) each time as a saviour to bring back life from the dormant state. The figures of human beings floating in between the two outer square boundaries of the *maṇḍala* represent the time — the continuous cycles of birth and death of living things on earth.

The figure of fish in a cycle represents the *matsya kalpa* (period), the end of the world, for a specific period, which got renovated by the fish incarnation of Viṣṇu. *Kalpa* is yet another measure of time. Purāṇas are named after *kalpa* like Matsya, Kūrma, Lakṣmī, Śveta Varāha, Śiva, Viṣṇu and Brahmā *kalpas*. A *kalpa* means a cycle of existence for a period of 4320 million years. Like now the current period is the Śveta Varāha *kalpa*. Brahmā's each term lasts for a period of 7 *kalpa*s and we are currently in the second half of the life of Brahmā. The reference point here is the moment of the commencement of creation of the universe by Brahmā.

The iconographic representation of the circle tangent with the square, and water-born plants and animals in the square also hints about the earth getting engulfed with water.

> *purā kalpa kṣaye vr̥tte jātam jalamayam jagat*
> — *Kathāsaritsāgara*

In olden time, life on the universe got diminished and ended, as the universe got covered by water.

The constituents of all things revolve around, and function for the spiritual factor, the consciousness. The experiences of the inner and the outer world are not complete without consciousness within us. This spiritual spark is represented in the *maṇḍala* as the central lotus by which the entire world of experience is sustained.

Another decorative *maṇḍala* in the pillar of same cave depicts a rare picture of a big fish being embraced by a hybrid form of man and fish. Philosophically it is linked with the episode of *Hari Purāṇa,* about Lord Viṣṇu incarnating in the form of fish to save the world during the *pralaya*. It may be the picture of Manu who is believed to be the forefather of Manu *kula* — the current human race, depicted as a hybrid form of fish and human, expressing his gratitude to Lord Viṣṇu for saving his race.

SCIENTIFIC PERSPECTIVE

The post-Vedic period (*c.* 600 BCE - CE 800) was the most flourishing and fruitful age because of the concerns with the development of science in ancient India. Science was dominated by the abstract philosophical theories and the systems of the Upaniṣads. The physical and the chemical theories of cosmic evolution as well as methodology of science were influenced by them. Over a period of time two theories got evolved regarding the birth of the universe:

1. The oscillating theory of the universe, according to which our present universe began with a big bang 18 billion years ago, is still expanding even now and in the future will stop, contract and end. A new explosion will occur and a new universe will be born out of the same matter.
2. The steady state theory, according to which the universe had no beginning and no end, but stays the same for ever.

The wonderful universe in which we live, its age, history, longevity, beauty and its violence were the most favourite topics amongst the philosophers all over the world from time immemorial. The Hindu philosophy strongly advocates about the repeated birth, death and rebirth of the universe and have given a divine orientation to it. *Brahman* represents our universe which has birth, growth, death or big crunch, all on the navel singularity of lord Nārāyaṇa. Nārāyaṇa represents eternity that has no birth or death according to steady state theory from whose navel arises another Brahmā, after the death of one. The word Brahmā is derived from the Sanskrit root *bṛh* — to grow and thus suggests a reality which is dynamic and alive. In the words of S. Radhakrishnan the word *Brahman* means growth and is suggestive of life, motion and progress. Vedas say that many Brahmās have passed away meaning universe is not created for the first time. This is, however an unseen principal of *adṛṣṭa* and human effort cannot account for it since it does not yet exist. The interesting fact according to Vedas is that humans are part of *yuga*s and the cosmic timescale.

Carl Sagan, the famous astrophysisist, has quoted that "Hindu religion is the only one of world's faith, dedicated to the idea that cosmos itself undergoes immense and infinite number of births and deaths and rebirths. It is the only religion in which timescales correspond to those of modern cosmology." The Western scientists popularised the theory of big bang for the birth of the universe and the beginning of time as crucial for the understanding of the origin of the universe. As explained by Stephen Hawking, if the birth of the universe was by big bang theory, the questions such as who set up the conditions for the big bang, and the events before the big bang were not answerable by scientific models.

The discovery of the expansion of the universe after the big bang changed the discussion about the origin of the universe. When the present notion of galaxies is considered and run back in time, it seems that all galaxies should have been on top of each other at some moment at which time the singularity of big bang occurred. The density of the universe and the space-time curvature was infinite, which breaks down all the known laws of science. It would mean that science alone could not predict how the universe began. The laws of physics are yet to determine how the universe began.

Regarding the future like death or dissolution — the crunch of the universe, which is again a singularity, occurs if the density of the universe is greater than a certain critical value according to the laws of physics. The gravitational attraction between the different galaxies slows down the rate of expansion and eventually stops, making the universe to contract and collapse into a big crunch, ending the "time." The events that occur "after" will be a part of another separate universe.

This, according to Stephen Hawking, is something like reincarnation.

Hindu philosophy and Vedas correlate the density that is explained by scientists to *dharma* — the moral and ethical values. When the negativity in value system goes beyond certain levels, the universe comes to an end, but the positivity is saved by Lord

Viṣṇu and he carries it over up to the rebirth of the universe in support of oscillating theory.

When the purpose of adopting fish as spokes for the body of the *maṇḍala* is analysed, which could have been just lotus petals or long strips for the body of the *maṇḍala*, the symbolism associated with fish has to be considered. The streamlined body of fish can easily move through the turbulence, for which reason Lord Viṣṇu incarnated as a fish, carrying the life force of mankind in seed form at the time of *pralaya*. Fish is an old and very suggestive symbol in the mystery language, as is also water. Fish was revered as creature of boundless liberty. The attitude of not reserving a space as their home in the ocean was viewed as an evolved psyche of liberation — *mukti* (compared to the release from ego) for which reason they were placed on the feet of Buddha symbolising restrainment from worldly desires. Similarly fish was the earlier emblem of Christ, symbolic of purity and Mesopotamians considered fish as god of waters and wisdom. The aspect of fish, which is highlighted in this *maṇḍala*, hints about auspiciousness associated with the symbol of fish. It also represents the mother goddess of primeval waters from which life grows (like the human foetus that grows in fluid medium). Fish had an impressive image all over the world. They appeared as saviours in Indian myth.

The *svastika maṇḍala* adjoining this may hint the state of storm indicated by the Marut gods in the corners that was followed by the universe getting engulfed by water at the *pralaya* and the significant role played by "fish" in reviving life in the universe after a dissolution period.

The very artistic and decorative *matsya maṇḍala* at the Bādāmi cave instigates everyone to ponder over the mystery behind the birth and the future of the universe on which we are living.

2.3. The Source of Energy : Nāga Maṇḍala at Bādāmi Cave (*Pl.* 14)

STRUCTURE OF THE MAṆḌALA

It is a circular *maṇḍala* the body of which looks like the ripples of waves in a pond. The *bindu* is not a dot, but a human form actualising the divinity. *Nāga*, the semi-divine being with the face and torso of a man, tail of a serpent, with a multi-hooded snake above his human head, depicts a god of hybrid form, between human and a snake, inhabiting the *pātāla* (the region below the earth). The *nāga devatā* has the upper limbs of a human, holds the tail part in his right hand. He wears a crown, ornaments on arms, neck, ears, a *yajñopavīta* and looks like a sovereign in the upper body, from the navel point. The lower limb is seen as a huge serpent, with distinctive scales and is coiled in 3½ circles. On the four corners are seen *apsaras*es (the celestial beauties), holding something like a full bloom lotus in their right hand, which is identical with the flower that the deity

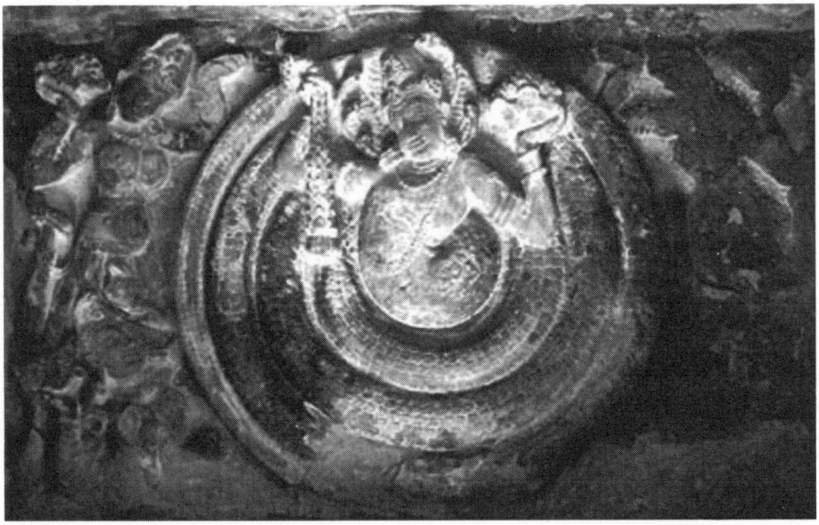

Pl. 14: Nāga Maṇḍala at the cave temple of Bādāmi.

is holding in left hand. The outer circle of this structure is decorated with scrollwork.

A PHILOSOPHICAL PERSPECTIVE

The central deity may be the representation of the atmospheric deity, dwelling in the atmospheric ocean. Right from R̥gvedic times, the *nāgas* and *nāginīs* as semi-divine forms were adored and respected in serpent forms. Later, among the snake cult followers, they enjoyed a revered status, with individualistic iconographic traits. The R̥gvedic *ahirbudhnya* (the serpent of the deep sea) also stands for an atmospheric deity, where snake is represented figuratively and is associated with *apsaras* (*nāgakanyā*) on either side. It is the representation of the folk divinity, a typical example of the hybrid iconographic trait. Considering the hybrid form of the central deity — the *nāga* king, one of the Purāṇic tales relates Nāgas as semi-divine race (the race of Kadru), inhabiting the waters, or the city of Bhogavatī, situated under the earth. They are fabled to possess a human face, with serpent-like lower extremities, like the Ananta (the king of Nāgas). In the secret doctrine, the word *nāga* stands for a serpent of wisdom. Nāgas were fabled to be wiser than serpents, and sons of will and *yoga*.

This *maṇḍala* of Bādāmi cave features a curvilinear design with an iconic representation. Such a *maṇḍala* is used in meditation, or in individual worship rites. It can be compared to a *devatā-yantra* for actualising the divinity. The deity's figure takes the place of the *bindu* (the sacred central dot) of the *maṇḍala,* which is the gathering up of forces, and the round — to the cyclical cosmic rhythm. In Hinduism, time and space are considered cyclical (*kālacakra*) and self-perpetuating. All existence is issued from a single source and ultimately returns to its point of origin. This concept is abstractly viewed as a Serpent God coiling into circles, and holding its own tail. The Nāgarāja (a cult god) for Hindus is the protector of *dharma,* is not a mortal king, or, of priest class, but the supreme, who alone is the guardian and master of the universe (for, Hindus are not followers of any accidental prophet, with historical reality, and limited mission of serving the immediate generation, with the best he had).

Śvetāśvatara Upaniṣad (1.3.4) explains that all who meditated according to the precepts of *yoga* saw the divine soul hidden deeply in its own three qualities of *sattva, rajas* and *tamas*. The divine who presides over all is perceived as a wheel with one axis and three tiers. The wheel is referred as the wheel of existence that comes into shape at the time of creation and revolves continuously till the end. The supreme deity is not only a part of the wheel but is the centre.

Perhaps the purpose of installing this type of *maṇḍala* is to enhance the function of purifying the mind and body through meditation. It is a concentration device, making concentric of the outflowing energies by turning them inward and focusing them to the central point. In this way the bio-cyclic energies are recycled. When a student of *yoga,* seated in the lotus posture, concentrates on the process of centring, this *maṇḍala* helps as a device of concentration. Hence, it is a *maṇḍala* for visual concentration that effectively draws the mind to the central source. It takes the mind directly to a trance-like state aiding the mind to realise the natural state of coherent and organised field pattern of orientation. To concentrate is to make sacred and devoting it to something. The territory of this type of *maṇḍala,* wherever it is and in whichever medium, helps in concentration and devotion. The five hoods may also hint to the awakening of the *kuṇḍalinī* (the latent and hidden psychic power) at the first five *cakra*s, which mean purifying the body of all its senses.

The deity is the personification of *bindu* of origin from which arises the eternal cycles of cosmic evolution and involution. The principal deity is conceived as unfurling itself from the *bindu* (moving through all *śakti*s or the body). The circular movement is meant to be visualised as cyclical rhythm of cosmos. The snake deity, either holding its own tail or swallowing its tail is symbolic of eternity and divine self-sufficiency. Holding the tail is also symbolic of involution that all meditation converges to the central deity.

The concept is as emanating from the *bindu*, the source of *śakti*, the epicentre of primeval energy in Indian cosmology of the Brahmā. The expansion can be designated as *vistāra* with *maṇḍala* as its logo, the *puruṣa*, representing the point of entry according to Indian aesthetics.

SCIENTIFIC PERSPECTIVE

This *maṇḍala* may suggest the cosmological model of the theory of big bang, followed by the big crunch. It holds that all matter and energy originated in the singularity at the beginning of the universe, that is a point in space-time at which the space-time curvature becomes infinite in density. Ever since the big bang, the universe has been expanding and cooling down. This singularity, at the end of the universe, is called the big crunch to dissolute. This is depicted by the head of spread of hood and the deity holding his own tail. It is the picture of the whole universe in its essential plan, in its process of emanation and of re-absorption. In other words, this *maṇḍala* represents the theory of evolution and involution, which characterise the *vikāsa* and *saṁkoca* — the expansion and contraction of the world process in support of the oscillating theory of universe. When viewed from the periphery to centre, the opposite direction, it is the involutory mode and that which is indicative of a higher state of consciousness. It is like ascending the ladder by suppressing the lower, to a field of unity. The personality changes from egocentric, fragmented awareness to a Cosmocentric wholeness. The *maṇḍala* is aimed at the goal of return to the supreme centre.

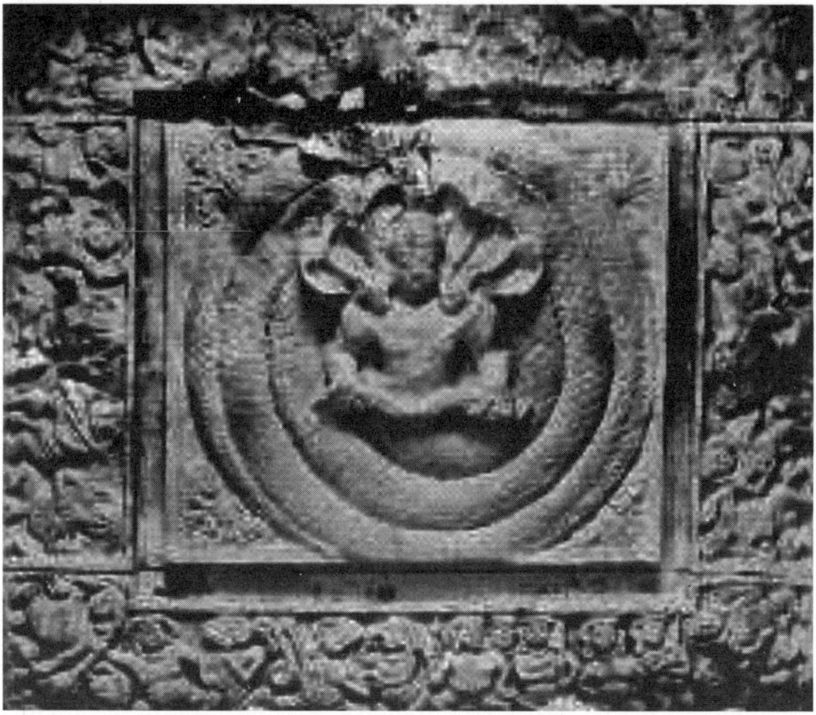

Pl. 15: Another *maṇḍala* of snake at Bādāmi cave temple.

The other perspective in the concept of this *maṇḍala* can be grouped under the doctrine of political *maṇḍala* — the sphere of circle. The underlying Hindu idea of the balance of power with the theory of sovereignty is also hinted. Here the sovereign is established at the *nābhi* — as the centre of gravity of the system, and he is the Lord of the *maṇḍala*. The concentric circles of the serpent, around the human body are like the wheel, the symbol of sovereignty — the territory around the *cakravartī kṣetra*; even the end part of the *kṣetra* is under the protection of the sovereign. Whichever way it is analysed, the ultimate focus of this *maṇḍala* is that all understanding, knowledge and principals; based on earthly consciousness, bow before the mystery of the centre, the point from which all goes forth and to which all returns. As is true of most of the maṇḍalic process, the end is a return to the centre or the beginning point, indicating the re-establishment of harmony — a state of union/liberation, meaning an entry into the point of origin.

This *maṇḍala* also leads one to visualisation and realisation of the source of energy within him, the *nābhi* (the seat of *Maṇipūra cakra*), the source from which the form-creating energy flows. In Hinduism, a coiled serpent is symbolic of the serpent power (the psychic energy of the *Kuṇḍālinī* power), in its coiled up or dormant state, wound into a "closed circuit." Another symbol of a coiled serpent biting its tail is symbolic of self-sufficiency, and when they coiled they formed spirals. Both circles and spirals were seen as symbols of eternity.

2.4. Maṇḍala of the Cosmic bi-unity at the Somanāthpur Temple (*Pl.* 16)

HISTORICAL BACKGROUND

Somanāthpur is situated in the Mysore district of Karnataka state, 32 km away from Śrīraṅgapaṭṭana on the banks of river Kāverī amidst lasting rural serenity. According to the epigraphical records, Soma, a *daṇḍanāyaka* (commander-in-chief) under the Hoysaḷa ruler Narasiṁha III (CE 1254-91), built the Keśava temple in CE 1268. It is an example of the fully evolved style of Hoysaḷa architecture, the most complete and symmetrical, although it is the smallest of the three great temples in Karnataka. Somanāthpur was an *agrahāra* (a great centre of traditional learning).

The temple is a famous one in Karnataka, highly ornate, unique in design, perfect in proportions, raised on a platform (*jagatī*) of 1 m high, and built in greenish chloritic schist also

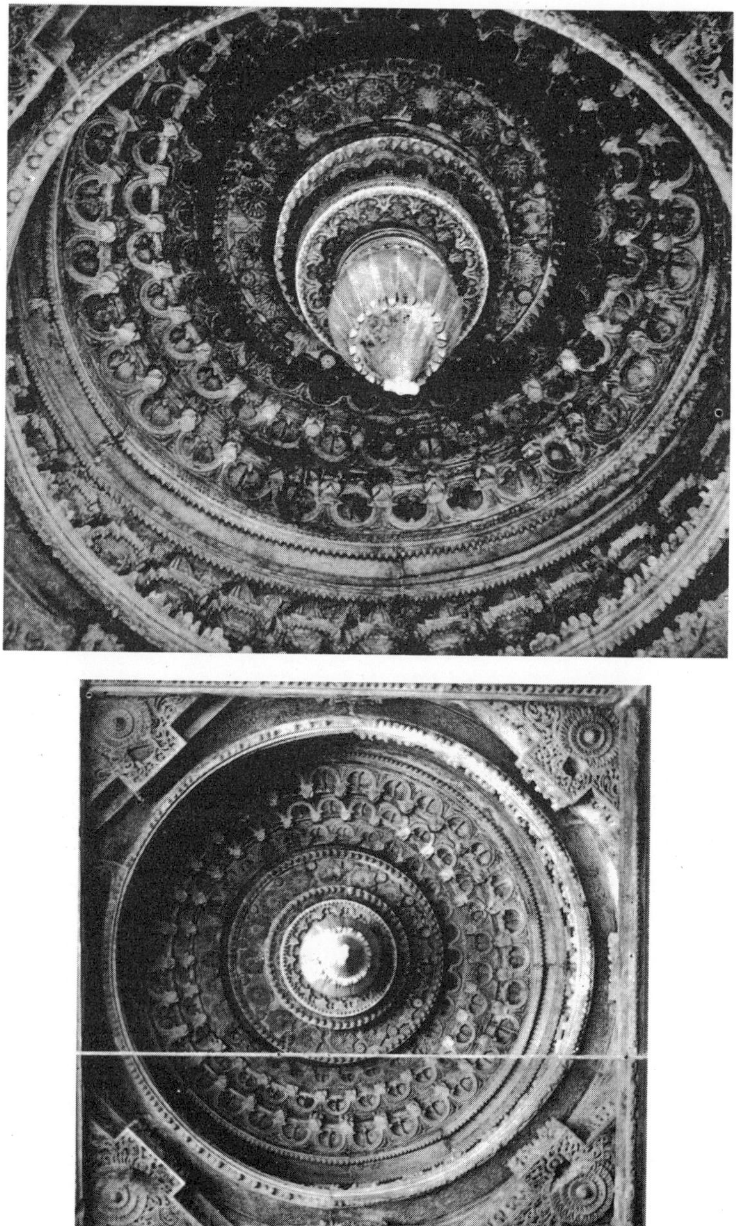

Pl. 16: *Maṇḍala* at the Somanāthpur temple.

called soapstone. All the three sanctums are stellar in shape and the platform follows the star shape. The temple is *trikūṭācala* (with three sanctums) and has three elaborately carved pinnacles with a common *navaraṅga* hall. The *navaraṅga* or the middle hall has six ceiling panels and the *mukhamaṇḍapa* or the front hall has nine. Everyone of them is nearly 3 ft deep and very artistically executed, no two of them being similar in design. The central ceiling (*bhuvaneśvarī*) has a huge circular *maṇḍala* enclosed in a square boundary. The three sanctums once housed the beautifully carved idols of Keśava, Janārdana and Veṇugopāla. But now the idol of Keśava is not there.

STRUCTURE OF THE MAṆḌALA

The *maṇḍala* of the *bhuvaneśvarī* of Somanāthpur temple is a huge circular *maṇḍala* with several concentric rings — the *valayas* as they are called. The central core is a conical lotus bud, hanging down like a pendant. This bud is encircled by sixteen-pointed petals. The special feature of this *maṇḍala* is that the petals in concentric circles are semi-circular in shape with the specific design of two halves inside separated by a bifurcation. Immediately after the lotus bud is a small circle of such rounded petals that is followed by a circle of miniature cones — the fractal representation of the central bud. The next circle has 16 lotuses (*padma*) alternating with 16 identical miniature lotuses. This is again encircled by a *valaya* of conical fractal designs, which are probably 108 in number.

The following *valaya,* constituting the body of the *maṇḍala,* is made up of three concentric circles, all with the same design of a semi-circular petal, with the specific design of two halves of an egg or a seed inside. Number of petals are 30 but the outermost one has 31 petals. This structure is enclosed in a thick circle, made of three concentric circles, a plain *vīthi* on either side of which are innumerable conical fractal representations.

This whole structure is enclosed in a square courtyard, the boundary. On all the four corners are the *padma* design, aniconic representation of *pañcāyatana maṇḍala*.

The special feature in this *maṇḍala* is that the petals in each circle are rounded in shape. Representation of round petals is seen when a *gaṇa* (a troop of demi-gods or attendants of the main deity) is indicated. The 16 petals according to the significance of numerology may indicate the *puruṣa* who consists of 16 parts (*kalā*).

A PHILOSOPHICAL PERSPECTIVE

As a special feature the *maṇḍala* has several fractal and self-repeating design of two halves in a round petal, along the circumference of the concentric circles. The halves when joined resemble an egg which is again a dominant, self-explanatory, meaningful symbol for the mystery of original creation. The egg or seed is an emblem of potentiality. On division it reveals the complementary forces necessary for the law of creation. The two halves in each petal is perhaps a representation of the cosmic bi-unity of Hindu divinities of male and female forces of creation. It may also be the representation of the equality that exists between the two cosmic energies of Śiva and Śakti in a symbolic form, conjoined in each round petal of the *maṇḍala* and representing unity in duality.

While thinking about the mysteries and multitude of the variety in creation, the ancient philosophers categorised the process of creation into three groups:

1. *Saṅkarṣaṇa* — meaning the act of drawing together, and contracting. All the five elements — the earth, water, fire, air and space were understood to be the essential components of all living forms, which was the most fundamental act in creation.

2. *Pradyumna* — meaning the God of love. *Dyumna* means splendour, energy, wealth and inspiration. The life force created by the five elements got divided into two principals that were equal but opposite forces of nature, recognised as the static and the dynamic forces or the male and female forces. The multitude of forms were created by the union of the male and female forces.

3. *Aniruddha* — meaning unobstructed and free. The living forms that were created by the union of the male and female principals gave birth to the multitude of living things in this universe and the process is an eternal one. In mythological connection, Aniruddha is the son of Pradyumna.

The picture of the *maṇḍala* can be read as the five elements (*śaṅkarśana*) represented as cones in four corners plus the central one, the petals with two halves as the male and female principles (*pradyumna*) and the multitude of petals as the uncountable living forms created by the union of the male and female forms (*aniruddha*).

The absolute reality — the *Nirguṇa Brahman* or Paramaśiva, represented as *mahābindu*, is by the combination of two halves, the pure consciousness and the power consciousness. According to the Sāṁkhya philosophy, the world consists of basic principles, which are made up of matter (*prakṛti*) and spirit (*puruṣa*). In this system, there is no creator, nothing divine, or more important. Life is created by both, which is an eternal law and uncaused. But Vedānta says that *puruṣa* is the energetic force in the universe, of which *prakṛti* is the dynamic part. *Prakṛti* is equated to nature, the great producer of beings, containing the *jīva* (the divine life force), in the *śarīra* (the body). They are two but essentially one, as one cannot survive without the other. This logic is perhaps the theme of the *maṇḍala*. The theory of *prakṛti* and *puruṣa* is a direct development of the idea of Ardhanārīśvara conceived as androgynous. *Puruṣa* and *prakṛti* (Śiva and Śakti) are the two aspects of *Brahman*, the *avyakta*. This can be compared to the "Matter and energy equivalent" according to Einstein's theory.

Bṛhadāraṇyaka Upaniṣad (1.IV.3), has interesting information regarding the androgynous aspect. Prajāpati, at the beginning of creation, felt alarmed at his own solitude when he realised that there was none other than himself. He did not feel joy as he was alone. He then desired to have another soulmate much like the husband and wife. So he divided the androgynous form into two parts like the two halves of the pea and the void was filled by woman. New life was born when he approached her. The idea remained throughout the centuries as the keystone of all Indian gnostic thoughts and was progressively clarified and expressed in symbolic form. The *maṇḍala* of Somanāthpur was designed probably with this theme.

In philosophical terms, the world stands on opposites. They complement and glorify each other and do not contradict. The universe is an expansion of the mystic combination of Śiva and Śakti equation. The two principles, though diametrically opposing, are identical halves essentially. *Śiva Purāṇa* compares these *puruṣa* and *prakṛti* forces to the moon and its beam, or *prakāśa* and *vimarśa* (light and its dispersal) of the light, which cannot be isolated. Śiva (*puruṣa*), the male energy, is the cosmic consciousness, as the static substratum to all phenomena. Śakti (*prakṛti*) is the female energy, though opposite, is complementary to Śiva, and is active, creative, mobile and dynamic, in contrast to the static force. The intense impulse is of procreation, in which Śiva and Śakti join to produce the *bindu*, the primordial seed of the universe. The inseparable relationship between matter and energy or the static and dynamic forces, is explained in Purāṇic and mythological stories as Lord Śiva and Pārvatī or Lord Viṣṇu and Lakṣmī, personifying the inseparable relationship of husband and wife.

The fully created cosmos (*sṛṣṭi*) is indicated to be arising from the male and female principles of the cosmic pair. The corresponding energy patterns are indicated to be existing right from microcosmic to macrocosmic, at all levels. The mutual dependency between the two forces is so great that they remain inseparable, since each requires the other in order to manifest its total nature. The "Cosmic bi-unity" is paralleled in different levels of universe as "Psychic bi-unity" in all categories of males and females.

The cosmic bi-unity was represented both in symbols and anthropomorphic form. Symbolically the *puruṣa* (the male force) is indicated as a triangle with apex upwards and *prakṛti* (the female force) is indicated as a downward triangle with apex pointing downward. The interlacing of two triangles meant the union symbolically. But in the Somanāthpur *maṇḍala* it is seen as two halves of a seed. In anthropomorphic form, an iconographical representation of this inseparability of forces is seen as Ardhanārīśvara in mythology, which is interpreted as the partial illumination of the whole. The circular *maṇḍala* represents that the whole universe lies extended between the two opposites, but complementary principles reasoning out that unity is the foundation of duality. All creations in the cosmos is the result of the creative play between the two forces is expressed beautifully through fractal, self-repeating representations of what is in nature at macrocosmic level, is the process at microcosmic level also. The only logic to account for the number of petals to be 31 in the girdle of three layers is that 31 is the number of *Atharvan* and *Kṛṣṇa Yajurveda* Upaniṣads.

Lord Kṛṣṇa says in *Bhagavad-Gītā* (13.20, 21) that *puruṣa* and *prakṛti* are like the cause and experience. *Prakṛti* is matter — the field, and *puruṣa* — the spirit is the knower. They are called the *kṣetra* and *kṣetrajña*, which are conceived as the two aspects of the lord and hence are without a beginning. The interplay and union project that creation continues to preserve and dissolve what is created by it. The play of matter and spirit is the cause of *saṁsāra*. This combination of matter and spirit is not an accomplished union but is only a mutual superimposition.

In between the first and the second layer of semi-circular petal layers are the motifs of big and small *padma*s. They are rationalised into the expanding and contracting state of mind as lotuses, representing the expansion and contraction of the *līlā*s (pleasures and pains) of the two complementary principles in the process of creation. (It is compared to the 16 digits (*kalā*s) of the moon and its light and dark phases. The moon in Hindu philosophy is compared to mind, its joys and sorrows experienced.)

These two different zones, separated by fractal circle, also hint that the law of bi-unity holds good at both the divine and human levels.

Beyond the three nested circles runs a passage called *vīthi*. Philosophically if the inner deity is compared to the *buddhi*, the *vīthi* is for movement of the *manas* and the square grid is compared to the body (*ahaṁkāra*). The outer square enclosure is the physical boundary often also termed as the *pīṭha* (the seat or throne of *maṇḍala*).

The central deity is surrounded on all the four corners, by four other deities of *pañcāyatana maṇḍala*. It is a symbolic and aniconic representation of the five deities of *pañcāyatana*, represented through lotus each with three concentric rings. The five deities represented in *pañcāyatana* are Gaṇeśa, Sūrya, Viṣṇu, Durgā and Śiva. Since the temple is built for God Keśava, the central deity is Viṣṇu. Meditating on these five deities is referred to as fivefold worship (*pañcopāsanā*), which is mostly represented in all *maṇḍala*s.

A SCIENTIFIC PERSPECTIVE

The circular *maṇḍala* is a symbol of universe. Hindu philosophy advocates that time and space are considered cyclical and self-perpetuating. The process of evolution and involution is not viewed as a linear motion of single direction but a circle of cyclic rhythms. The planets and constellations move in orbits to trace the expanding and contracting spheres. These curvilinear cosmic images are indicated in the roundness of the petals, surrounding each unit of Śiva-Śakti principle.

A comparative picture that can be drawn between the details of the *maṇḍala* and the constitution of matter is that — matter existing anywhere in the universe can be divided into particles, each called an atom (compared to the circular petals of the *maṇḍala*). In India, every rational school of philosophy whether Hindu, Jain, or Buddhist had something to say about the nature of elementary particles. Vaiśeṣika, which is one of the six Hindu schools of philosophy of orthodox Vedic system of logic, espouses a form of atomism, and postulates that all objects in the physical universe are reducible to a finite number of indivisible atoms, which are continuous in a matter (originally proposed by the sage Kaṇāda, around the sixth century BCE). Later philosophers elaborated further on this notion that atoms could combine either in pairs called diads or in threes called triads which act as the determining factor for different physical properties of substances found in nature. The *maṇḍala* can be considered as a picture of the earlier atomic theory and the molecular theory of matter. The atom turned out to be not the end of the road, but had component parts (the positive and the negative), because the two identical halves present in each petal clearly indicate that they are two opposite forces, two unlike charges that are attracted or else they would have been placed in a consecutive pattern. According to the laws of electromagnetism, in the primary form, all matter is made up of particles that can be compared to the rounded petals.

Every particle has two types of charges, which, by convention are labelled positive and negative. Like charges repel and unlike charges attract. These charges are never created or destroyed and they just exist like that in nature.

The ideas about atoms were mainly speculative. The old atomic theory is unable to explain the new facts. It should be viewed as a hypothesis that was put forward as a metaphysical one and not as a scientifically verified principle. The *maṇḍala* is more a conceptual scheme adopted to explain the facts of nature.

At mythological level and anthropomorphic form, this concept is seen as the Śiva-Śakti forces, as the two halves of Ardhanārīśvara, and in non-mythological level, it explains the non-separability of positive and negative forces for the continuity of equilibrium. Separation indicates a state of chaos and disequilibrium. (At mythological level, it is explained as Śiva lying down as a corpse, when separated from the Śakti.)

The *maṇḍala* is a striking representation of the cosmic bi-unity, the union of opposites and the Śiva-Śakti equation that contains a constant tendency towards fusion of the two principles to initiate another stage of growth. The polarity is also explained for the potential or static force uniting with the kinetic or dynamic force, in an abstract form in the *maṇḍala*.

Despite the fact that universe is so homogeneous on a large scale, it contains local irregularities. These are thought to have developed from the interstitial force of gravity. The expanding and the contracting *padma*s in the third circle hints about the irregularities in the density of matter distribution.

FRACTAL REPRESENTATION

The Śiva-Śakti equation and the central deity as a cone are represented as fractals of self-repeated motifs in the concentric layers at different levels and in varying sizes. The inner circle has smaller cones and the same cones are seen on the outer concentric layers, which are identical with the central design, but are miniature in form. These fractals reinforce the Hindu thought that cosmic order is identical at both macrocosmic and microcosmic levels, which bring about a feeling of unity with the cosmos and its ruling power. The two identical halves in each round petal signifying the male and female forces, are also repeated as fractals, in all the concentric circles, to suggest the aspect of the cosmic bi-unity that is at macro and microcosmic levels. The realisation of oneness by setting out to dissolve the boundaries between man and divine is beautifully expressed in the fractals of the *maṇḍala*.

2.5. Rhythm of Life in the Maṇḍala of Keśava Temple, Somanāthpur (*Pl.* 17)

HISTORICAL BACKGROUND

Somanāthpur is situated in the Mysore district of Karnataka state, 32 km away from Śrīraṅgapaṭṭana on the banks of river Kāverī amidst lasting rural serenity. According to the epigraphical records, Soma, a *daṇḍanāyaka* (commander-in-chief) under the Hoysaḷa ruler Narasiṁha III (CE 1254-91), built the Keśava temple in CE 1268. It is an example of the fully evolved style of Hoysaḷa architecture. Somanāthpur was an *agrahāra*, a great centre of traditional learning.

The temple is a famous one in Karnataka, highly ornate, unique in design, perfect in proportions, raised on a platform (*jagatī*) of 1 m high, and built in greenish chlotic schist also called soapstone. All the three sanctums are stellar in shape and the platform follows the star shape. The temple is *trikūṭācala* (with three sanctums), and has three elaborately carved pinnacles with a common *navaraṅga* hall. The central ceiling (*bhuvaneśvarī*) has a huge circular *maṇḍala* enclosed in a square boundary. The three sanctums once housed the beautifully carved idols of Keśava, Janārdana and Veṇugopāla. But now the idol of Keśava is not there.

STRUCTURE OF THE MAṆḌALA

The central dot or the sacred *bindu* in the conical lotus bud is like a pendant, from which arises the 12 radiating spokes of a wheel. This circle of wheel is enclosed in an octagonal boundary that is indicative of the eight cardinal directions and space in infinity. Around this, three distinct lines like creepers are drawn in an interwoven design to create a pattern. It is difficult to trace the beginning or end of the lines as it looks like a close circuit diagram. These three lines have self-repeating designs of scrollwork all through, giving a picture of fluid but rhythmic movement. This is enclosed in an outer circle, which has conical fractal miniature representations identical like the central cone. The ancient art of knot pattern without dead ends, with overlapping technique of geometric designs such as square and circle is beautifully carved in the medium of stone. The whole structure is enclosed in the square courtyard (*bhūpura*).

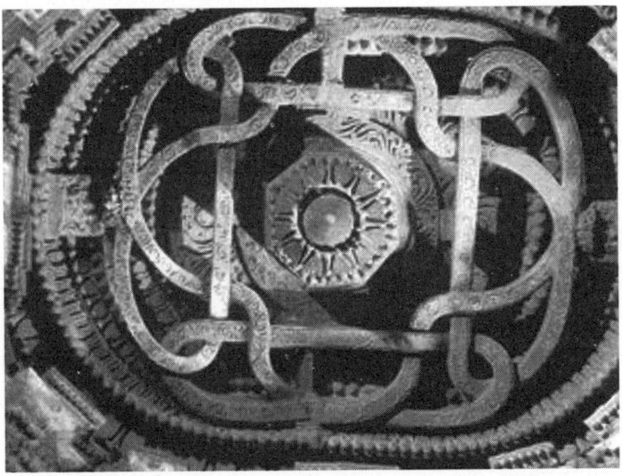

Pl. 17: Rhythm of life in the *Maṇḍala* at the Somanāthpur temple.

A PHILOSOPHICAL PERSPECTIVE

The core of the *maṇḍala*, the central dot and the conical bud symbolise the spiritual plane and the deity, which is free from dimensions. It is the gathering centre, in which the outside energies are drawn. The dot looks like nothing, yet it is everything — the essence of cosmic order. This *bindu* — the source of all energy is encircled by a wheel of 12 spokes. Twelve is the number of sun according to the Hindu sacred numerology and represents the 12 months of the year or the 12 zodiacal signs and the continuous revolution of months, making a year. Interspersed with the spokes are the miniature *padma*s that look like stars, which symbolise the 24 epithets of Lord Viṣṇu, the presiding deity of the temple. The octagonal boundary is again symbolic of eight directions or infinity.

Encircling this are the three interwoven patterns, of which it is hard to trace the beginning and end. A detailed study of this design reveals three basic shapes, a square that is followed by four-petalled figures and four lobes-like structures interlocking the square to the petals on all four sides. All of them looking like knotwork of loops are inscribed in a circle. Square design symbolises the earth or the body, stability and *sr̥ṣṭi*. Enthusiasm, the sign of life, is symbolised by the four petals — like the psychological vibrations associated with symbolism of *Mūlādhāra cakra*. The representations of life and enthusiasm are interlocked to symbolise that life and enthusiasm are interdependent, inseparable and are the fuel to keep the life going. The surrounding circle represents *laya,* the ultimate merging. These can be compared to the three phases of cosmic process — the creation, sustenance and dissolution. In other words, they are the interrelated activities of basic faculties of reproduction, maintenance and self-realisation. The square is symbolic of the physical boundary of the body, the petals are an expression to the psyche of the human desire for preserving and expanding on what they already have. Human mind longs for boundless expansion but encounters death before it is reached as desires are infinite in nature. Life and preservation are like two forces that make humans exist, as when the love for living and preservation of body is lost, it encounters death and dissolution. The brevity of human life, the fear of death and the hope of rebirth were major symbolic themes in ancient culture and philosophy. The wholeness of living things involves an interrelated activity of all the three forces. On the entire three interwoven patterns are spiral designs in continuous mode that are indicative of the pulsating cycles of energy, the continuous and ongoing progressive movement of life force. Each design hints that life just exists, grows and merges with the next generation and ultimately ends with the *pañcabhūta*s after giving birth to its younger replicas. The continuous mode of scrollwork design hints that they are not the isolated grains of matter, but are the Probability Patterns and interconnections in the inseparable Cosmic Web, revealing their dynamic character. The events at all moments and locations in space-time are directly perceived and governed by the supreme power, shaping the material space-time history. Life on earth is a continuous and eternal movement, which has neither beginning nor end, and the central deity "sun" is the only constant factor, the donator of energy for all living beings and hence revered as God. The theory of emanation (that which flows from a source) where the light coming from the sun eternally leaves the sun unchanged is also pictorised in the *maṇḍala*. In this context, the sun can be compared also to the *ātman* or the *Brahman* — the imperishable and the changeless one (*ādhidaivata* as it is called) — while the matter that is conceived to have formed of the five elements — *pañcabhūta*s — is ever changing and perishable in nature (*ādhibhūta*). The *maṇḍala* suggests a universal theory that the activities of the world like birth, maintenance and multiplication are based on the energy drawn by sun God. In the great statement of *Kaṭhopaniṣad* (2.9.15) the divine is defined as that which is self-luminous, shining and causes everyone to shine: "All shine after him who shines:" The definition of God, the controller of all the cosmic order which knows no destruction, is represented in Hindu philosophy in any form as a man, woman, anything or any symbolic figure.

The aspect of "Life" in the *maṇḍala* is seen in the context of cosmos and not with a particular living object. The eternal truth that Life on cosmos is going on from millions of years and will run for an indefinite period is represented in the continuity of scrollwork design that is indicated and drawing energy from Sun God constantly. The truth of the substratum, right from the lowest of worms, to the highly evolved form, everywhere and at all times that universe creates living things, preserves it and destroys it, is the beautiful concept that is expressed through this artistic diagram, which is beyond one's ability to describe in words. Only the manifestations of life on earth are varied according to the grossness or the subtlety of the form. The labyrinth design of intricate passage, with decorative loose knots represents infinity or longevity of the energy bundles. Such designs in which it is hard to find the way out are used in temples to symbolise initiation routes.

This *maṇḍala* reinforces the royal secrets and the secret of secrets that is explained in *Bhagavad-Gītā* regarding the impermanence of all forms that life is *anityam, asukham,* and *lokam.* "Nothing is permanent in the world, life, joys and sorrows are all temporary phases." Change is the only certainty. Humans are constantly changing with time. So any perceived continuity or seeing constancy is just an illusion of the perception. When ancient scriptures comment on the illusory nature of all creation, they are alluding to the impermanence and deception created by sensory perceptions. The continuum of existence is only a mirage. Understanding the primordial symbolism of this *maṇḍala* can lead not only to greater awareness that every event is part of a single process, but also to a transformation of the ways in which a man responds to the world — transmutating him to a spiritual sphere of understanding what is unchangeable, permanent and eternal.

A SCIENTIFIC PERSPECTIVE

This *maṇḍala,* when viewed with a focus on its symbols, provided a base structure revealing harmonious interaction of various energy forms. Life here is viewed as a force and energy, that has been existing, growing and dissoluting on the universe and hence it is flowing. It is without an *ādi* (beginning) or *anta* (end). Only sun is the constant force. The 12 spokes confirm that the central deity is sun.

Mankind has been dependent upon energy from sun's lights both directly and indirectly. Our awareness of the value of sun's rays revolves around the manner in which we benefit from the energy. When the origin and sustenance of individual life is rationalised, comparing it to individual design on the three interwoven lines, it is analogous to the law of conservations of energy, which is one of the most significant laws of nature.

Sun is the constant donor of energy. Scientifically it is said that sun exists for 10 billion years. Every living thing that is born of the *pañcabhūta*s receives the heat and light energy from the sun and grows. Here again we can recall the saying of *Bhagavad-Gītā* (8.3) that all actions take place in time by the interweaving of the forces of nature. When it dissolutes, that life energy is released back to the universe as the same five elements. Hence there is no loss of any energy. Law of conservation of energy states that energy can neither be created nor destroyed. Total energy of an isolated system is constant, but can change its form, from one to another. The life energy begets another living replica and the static energy is transferred to potential energy. This emphasis on movement, flow and change is not only characteristic of Eastern mystical traditions but has been an essential aspect of the world view of mystics throughout the ages. This process that is timebound is going on and on in nature, which is indicated through the running packets of scroll design on the body of the *maṇḍala* suggesting the viewpoint of connection. The rectangular conduits in which the scrollwork designs are engraved may also represent the idea of wave guides, which are used as the most effective and efficient way of energy propagation.

The "steady state theory" also known as the infinite universe theory or the continuous creation theory deals with the study of the universe and its origin. According to this, the universe is the same everywhere and for all time — both past and future. Even though the universe is expanding, it does not change its look over time as it has neither beginning nor end. The *maṇḍala* gives a clear picture of this theory. This logic accounts for the harmony and equilibrium that is existing in nature.

According to the Indian evolutionary theory, the cosmos is to be viewed as a continuum. All that is born develop, age and dissolve into the primordial reality that gave birth. This dynamism is expressed in Hinduism through figure of Naṭarāja. Lord Śiva (the cosmic dancer) is perhaps the most perfect personification of the theme of rhythm and the participation of all forms in the rhythm of the dynamic universe. The continuity of cosmic order is like a circle with neither a beginning nor an end and there is no period when the universe got static. This ongoing process of the cosmic order is explained graphically in the *maṇḍala*.

The central deity is conceived as a conical pendant, with a dot. The same motif is repeated in miniature shape at great numbers in the *maṇḍala*. We can see them in a circle around the radiating spokes of the inner circle. The outermost circles are full of this particular motif. The self-repetition of a motif at various levels in varying sizes but identical in pattern is an aspect of fractals in scientific terms. (For details on fractals, see the section 1.10, on fractals) This is to reinforce the presence of the deity at macro and microcosmic levels of cosmos, establishing oneness with the central deity.

The *maṇḍala* at Keśava temple, Somanāthpur, appears to be a symbolic picture of the movement of life of a living organism at microcosmic level. It is seeing life from the context of the cosmos for an easy understanding of the law of nature. It is an aid to realise through knotwork for what life is in its eternal connections and flow of unity, holding things together. It is perhaps a figure to indicate that the life force or activity in cosmos is to be viewed as continuum, which is dependent eternally on the centre, the Sun. All actions in the world are by the life force, for life and through life. Beings create beings. Each member is connected in spirit and is always next to each other. All that is born develop with age and finally dissolve into the primordial reality that gave birth. In this uninterrupted cosmic order, there was never a specific beginning nor will there be a last, which is in support of steady state theory of universe — or a period at which universe will remain in a static phase of total integration or total disintegration. Nyāya Vaiśeṣika says that knowledge, even in a small aspect of cosmic order, leads one to *mokṣa*. *Maṇḍala*s in temples, when viewed with an analytical thought, reveals the secrets of the cosmic order.

2.6. The Birth of the Universe in the Maṇḍala of Belavadi Vīranārāyaṇa Temple (*Pl.* no. 18)

The size and age of cosmos is beyond ordinary human understanding. Even to comprehend that our tiny planetary home earth is lost somewhere between the immensity and eternity of cosmos, needs lot of understanding of astronomical information. In the two *maṇḍala*s of Belavadi Vīranārāyaṇa temple an attempt is made in the first one probably to present a picture of the birth of the universe and the relationship of time and space associated with it. The second one is probably exploring the astronomical time cycles according to the ancient Hindu philosophy. It looks like a speculation that God has created everything and the universe we are living with all the manifestations of matter is the evidence of God.

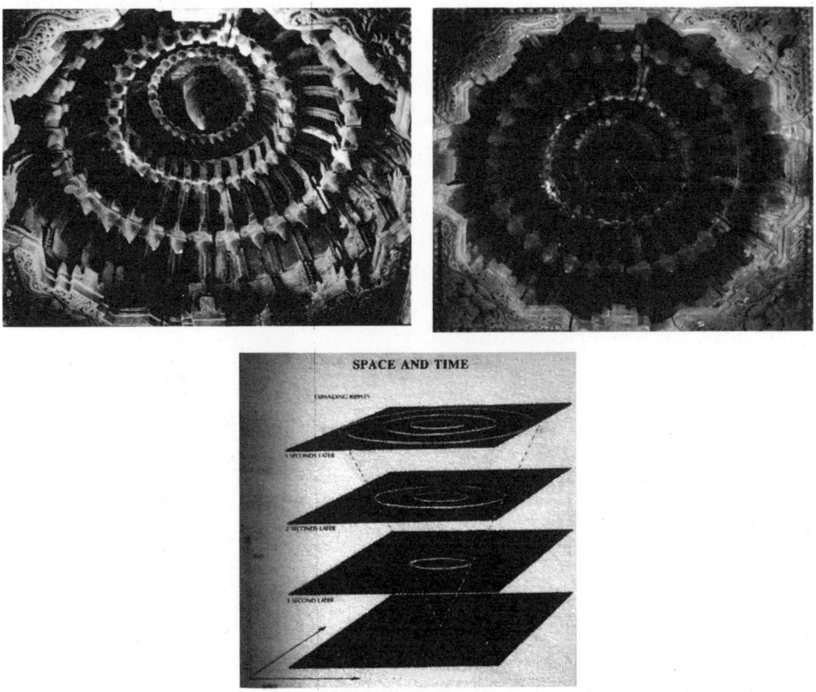

Pl. 18: *Maṇḍala* at the Belavadi Vīranārāyaṇa temple.

The first one of the two *maṇḍala*s is a beautiful design, resembling the umbrella spread of star sparklers. It is in the ceiling of the *raṅga-maṇḍapa* of the temple. A *maṇḍala* with the same design can also be seen even in the roof ceiling of Somanāth-pur temple.

HISTORICAL BACKGROUND

Belavadi is located 29 km south-west of Chikmagalur town, and 10 km north-west of another famous Hoysaḷa temple of Halebiḍ. The temple was built in CE 1200, by the Hoysaḷa king Vīra Ballāla II. It is a Vaiṣṇavite temple, exhibiting the perfect Hoysaḷa architectural idiom. This very ornate temple has a unique plan with two shrines facing each other, on either side of a spacious *maṇḍapa* hall, containing three bays. The third shrine is an old construction. All three shrines have the deity Viṣṇu in different forms of Veṇugopāla (Kṛṣṇa with flute), Yoga Narasiṁha in sitting posture and Vīranārāyaṇa. Each shrine has a complete and well decorated superstructure, making it an ornate *trikūṭa* (three towers) temple. The temple built in soapstone — the chloritic schist, is well known as the largest example of Hoysaḷa architecture. It looks different from the Belūr temple, which is known for intricate sculptures.

STRUCTURE OF THE MAṆḌALA

Lotus buds in varying sizes is the main feature of this *maṇḍala*. The central point in the shape of the conical lotus bud is fixed on an octagonal base. Encircling this are three distinct layers of consecutive circles, decorated with the replicas of the central conical bud in miniature forms that are 32 in number in each circle. The cones of each circle are connected to the central one by a longitudinal strip, resulting in 32 equal divisions covering all 360° of the *maṇḍala*. The three-tiered *maṇḍala* is enclosed in a square *bhūpura* courtyard, the corners of which are decorated with *kīrtimukha*s and laced with scrollwork design. The highlight of the *maṇḍala* is that the cones in consecutive circles are in an increasing order of size.

The structural details when analysed look like a theme on the birth of universe, about which ancient saints as far back as Ṛgvedic period (5000 BCE roughly) had put forth their views.

PHILOSOPHICAL PERSPECTIVE

The central conical lotus bud of the *maṇḍala,* representing Lord Nārāyaṇa (as the temple is dedicated to Vīranārāyaṇa) is the aniconic representation of the god, and is mounted on an octagonal base that is indicative of the eight directions. Each of the three concentric circles around the central bud has 32 miniature replicas as the fractal representation. According to the sacred numerology, 32 is indicative of 32 placements of numbers rising from one (*eka*), to infinity, like *eka, daśa, śata, sahasra* . . . up to *parārdha* which was considered to be infinity beyond 10 to the power of 32. Since it is a circle, the first point *eka* cannot be defined. The three tiers probably represent the three worlds of *bhū, bhuvar* and *suvar* — the earth, sky and ethereal zones in which the *Brahman* transforms himself into the world. Hindu myth of *līlā* — the divine rhythmic play that goes on in endless cycles of the one becoming into many and the many returning into the one is explained in this *maṇḍala*. Here the universe is explained as a rhythmically moving cosmos in organic state. In the Ṛgvedic hymn of Puruṣa-Sūkta (10th *maṇḍala*), the cosmic form of the *Puruṣa* (the supreme power of the cosmic man), is described as Lord Nārāyaṇa who is omnipresent and omniscient.

The Upaniṣads attribute the creator of this universe to be the *Brahman* (the *puruṣa*) on the consciousness basis. *Brahman* is the sole creator and the cause in the whole expansion of the world (the *brahmāṇḍa*) and its material. The beginning of the creator is described in *Taittirīya* and *Bṛhadāraṇyaka Upaniṣad* as *Svayambhū* "that created by itself." *Brahman* creates the world and then enters in it, pervading all things like the salt that is dissolved in water pervades the water. While discussing about how the relationless *Brahman* is related to the world, it is presumed that the world of relations does not in any way affect the nature of *Brahman,* as *Brahman* can and does exist apart from the world of relations. Many passages of Upaniṣads declare that world is only a development of the absolute spirit, and does not insist on how and when God created the world as it means he is bound by an account of time and space. World is only an expression of the supreme power, whose nature is a system of spontaneity or self-evolving autonomy. Self-expression becomes the essence, with the idea that the world is God's revelation of himself. His joy assumes all these forms.

The cosmic form of this power is described in *Bhagavad-Gītā* (ch. XI), where the vastness of the concept of the *puruṣa* and the significance of its sheer dimensions are explained. It explains that lord is one dynamic truth who is boundless in form on every side, with neither a beginning nor an end. He is a mass of radiance, shining everywhere, all round like a blazing sun. From this sea of substratum, like the appearance of waves, the pluralistic world of phenomena arises, exists and merges into it. The spark of life in everyone that is present as conscious principal is indicated to be present in the entire world of objects. "By you alone the space between the heaven, earth and all the quarters of the sky are pervaded." The concept of the universal oneness is expressed in the present *maṇḍala* in a coded form using fractals. The concept of *puruṣa* in the centre, who is perfect in form, creates perfect things. Even when infinite parts are drawn from it, it still retains a perfect form — as described in the *śloka*:

> *pūrṇam ada pūrnaṁ idam, pūrṇāt pūrṇam udacyate* ।
> *pūrṇasya pūrṇam ādāya, pūrṇamevā vaśiṣyate* ॥

The *puruṣa* who is *pūrṇa* (perfect) in the centre, is depicted to create uncountable perfect forms in all directions according to the *maṇḍala* of this temple.

Puruṣa-Sūkta explains the form of the soul of the universe, to be with thousand heads, thousand feet and eyes, giving the concept of *virāṭ* — whose limbs are the cosmos. (Thousand is to be viewed here as a plural number, uncountable or infinite and not for the numerical value of a thousand.) This popular *śloka* speaks of the Supreme Being, as the creator of the universe, and how man is related to both the God and the universe.

> *sahasra śīrṣā puruṣaḥ sahasrākṣa, sahasrapāt* ।
> *sabhūmim viśvato vṛtvā atyatiṣṭa daśāṅgulam* ॥

The *puruṣa* also transcends covering the earth from every side like the clay pervades the pot, and stands like a milking cow in the heart region, which is not more than *daśāṅgula* (10 *aṅgula*s) (*aṅgula* is a small unit of measurement). The expression can also be compared to the *Hiraṇyagarbha* the cosmic womb from which the energy of all life force is born.

Puruṣa is the central conical lotus bud and is present in the infinite parts as lotus buds that are represented as self-repeating fractals in the *maṇḍala* of Belavadi Vīranārāyaṇa temple.

The concept naturally leads to an inquiry, since when and from where did it start. The aspects of time and space get associated. When the conical buds of the *maṇḍala* are viewed as the space (matter) and the long strips emerging from the centre are viewed as time, the *maṇḍala* can also be the aniconic representation of Lord Nārāyaṇa in his *yoganidrā*.

In the iconic representation in the *garbhagṛha* of Hindu temples, on whose waking up the world began to manifest from smaller forms of life to the complex and bigger forms, Nārāyaṇa (the creative power of the cosmos) is personified as the lord sleeping on the coils of the huge serpent Ādiśeṣa or Ananta. (*Śeṣa* in Sanskrit means what is remaining. The living forms were contained in seed form in the snake's body that was controlled by Nārāyaṇa.) Sleep is associated with the cessation of movement and the coiled non-moving snake to the non-moving concept of time. As the creation had not yet begun the sea was shown still without waves or currents, with the non-manifestation of the *pañcabhūta*s. The creation, according to Vedic literature, began only when lord Nārāyaṇa woke up from his dreamless slumber (the *yoganidrā*). His consorts Bhūdevī and Śrīdevī — the iconic representations of earth and its quality of bounty, are depicted as sitting by his feet and waking him up to say that the earth, after its manifestation, is now ready to bear the living forms. The time started rolling from then and the space began to unfold in all its multiplicity. The waves appeared in the sea due to the manifestation of the five elements causing the churning up of the ocean. The source of creation and its manifestation as an absolute domain outside time and space is traced in a symbolic way in the *maṇḍala*.

Nārāyaṇa's *yoganidrā* is represented symbolically in the central cone of the *maṇḍala*. The octagonal base is indicative of the cardinal directions meaning that the progress was in all directions. The long strips are indicative of the time factor that originated from the central deity and the smaller cones represent the manifestation of matter.

The picture of the other *maṇḍala* of the same temple (*Pl.* 19) hints about the measurement of the time of Brahmā (the creator who is again personified to be emerging from the navel of Nārāyaṇa), his active and rest periods. After the reign of one Brahmā Lord Nārāyaṇa goes into *yoganidrā* symbolic of the involution or the big crunch and another Brahmā emerges from his navel. The *kīrtimukhas* are placed in all the corners of the *bhūpura* courtyard (for details, see section 1.8, on *kīrtimukhas*).

This concept differs from the idea of big bang from which the universe evolved according to the Western philosophy.

A SCIENTIFIC PERSPECTIVE

The design can be read as a scheme which can be correlated to a pictorial and symbolic representation of the birth of the universe, its expansion in the pluralistic form, and hints about the merging after the big crunch to its source. One of the cosmological models "Big Bang theory" says that 18 billion years ago all the matter of our present universe was originally packed in the primeval fireball, which exploded with a tremendous bang and formed galaxies years later. Galaxies have continued moving away. The question of whether the universe had a beginning in time, its limited space and density was extensively examined by philosophers and scientists all through the ages. Since this was a debate involving time and space, the concept of time had no meaning before the beginning of the universe. In 1929, Edwin Hubble experimentally established that the universe is expanding. To quote the words from the book *A Brief History of Time* by Stephen Hawking, chapter 1:

> that in 1929 Edwin Hubble, who spent most of his life studying galaxies and made the landmark observation through a telescope that velocity of recession is proportional to the distance from us, and wherever you look distant galaxies are moving rapidly away from us. In other words the universe is expanding. This means that at earlier times objects would have been closer together. In fact, it seemed that there was a time about ten or twenty thousand million years ago, when all things existed almost in the same place, the universe was infinitely small with infinite density. This discovery brought the question of the beginning of the universe into the realm of science.

Most astronomers agree that the universe is expanding and evolving into emerging forms expressing its creativity through quantum leaps but the expansion to where and from what is not sure. One implication of this cosmological theory is that the universe may grow cold, dark and die destroying all the life on earth with the continuous expansion which is called an open or flat universe. Alternatively some scientists believe that the universe will eventually stop expanding and begin to contract, calling it a closed universe. This is what is explained in the "oscillating universe theory" where the periods of forward and backward motion of the expansion and contraction of the universe are discussed. However, they also speculated with a philosophical appeal to the people who like the idea of a never-ending universe that the big crunch would not signal the end. Perhaps another big bang would follow the big crunch giving birth to a new universe of possibilities in never-ending cycles of the expansion and contractions of the oscillating universe.

Regarding the matter in the universe, the observation from the Hubble space telescope indicates that matter in the universe has a uniform distribution of matter in a homogeneous way. This theory correlates very well with the structure of the *maṇḍala* where the conical fractal buds, the matter, are shown distributed equidistantly all over the circle. The increase in the size of buds in the concentric circles also hints about the theory of expansion.

The picture of the *maṇḍala* owes the origin of the universe to the cosmic power in the centre and the time started ticking from then onwards, which is indicated by the long strips radiating from the centre, and which are all round the central core, expanding simultaneously with matter (shown as fractal cones). According to the theory of relativity, the intimate connection of the space-time is explained as a four-dimensional continuum and space cannot be dealt without time and vice versa. The inter-relation and unification between time and space which has equal footing and connected inseparably is noticed in the Vaiśeṣika treatise. Space deals with visible objects while time that is eternal deals with succession of things produced and destroyed. Things move by virtue of time and hold together by virtue of space.

The eminent scientist Brian Greene, in his book *The Elegant Universe* (part II, ch. 2) describes the expansion of space with matter after the big bang as stretching of "space fabric." According to him if the fabric of space is stretching, thereby the distance between the galaxies that are carried along on the cosmic flow is increasing. We can also imagine running the evolution backward in time, to learn about the origin of the universe. In reverse, the fabric of space shrinks, bringing all galaxies closer and closer to each other. As the shrinking universe compresses the galaxies together with stars disintegrate, temperature dramatically increases and as an outcome, hot plasma of matter's elementary constituent is formed. In the process of compression, the matter in cosmos is compressed gradually from the size of an orange, to a lemon, a pea, grain of sand and yet to the tiniest size, still extrapolating all the way back to the beginning. The cones of the *maṇḍala,* which are biggest in the outermost circle is depicted smaller in the middle zone and further smallest in the inner circle, where the matter is placed compact and closest to each other. This picture is similar to that of big crunch, *pralaya,* as it is called in Hindu scriptures. The hot plasma that forms due to excess heat of the crunch merges with the central core, giving way later for another big bang for the creation of the universe.

This concept of big bang is viewed as a cosmological expansion, the unfurling of matter and energy with a ratio of time like a wave pattern and the big crunch with the universe collapsing into dimensionless singularity when viewed in a reverse pattern, are artistically carved in the *maṇḍala* of Belavadi Vīranārāyaṇa temple. Even though there is no epigraphical documentation in support of the theme of the *maṇḍala,* the parallel lines of scientific and philosophical theories can be visualised in the *maṇḍala* design. Both philosophers and scientists speculate endlessly about things that have not been experienced or documented. Only philosophy can answer some unique questions about the birth of universe, the purpose of God behind dissolution, or why we exist and how we merge ultimately with the central power, etc.

2.7 The Astronomical Time Cycles of Ancient Hindu Philosophy in the Maṇḍala of Belavadi Vīranārāyaṇa Temple (*Pl.* 19)

HISTORICAL BACKGROUND
(ref. *Pl.* no. 18 for details on Belavadi temple)

The temple is dedicated to Lord Nārāyaṇa. The central deity of the *maṇḍala* appears to be the "Sun" — as Sūryanārāyaṇa. Both the deities, Sūryanārāyaṇa as well as Ugra Narasiṁha, who is installed in one of the three shrines, are associated with the aspect of *tejas*. The *maṇḍala* has 12 spokes, and designed like a *padma* with 12 petals. According to the symbolism of Hindu numerology, 12 is the number symbolic of cosmic organisation, of sun god, 12 images of sun as the 12 *āditya*s, the 12 zodiacal signs and the 12 months of the year. According to *Ṛgveda* (1.155.6), Lord Viṣṇu is conceived as the manifestation of the Sun. He is called *Śipiviṣṭa,* i.e. clothed with the rays of light and enveloping the earth on all sides, with the *mayūkha*s (rays of light). Hence Sūryanārāyaṇa is an epithet of Lord Viṣṇu.*

STRUCTURE OF THE MAṆḌALA

The beautifully designed *maṇḍala* looks like a star radiating the brightness of the inner deity. The conical central lotus bud of the *maṇḍala,* hanging down like a pendant is enclosed in a square boundary. The inner deity is encircled by four concentric circles, each one designed like a *padma* or wheel of 12 petals with sharp edges. For meditation on Gods bestowing good fortune, the petals are designed with pointed tips (Ref. ch. 1.7 for details on shape of petals). Of the four concentric circles, the first three

---

* The peacock's feather which decorates the crown of Lord Kṛṣṇa is symbolic of the aspect of *Śipiviṣṭa*. *Puruṣa* can be identified with the triangular design that is in the feather. Deep inside is the core blue design of cosmic bi-unity which means "life" and it is enveloped on all sides by the filaments like rays. It is because of this comparison, peacock feather is revered in India.

circles have 12 representations of small cones as fractal motifs, identical with the central one. The circles and the cones increase in their size representations. The fourth outermost circle has small and miniature cones in each petal in continuous mode. It also has four square blocks, facing inwards which have circular designs in the middle. Above these four blocks is the design of *kīrtimukhas*. From the inner deity arises 12 spokes, or rays running up to the outermost circle, passing through the base part of each petal. The fractal cones are arranged on these rays. The *maṇḍala* is designed in a stellate plan, observing a right-angled corner of the buttresses.

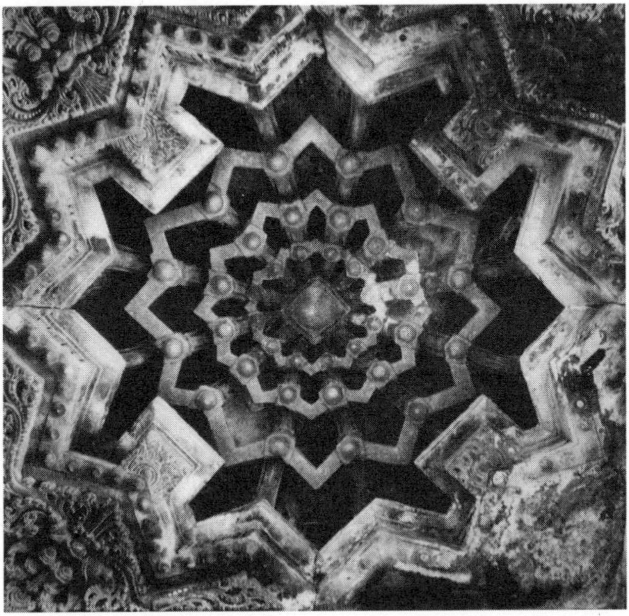

Pl. 19: The astronomical time cycles of ancient Hindu philosophy in the *maṇḍala* of Belavadi Vīranārāyaṇa temple.

PHILOSOPHICAL AND SCIENTIFIC PERSPECTIVES

According to the iconographic representation of the *pañcabhūtas*, the stellate designs of the *maṇḍala*, with interlacing triangles and starry designs, indicate the theme of *maṇḍala* as related to the element *tejas*. The triangular petals with angular tips are indicative of the radiating power of the associated deities, and also for the meditation on gods bestowing good fortune. Analysing the significance of the symbolism of number 12, the whole *maṇḍala* is in the honour of Sūrya, the sun god, the source of all spiritual and earthly light. Sūrya is revered as the central deity with the number symbolism of 12, the other celestial bodies conceived as zodiac signs and the 12 *āditya*s to be around him in their revolutions. The 12 petals and conical fractal representation may be the representation of 12 *āditya*s — namely Mitra, Aryamā, Tvaṣṭā, Dhātā, Varuṇa, Sūrya, Vivasvān, Viṣṇu, Bhaga, Pūṣā (Pūṣan), Savitā and Aṁśumān — who are like other solar divinities of the sky. They may also represent the 12 zodiacal signs, the 12 months of the year. The fourth circle has the representation of the eight (*prahara*s or *yāma*s, three hour divisions as they are called) fractal symbols of the cones in each petal, all revolving in a cyclic order eternally around the sun. The month is determined by the entrance of sun into the sign of the zodiac. This is one of the ways for reasoning the significance of the 12 fractal representations in each wheel.

The theme of the *maṇḍala* appears to be the cycles of time zones, as the expanding and the involuting circles can be correlated to the movement of time in connection with the cycles of day, night, months, years, etc. Time is a basic component of our measuring system and a major subject of art, philosophy and science.

The peak and base of petals in each circle is indicative of the two factors of night and day, related to time divisions. The unit of time, however big or small, has two components separated by an overlapping period:

1. Peak represents day time and base is night time. Day time is the active or the brighter period and night is the

creative period, as the mystery of creation, and the maintenance of life takes place in darkness. Philosophically it is called as the *suṣupti*, where the soul is considered to be one with the *Brahman*, for which reason, they are indicated to be merging with the central deity through the spokes to experience the rejuvenation. Ch. VIII, 18 of *Bhagavad-Gītā* explains that "at the approach of night they merge verily into That alone, which is called the unmanifest, and when the new day of time begins, I bring them again to light."

2. The peak and the base indicate the two *pakṣa*s (fortnights) of the month like *śukla pakṣa* (bright phase) and *kṛṣṇa pakṣa* (dark phase). Thus each petal of the wheel represents the duration of a month with the two *pakṣa*s and a cycle of 12 petals is one year.

3. Six petals together is the representation of *ayaṇa*s — the *uttarāyaṇa* period, where the progress of sun is to north of the equator, the summer period, and the *dakṣiṇāyaṇa*, where the movement of sun is in the southern direction. At cosmic levels of the *maṇḍala* diagram, it is viewed as the day and night durations of Brahmā.

The four square blocks in the outermost wheel can be considered for aspects like:

1. It may represent the four *prahara*s of the day, and the four *prahara*s of the night. The units of four *prahara*s are the dark side, the period of awakening, the period of movement, and the bright side.

2. They may represent the quarterly divisions of seasons of one-year cycle.

3. It also represents the *caturyuga*s — the four *yuga*s, namely Satya, Tretā, Dvāpara and the Kali cycle, and one cycle

of *yugas* is called *mahāyuga*. *Yuga* is a specific age of the world.

The study of this *maṇḍala* is to indicate how concentric circles can generate multi-dimensional figures of the same shape, regardless of its original size. The diagram is so constructed that the devotees understand and meditate on the particular pattern of force that is governing the universe.

Two views are put forth by the author considering the *maṇḍala* on the basis of time zones and the calculation of *yugas*.

The four wheels, observed in increasing order in the size of petals and the fractal cones, indicate the four different time zones of Hindu calendar of human, *pitṛs* (forefathers), *deva* and the Brahmā time cycles.

Reckoning of Human Time

The innermost wheel is the representation of the 12 months, each of 30 days and a cycle representing one human solar year. The 12 peaks and bases are indicative of the *śukla* and the *kṛṣṇa pakṣas*. The fractal representations of the central deity can be seen at the base of petal.

Reckoning of Pitṛ Time

The second wheel depicts the time cycle of *pitṛs*. One month of humans is equal to one day of *pitṛs*. The *śukla* and *kṛṣṇa pakṣas* of inner circle are like day and night of *pitṛs*.

According to the customs of Hindu rituals, *pitṛs* enter into the realm of God after the 12th day of their death.

Reckoning of Devatā Time

The third wheel represents the time cycle of *devatās*. One human year is equal to one day of the *devas*. The *uttarāyaṇa* and *dakṣiṇāyaṇa* periods of human year cycle of six months each is equal to a day and night of *devas*. One month or 30 days of *devas* is equal to 30 human years. One cycle of a divine year means 360 human years and one divine year is equal to (360×12) 4320 years of humans.

In Hindu philosophy, an epoch or Era with a cycle of four ages (*yugas*), is called a *mahāyuga*. *Yugas* are four, namely Satya, Tretā, Dvāpara and Kali together making a period of 12,000 divine years. But the time divisions are not the same for all four. The divisions go in the ratio of 4:3:2:1, which also accounts for the difference in the size ratio of the circles in the *maṇḍala*. Depending on the moral values and duration, it is equated with the Roman time chart of Golden, Silver, Bronze and Iron Ages.

Satya or the Kṛta yuga	=	4,800 divine years or 1,728,000 solar years (4,800×360)
Tretā yuga	=	3,600 divine years or 1,296,000 solar years (3,600×360)
Dvāpara yuga	=	2,400 divine years or 8,64,000 solar years (2,400×360)
Kali yuga	=	1,200 divine years or 4,32,000 solar years (1,200×360)

Together it is 12,000 divine years or 4,320,000 human or solar years.

One cycle duration involving all four *yugas* is called a *mahāyuga* which is indicated as the one cycle of the outermost wheel of the *maṇḍala*, with the four blocks. Each divine *yuga* is represented by the symbolic baleful figure of the lion-faced *kīrtimukha* on the outer side of the last wheel (for details on *kīrtimukhas*, see section 1.8).

The above-mentioned time chart is according to *Manusmṛti*. But the archaeological proofs match approximately with the number of divine years and not the solar years. The mystery of this timescale is a controversial topic.

Reckoning of Brahmā Time Cycle

One thousand *mahāyuga* cycle is equal to 1 day of Brahmā, which is called *kalpa*, equal to 4.32 billion years. This is indicated on the outermost wheels by four conical fractals, *praharas* or *yāmas* in the ascending phase of the petal and the other *kalpa* of 1,000 *mahāyugas* make the night of Brahmā, which is indicated as the descending four fractal cones. One complete day of Brahmā is thus 8.64 billion solar years.

50 years of Brahmā is called a *parārdha* and Brahmā's one life-span is two *parārdhas* (or 100 Brahmā years) which is called one *mahākalpa.*

As is confirmed in *Bhagavad-Gītā* statement — *sahasra yuga paryantam ahar yad brahmaṇo viduḥ* (a day of Brahmā is of 1,000 *mahayugas*).

Thus the daytime of Brahmā is 4.32 billion years, a *kalpa.*

71 *mahāyugas* is called a *manvantara* and is ruled by a Manu.

The Hindu sages identified the rhythmic evolution of the cosmos as a whole as the divine play (*līlā*). They pictured the universe as periodically expanding and contracting and gave the name *kalpa* and *mahākalpa* to the unimaginable time span between the beginning and the end of one creation.

According to *Manusmr̥ti* (ch. 1.73), one who has the knowledge of the days and nights of Brahmā, up to 2,000 cycles of *mahāyugas* is elevated to the status of *kālajñānī*. The *maṇḍala* of this temple is a sincere attempt to enhance the knowledge of devotees.

The second way of analysing the theme of *maṇḍala* is that the four concentric wheels represent the four *yugas*.

The outermost wheel corresponds to the Satya yuga, the golden age of truth and purity, the duration of which is the biggest extending to 4,800 divine years. It may also indicate a *mahāyuga*, a turn of the four *yuga*s together, when the expression of the four blocks is considered.

The third wheel in the descending order of duration represents the Tretā yuga the period of threefold objects of worldly existence like *dharma, artha* and *kama*, collectively (the period of the mythological king Lord Rāma) which was for a period of 3,600 divine years.

The second wheel corresponds to the Dvāpara yuga — the period of doubt, suspense and uncertainty, the period of Lord Kṛṣṇa, which ran for 2,400 divine years.

The innermost wheel corresponds to the Kali yuga — the period of strife, disorder and clash, which is running now and that extends for a period of 1,200 divine years.

Just like the cycle of day and night is caused because of the revolution of earth around the Sun so too is the *yuga* cycle caused by the celestial motion.

Brahmā represents our universe which has birth, growth, death or big crunch, all on the navel singularity of Lord Nārāyaṇa. Nārāyaṇa represents eternity that has no birth or death from whose navel arises another Brahmā, after the death of one. The word Brahmā is derived from the Sanskrit root *bṛh* (to grow) and thus suggests a reality which is dynamic and alive. In the words of S. Radhakrishnan the word *Brahman* means growth and is suggestive of life, motion and progress. Vedas say that many Brahmās have passed away meaning universe is not created for the first time. The interesting fact according to Vedas is that humans are part of *yuga*s and the cosmic timescale.

Carl Sagan, the famous astrophysist, has quoted that

> Hindu religion is the only one of world's faith, dedicated to the idea that cosmos itself undergoes immense and infinite number of

> births and deaths and rebirths. It is the only religion in which timescales correspond to those of modern cosmology. Its cycles run from our ordinary day and night to the day and night of Brahmā, that is, 8.64 billion years — longer than the age of earth, or sun or about the time since big bang — and there are much longer timescale still.

Such a timescale is beautifully represented in the *maṇḍala* of the Belavadi Vīranārāyaṇa temple.

- Our current date can be understood viewing the *maṇḍala* picture. The current Kali yuga (Iron Age) began in 3102 BCE of proleptic Julian calendar.
- The eternal time frame is considered as the life of Brahmā (the creator), which is 100 years in Brahmā time. Presently we are in the 28th Kali yuga of the first day of the first year of *Śvetavarāha kalpa* of the second *parārdha* of Brahmā in the reign of the 7th Manu Vaivasvata. This is the 51st year of the present Brahmā and 155 trillion years have elapsed since he took over as Brahmā.

2.8. Manifestation of Sound in the Maṇḍala of Vīrabhadra Temple, Keladi (*Pl.* 20)

HISTORICAL BACKGROUND

Keladi was the first capital of Keladi Nāyakas. The place is 6 km to the north of Sagar taluka, Shimoga district of Karnataka state. At almost the northern end of the village, there is a large courtyard which is enclosed in modern tiled veranda. In the middle of the courtyard stands a temple complex of three temples. Rāmeśvara temple is in the centre, Vīrabhadreśvara temple is to the right and the Pārvatī temple is to the left. The Rāmeśvara and Vīrabhadreśvara temples are a mixed pattern of Hoysaḷa and southern or Draviḍian style. The Pārvatī temple is a small building which has old back portion built of stone and the front modern portion built of brick. There is also a well-maintained Keladi Museum, which has a collection of copper inscriptions, palm leaves and coins from Nāyaka's period.

The builder of this temple, Vīrabhadra Nāyaka, ruled the place between CE 1629-45. In spite of being troubled by the rival chieftains, Vīrabhadra Nāyaka built the enchanting temple at Keladi. Keladi Nāyakas were an important ruling clan of post-medieval Karnataka. They initially started to rule as the feudatories or vassals of Vijayanagara Empire. After the fall of the empire in CE 1565, they gained independence and ruled significant parts of Karnataka including Shimoga (Shivamogga) and the whole coastal districts till CE 1763 and were overthrown by Hyder Ali. Nāyakas of Keladi played an important role in the history of Karnataka during the period of confusion and fragmentation that prevailed in south India.

STRUCTURE OF THE MAṆḌALA

The five-tiered *maṇḍala* looks like a twisted band of designs, which is decorative, and ornate. The innermost point, the sacred *bindu* is encircled by five consecutive layers of concentric circles. Each *valaya* has petals of a specific design, which run in mathematical progression of 16, and the petals are varying in size and length.

The innermost circle encircling the *bindu* makes the first ring of 16 petals radiating from the centre. The second circle also has 16 petals that look like a continuation with the first circle, but are bigger in size and look convex in structure with a hump in the middle of each petal. Petals in these two rings have round tips.

The third *valaya* has 32 petals with a distinctive high crest or a curve in the middle, the petals being oriented in a clockwise direction. The petals are bigger than the previous circle.

The forth *valaya* has 64 petals, doubled from the previous circle of 32 petals. The petals are longer, with pointed tips and the orientation of the petals is in anticlockwise direction, with a hump in the middle of each petal.

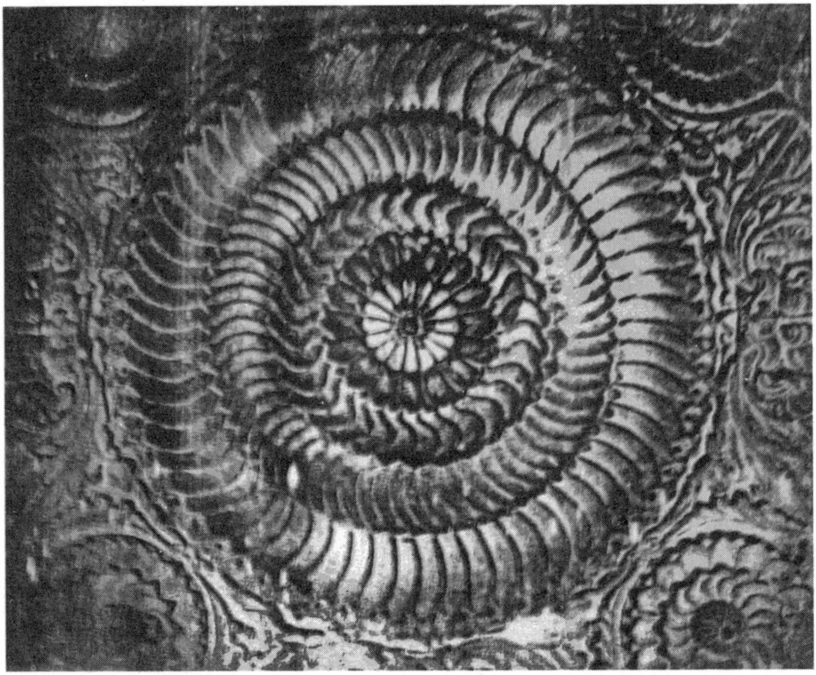

Pl. 20: *Maṇḍala* at the Vīrabhadra temple, Keladi.

The fifth *valaya* has 64 petals which are long with pointed tips, oriented in clockwise direction, with a crest in the middle.

The *maṇḍala* on the whole gives the picture of a wave pattern in which the number of petals is in the mathematical progression of number 16 and a specific equation is followed regarding the length of the petals. The circular *maṇḍala* has smaller *maṇḍala*s of three consecutive layers in all the four corners, totally making it a group of five *maṇḍalas*, while the four sides are decorated with *kīrtimukha*s and scrollwork design.

A PHILOSOPHICAL PERSPECTIVE

The five lotus designs indicate that it is a *pañcāyatana maṇḍala* (ref. ch. 1.8 for details on *pañcāyatana*) with Lord Śiva in the centre, to whom the temple is dedicated. The other smaller *maṇḍala*s are representations of God Gaṇapati, Sūrya, Viṣṇu and Durgā, which indicates the equality observed by the respective cult worshippers and the central one indicating the deity for whom the temple is built.

The analysis of this *maṇḍala* is based considering the number significance of 16.

Sixteen is a sacred number of the *viśuddha cakra* of *kuṇḍalinī cakra*s, which is associated with the element (*tattva*) of ether (sky), which is considered as the zone of purity and non-pollution. According to the psychological attributes of *kuṇḍalinī cakras*, *viśuddha* stands for communication and inspiration, and the faculty of sound (*śabda*) is activated at this level of consciousness. The faculty of speech, after undergoing the previous phases of the vital air undergoing a process of transformation with knowledge and articulation with the oral organs, emerges out in a clear, audible and understandable mode of speech. *Viśuddha* means that which is pure and clear and hence *viśuddha cakra* is supposed to open the gateways of communication to the *jñānaloka*, connecting the body to the spiritual world. The multiplication of 16 petals in progression in the ratio of 1:2:4 indicates sound vibrations representing varying intensities of energies, working at different levels. The mysterious power of sound and the activity of communication make it a dwelling place of Goddess of knowledge. In the author's opinion, this *maṇḍala* is perhaps the representation of *vāṅmayī sudarśana-yantra* — a *yantra* which is associated with the energy of sound and *mantra*, where the sonic vibrations of reciting a *nirguṇa mantra* (which does not invoke a specific deity, but aimed at merging with the infinite nature of cosmos), like *AUṀ*, is depicted as vibrations of *śabda* energy reaching infinite regions. Such words of power which are encasements of spiritual energy and potent to transform levels of spiritual energy are probably viewed in the *maṇḍala* with its physical properties of sound wave and the space-time dimension. The prefix *su* in *sudarśana* stands for that which is good, perfect, thorough, and *darśana* stands for that which is easily seen, with particular reference to the experience of Lord Śiva or the *sudarśana cakra* of Lord Kṛṣṇa.

Regarding the shape of petals — the divisions in each concentric circle, the first two circles near the centre have 16 petals of rounded tips, the shape is indicative of the installation of the troup of deities, the *lokapāla*s. The last two concentric circles have 64 petals each, that have petals or divisions that are small in width, with long and pointed tips like a needle, which is called *animnonnatata agram, samam*. According to the shape of petals this is indicative of liberation, and the energy becoming small as an atom.

The sacred texts of India teach that sounds hold the key to the mysteries of the universe, to the creation and the constant changing of our world. They put much emphasis on *mantra*s and sacred music for a blissful state of mind as they have the ability to awaken the divine energy in humans.

SCIENTIFIC PERSPECTIVE

The *maṇḍala* of Keladi Vīrabhadra temple depicts a wave pattern. Waves are everywhere, sound waves, visible light waves, radio waves, water waves, etc. It is interesting to know how ancient Indian thinkers thought about the propagations of sound.

Praśastapāda's (an ancient philosopher) hypothesis was that sound at any moment, formed a circle in *ākāśa*, and the propagation of sound was carried on in air by means of ever-expanding circles as in the case of ripples in water. The

Mīmāṁsakas, on the other hand, explained the physical aspect of sound and the mode of its propagation as being due to condensation and rarefaction of air molecules (that can be compared with the petal divisions ratio in the consecutive bands of the *maṇḍala*). This was also the view of Bhartṛhari, of fourteenth century CE, the velocity of sound on the basis of movement of air waves — the vehicles of sound is explained.

The earliest Indian rationalists also attempted to provide theories on the nature of sound and light. Sound pitches (*śruti*) were seen as caused by the frequency of vibrations.

Sound is characterised by the properties of waves called the frequency, wavelength, period amplitude and speed. Visualising sound and light as waves is an ancient and cosmological aspect in Hindu philosophy. Sound waves have compressions and rarefactions, and travel from one location to another. One crest of high density displacement of particles or positive phase is followed by another crest, of compression but separated by a rarefaction, which is a low density displacement of particles or a negative phase of compression. Sound propagates as waves of alternating pressure, causing local regions of compression and rarefaction. So a wave is a repeating and a periodic disturbance that travels through a medium, transporting energy from one location to another.

The *maṇḍala* is a picture of a frozen wave pattern as conceived in olden days, where the wave is depicted to be staying in one place. It is an effort in the medium of art, to visualise the concretisation of sound vibrations in a two-dimensional representation, depicting a region containing sound waves, that are perfectly uniform in distribution. It shows the source as a point source — the *bindu*, from where the sound radiates as if from a single point. Like in any stationary wave pattern, sound waves too have an alternating pattern of nodes and antinodes.

The point of no displacement is a node and a point that undergoes displacement in an antinode. (For details see section 1.3 on wave patterns.) In the *maṇḍala,* the region in between two consecutive bands is the nodal region and the midpoint of a crest or a trough is the anti-nodal region. Nodes and anti-nodes are parts of a stationary wave. (Sound wave is created by a vibrating object and propagated through a medium.) The symmetrical nature and properties of sound waves, the harmonic progression with the behaviour of sound waves, the mathematical and numerological progression of the vibration ratio of octaves with wave interactions are the themes of this *maṇḍala,* which is explained in a pictorial form that can be called a "frozen pattern of *nāda.*"

It is like visualising the dispersal of sound waves in an artistic and decorative way. The conclusion is drawn by the author, basing the logic on number 16, of *kuṇḍalinī viśuddha cakra,* which is related to the faculty of sound. The mode of expansion of sound as any other form of energy in a wave pattern expressed through the mathematical and structural progression of petals that are indicated in this *maṇḍala* is compared with the properties of sound like wavelength, pitch, etc. The vibrations of energy of sound related to the recitation of a *bīja mantra* like *AUṀ* or any other sound, the vibrations of which, when recited with purity of thought (*viśuddha* means that which is pure), travel to infinity. It is explained in the *maṇḍala* that sound waves travel in a parallel manner in all directions, with equal distributions of energy from the source, i.e. its isotropic source. The dispersal of sound is suggested in a longitudinal wave pattern, each individual wave with its crests and troughs makes the bands look oriented in clockwise and anticlockwise direction. The sculptor or the artist of this *maṇḍala* has chosen this device to indicate the trough and crest pattern of sound waves. Sound waves are concretised and represented in the form of undulatory lines of travelling longitudinal waves or the progressive wave pattern. (Longitudinal wave is the wave pattern where the motion of the particles of the medium runs parallel to the direction of the energy transport.) The distance between the two successive regions of maximum compression or rarefaction being in same phase that is equal to the wavelength is also indicated in the crests of expanding circles. The wavelength is designed shorter, higher in energy at the source of sound and it increases with distance according to the wave pattern theory, where the energy becomes fainter on reaching infinity.

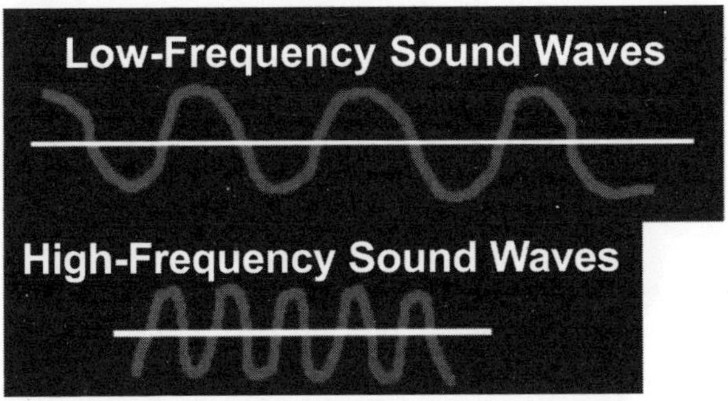

Pl. 21: Associated wave curves of low and high frequency sound waves.

The wave suffers a decrease in amplitude — the measure of energy in a sound wave, which amounts to the fractional change for unit of distance covered. For example, if the wave decreases from amplitude 2 to amplitude 1 over a distance of 1 m, the amplitude drops to ½ after covering another metre of distance. This reduction in amplitude is exponential. The distance is represented in the *maṇḍala* through the length of petals in the ratio of 1:2:3, and the intensity by the number of petals in multiplication of 16. The sound from a point source obeys the inverse square law. The intensity in decibels is calculated by comparing the intensity to the threshold of waves. Numerically it is confirmed that doubling the distance drops the intensity in

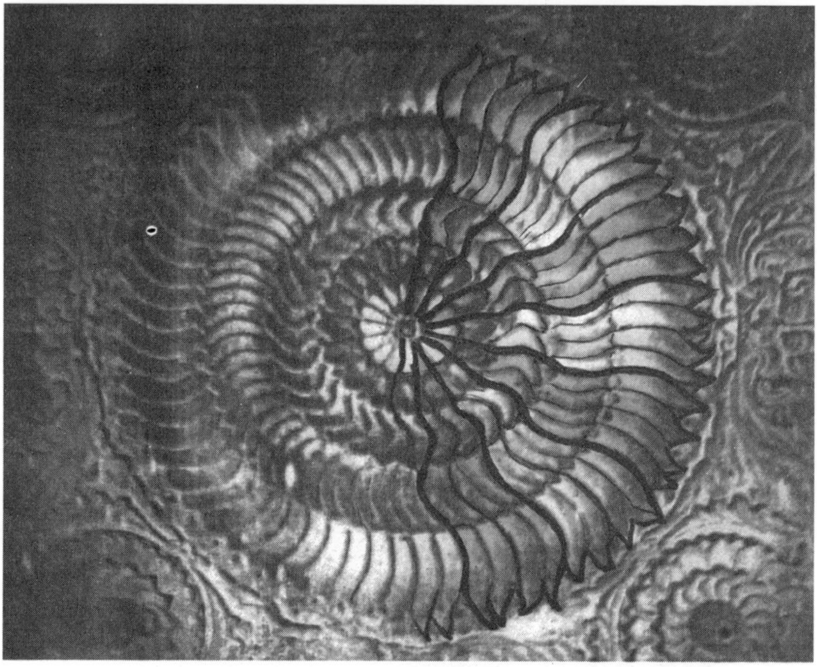

Pl. 22: Application of the ratio of the sound frequency.

the ratio of 1:2, indicated by the number of petals in the ratio 16:32:64, and absorption makes the sound waves gradually weaker also.

Regarding frequencies of sound waves, any two sounds whose frequencies multiply in the ratio 1:2, are said to be separated by an octave. The ratio of a note to its octave is explained through the multiplications of number of petals, 16–32 and 64.

Even though the *maṇḍala* has five bands, it can be considered as three because the smaller two bands have 16 divisions, the middle one has 32 and the last two have 64 petal divisions. The middle band is designed like a bridge, which is also true with the hearing organ. The three divisions when compared to the design of the organ of hearing — the ear — also have three zones like the external, the middle and the inner (ear). The sound vibrations, received by the external ear passes through the middle ear getting intensified and reaches the brain part (compared to the inner core) through the inner ear, cochlea. The structure of the longitudinal section of cochlea that is like a golden spiral with three canals running inside might be the inspiring factor for the design of this *maṇḍala*.

Another interesting factor in support of the sound wave pattern theory is its regularity of petal pattern. When the crests of two consecutive waves meet, they result in a super stronger wave, which is conveyed in this *maṇḍala.* When the contours of the two waves in a band match, it is harmony, resulting in a pleasing sensation. (When the crest of a wave coincides with the trough of a wave, the two waves cancel each other rather than making a strong wave.) This is called the phase of a wave. The position of its cycle, at a specific time, or measure of whether it is at crest or a trough or in between can also be understood by calculating the wavelength in this *maṇḍala*. It can be interpreted that when *mantra*s are recited with harmony of body and mind, the vibrations of sound waves travel stronger establishing equilibrium. When body and mind are in disharmony, then there is no desired effect of the sound or *mantra* chanted or produced.

The mathematical explanations on behaviour, for the equation of motion, as explained by E.C.G. Sudarshan in an essay on "cosmos of spirituality" that "when waves spread out moving from one localised region to another, their energy and motion also spread out larger and larger distances, while their intensity correspondingly decreases" are beautifully demonstrated in the *maṇḍala*. The low frequency wavelength is shorter near the source of sound. The higher frequency sound with longer wavelength and more spread out is depicted in the outer layer of the *maṇḍala*.

Sound was understood to have its own reflections. Echo or *pratidhvani* was a reflection of sound in the same way as an image in water or in a mirror, due to the reflections of sound. The smaller wheels of similar pattern on the four corners play a dual representation of *pañcāyatana* as well as a hint for the echo pattern. The sending back of the sound waves — a repetition and imitation of the last word in a soft tone — a property of sound waves when they hit an obstacle in any direction is cleverly depicted through the *maṇḍala*.

The musical sounds as distinguishable pitches were called *śruti*s. These were believed to be associated with the magnitude, momentum (*vega*) and the frequency of vibration (refer *Pl.* 22) (*kampana saṁkhyā*). The ratio of a note to its octave in respect of pitch was given as 1:2, which is hinted in the mathematical progression of petal divisions as 16-32-64. An indefinite number of *śruti*s could be interposed between a note and its octave.

A pictorial representation of these thoughts, where the physical sciences were not yet formalised, nor separated from the other branches of knowledge, is consciously attempted in the ceiling of Vīrabhadra temple at Keladi in a vague and approximate way. The understanding of physical world is not complete, till we understand the nature, properties and behaviour of waves.

2.9. The Power of Light in the Maṇḍala at Beḷūr Cennakeśava Temple (*Pl.* 22)

HISTORICAL BACKGROUND

The Cennakeśava temple at Beḷūr was constructed in the year 1117, by the great Hoysaḷa ruler Viṣṇuvardhana also called Bittideva who reigned during CE 1108-42. It is a typical and the first statement of Hoysaḷa school of architecture. Beḷūr is a small town in the Hassan district of Karnataka state, 155 km away from Mysore, or 224 km away from Bengaluru. The temple is dedicated to the Vaiṣṇavite god Vijaya Nārāyaṇa, also called Cennakeśava, bearing the image of that deity in the sanctum. The temple is in a stellate plan, the sanctum built on a raised terrace. The outer walls of the temple are with profuse sculptural details and jewel-like delicacy carved in soapstone. The temple consists of a *mukhamaṇḍapa* a *navaraṅga* with a dancing platform, a vestibule (*antarāla*), and the sanctum (*garbhagṛha*), all set in an axial strike. The temple has three entrances led by a flight of steps to the *navaraṅga* hall. The ceiling of the central bay between the side doors of the *navaraṅga* hall is one of the marvels of Hoysaḷa art. It is called *bhuvaneśvarī* — representation of the universe, seen as a huge circular *maṇḍala*.

STRUCTURE OF THE MAṆḌALA IN THE CEILING

The ceilings of the temple hall have a variety of exquisitely carved designs. The finest one of these is the central dome — which has concentric circles, enclosed in an octagonal boundary, that is again enclosed in a square courtyard. The whole structure is supported by four pillars, on the corners of the square. The central *maṇḍala* measures 13 ft in square, and 6 ft in depth and the square boundary measures 19.3 ft. The central sacred core is a small circle, with the icon of Lord Narasiṁha in the centre. The three concentric circles are extensively decorated with scrollwork, and pictorial with figures of Lord Kṛṣṇa. It is interspersed with elevated circles like boundaries — which appear in total like the circular ripples that can be seen in a pond.

A PHILOSOPHICAL PERSPECTIVE

This *maṇḍala* has been analysed comparing it to the structure of the *sudarśana yantra*, as the details of the *maṇḍala*, the central deity, and the pictorial representations, resemble the structure of this *yantra*. According to *Ahirbudhnya Saṁhitā*, when the central deity

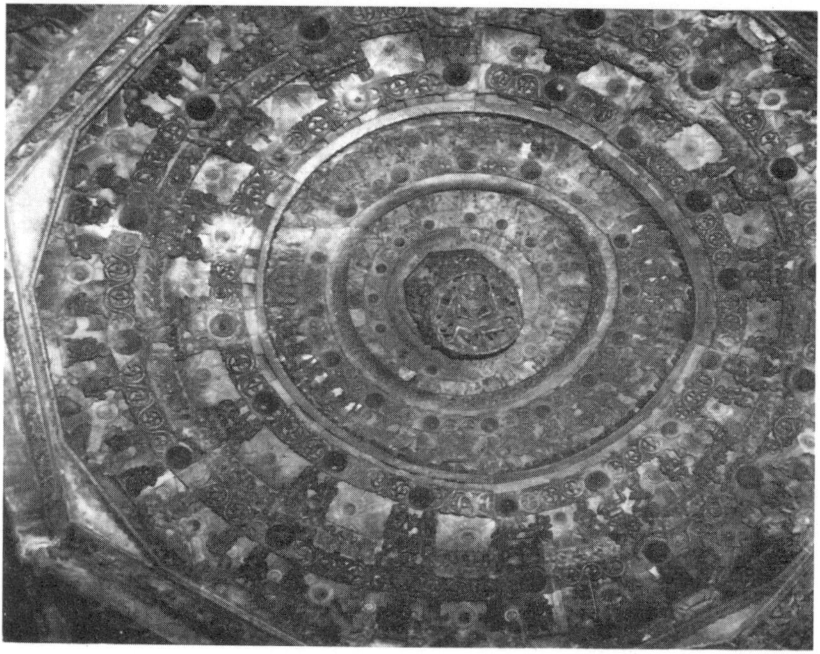

Pl. 22a: *Maṇḍala* at the temple of Beḷūr.

is either Narasiṁha (a deity in half-lion and half-human form which may also be symbolised as an upward triangle indicative of the element *tejas*) or Lord Sudarśana, symbolised either as two triangles interlaced in upward and downward direction or as the iconic form of the discus of Lord Viṣṇu, who is personified as one with 16 arms with sacred weapons, symbolising limitless power, the *maṇḍala* is a representation of *sudarśana yantra.*

In the *maṇḍala* of Beḷūr Cennakeśava temple, the central deity Lord Narasiṁha is represented as a violent and wrathful deity, in a combined form of a lion and a human. Wrathful deity (*ugra*) suggests the mighty struggle involved, in overcoming one's alienation. The terrific form characterised by the long and sharp nails, large number of hands carrying weapons of war, the wide and circular eyes, image adorned by human flesh (or the human bones or skulls worn as decoration on the garland or the crown, as seen in some images of Goddess Durgā or a form of Śiva), the dead body of the demon, are all indicative of the victory after the violent war. Traditionally wrathful deities are understood and worshipped to be aspects of benevolent principles, fearful only to those who perceive them as alien forces. King Viṣṇuvardhana, after adopting Vaiṣṇavism, chose Viṣṇu as *iṣṭadevatā*, and installed Lord Narasiṁha, an incarnation of Viṣṇu, in *ugra* form as the central deity of the *maṇḍala*. Before the setting up of an *ugra* image, the *śāntamūrti* or the pacific form (as seen in the *garbhagṛha*) or at least a water tank has to be installed to counteract the terrific effects of the wrathful deity. The *tantra*s claim that the devotee who worships *iṣṭadevatā* (chosen deity), which is another name for *Brahman*, in the prescribed manner, lives a happy and contented life, uplifting himself spiritually and psychologically to the level of his chosen deity. Probably King Viṣṇuvardhana imagined himself to be like Lord Narasiṁha, to his enemies. This *maṇḍala* was installed in the temple, after he declared his kingship and victory over his enemies — the Cāḷukyas.

A *sudarśana yantra* is used seeking unlimited release of power especially by kings and those who are ambitious of attaining kingship. *Ahirbudhnya Saṁhitā* gives a clear picture of the purpose and the fruits of installing a *sudarśana yantra* by kings. It quotes:

> Hear, the peculiarities of the protective prescription for kings — O Nārada. He who desires kingship, he who is deprived of kingship or he who is overpowered by other kings, should worship the four-armed Lord Nārāyaṇa, with all the prescribed ornaments and jewellery, in the prescribed manner, and install the lord in the *yantra*, in a temple. Only this instrument ensures him a sound kingship, bestows the attainment of everything, for a happy and contented life — when it is worshipped everyday respectfully.

Both *Ahirbudhnya* and *Parameśvara Saṁhitā* give elaborate description of the temple, or the pavilion (*maṇḍapa*) that should be built for the worship of *sudarśana yantra*, and about the solid medium as metal or stone, that should be used for this *yantra*. It also emphasises on the installation of this *yantra* prior to the establishment of the statue of Viṣṇu in the temple. Saint Rāmānuja influenced the King Viṣṇuvardhana to adopt to Vaiṣṇavism, and his patronage counted a great deal for the success of Vaiṣṇavism, down south.

Regarding the other details of the *yantra*, it is a full iconic representation observing the iconographic prescriptions of the Āgamic texts, with the presiding deity as a figurative symbol in the centre. The three concentric circles suggest the concept of expansion. Knowledge is continuous. It pervades space and time. The outer or the third *valaya* is large, with netted grid of circles. All the bands have pictorial representation of deities and the *līlā*s of Lord Kṛṣṇa, which may be either according to the *Harivaṁśa* or *Viṣṇu Purāṇa*. According to Upaniṣads, *Brahman* or Śrī Kṛṣṇa performs his *līlā*s with his eternal *parikara*s (playmates or associates) in his own *dhāma* (abode) known as Gokula, Vṛndāvana, or Braja, which is a particular expression of his *ādhāra śakti*. His self-sufficiency and self-complacency does not suffer on account of his pastimes with his associates as they, being his own manifestations or of his *śakti*s, are not different from him. They serve him with intense love in his *līlā*s, which therefore are exceedingly charming both to him and his associates — an expression of mutual love and happiness. The love of Vṛndāvana associates is intense enough to inspire in them a sense of "mineness" (a feeling of "He is mine"). A pictorial depiction of the Kṛṣṇa-līlās in the *maṇḍala* is thus charming and blissful.

The pictorial representation of *mantra*s is also explained as safeguards, the *rakṣā*, to hold the central power intact. *Ahirbudhnya*

Saṁhitā explains the *rakṣā* that can be in two forms, called *jyotirmayī* (associated with the congregation of the energy of light), and *vāṅmayī* (associated with the energy of sound or language). *Jyotirmayī* — that which is full of *tejas* or light, is related to the power of sight, the form (*rūpa*), for which reason a pictorial form is used. The light that is emanating from the truth is its own light and radiance (*sva tejas*) and the life is sustained in the world of names and forms. The *mantra*s are not inscribed in the *maṇḍala*, but one can probably recite on visualising the pictorial representations. The *mantra*s are words of power, sealed with hidden latent power that has the ability to awaken the divine energy. They are called *saguṇa* when it is designed to activate the devotee to a specific deity by a direct addressing, much like *kṛṣṇāya namaḥ*, and it is *nirguṇa mantra* which is formless, non-specific of any deity but with a purpose of merging with the absolute and infinite nature of the universe — like *OṀ*. The *maṇḍala* at Beḷūr temple can be classified under the former category.

Bhagavad-Gītā (ch. 11/17) explains the divine as a mass of radiance, shines everywhere all round and glowing like sun. This light is not to be taken in the physical sense of the term but viewed as flashes of light of consciousness that illuminates the interior. Light and consciousness are inseparably connected and light is the spiritual manifestation of divine reality. That the divine light of consciousness, when beamed through the eyes of viewers, illuminates the forms and shapes of the universe is demonstrated in the creation of this *maṇḍala*.

Ahirbudhnya Saṁhitā emphasises that a mere visualisation of this *yantra*, or concentration upon it, is sufficient to reach an aspired goal, like success in a battle, or dispute, and destroy all calamities. There is nothing that cannot be obtained by visualisation or recollecting this *yantra*. This dynamic *yantra* also represents a whirling wheel of the sacred flame that keeps all negativity, misfortune and ill-health at bay. While just visualising it also the devotee focuses on the centre of the sacred circle of sun — light.

The purpose of giving a pictorial form of Narasiṁha in the centre is that Lord Narasiṁha is symbolic of *tejas* (light) — as there is the immediate destruction of darkness or the *māyā* in the act of killing the demon, symbolic of an emergence from the psychological state of darkness. Light and consciousness are inseparably connected in Hindu philosophy, and the spiritual manifestation of divine reality is picturised in the *maṇḍala* of Beḷūr temple. Knowledge of eternity is compared to the knowledge of supreme light. The various activities of Lord Kṛṣṇa, as *avatāra puruṣa*, as a child, youth, and a teacher, are to emphasise that the supreme power is the foundation and the substratum that is supporting the cosmos — the *maṇḍala* and the universe. The concept of Puruṣottama, the Supreme Being is conceived with intellectual penetration. The episodes relating to Lord Kṛṣṇa also adds charm, like the waves add charm to a sea. The depiction of the episodes of *Mahābhārata* serves the useful purpose of stimulating devotion, prompting religious art, creating mythological literature enabling one to admire the heritage part of *Mahābhārata*, along with the symbols of spiritual ideas — like the repeated fractal representation of the deity in the circular bands. In the *yoga* of individual and ultimate consciousness in *Gītā*, Lord Kṛṣṇa says that "He is the illuminator of all light and resides as knowledge in all human beings." Perhaps this reality is conveyed in the *maṇḍala* through fractal representations.

Until and unless it is viewed with this insight, the *maṇḍala* is reduced to a mere design.

The episodes of *Mahābhārata* are interspersed with *gandharvas*, flying with garlands, *gandharvas* giving heavenly music with various instruments, and celestial dancers in dance postures, to indicate the celebration of divine joy and bliss. The concentric circles are also decorated with intricate scrollwork, and conical fractal representations, encircled by rays or spokes of a wheel. These may represent the *dhāraka yantra* — which has the representations of the *pañcatattvas* like earth, fire, etc. The power of *sudarśana yantra* is considered to be so great that it always goes with the *dhāraka yantra,* with the syllables of Narasiṁha *mantra* on the spokes. This combination keeps the power of *sudarśana yantra* in check.

The *maṇḍala* is enclosed in an octagon, which can be compared to an eight-petalled lotus — that is symbolic of expansion of knowledge reaching all the eight directions. The outermost panels have figures of king and queen, seated in a court, watching a wrestling match, or enjoying dance and music of artists, to represent the celebration at human level. The *maṇḍala* is enclosed in a square boundary, the *bhūpura,* which is the courtyard, or the palace, where the deities live. This is supported by ornate pillars, on the four corners, with a figure of an *apsaras* atop.

Note: The author observes a similarity in the domical ceiling between the Santa Maria Basilica and the *maṇḍala* of Beḷūr temple, though the former is a painting and the latter is carved in stone. Both are encased in an octagonal frame, one allowing light in natural form and the other indicating light in an anthropomorphic form of Lord Narasiṁha. The concentric circles in the dome of Santa Maria Basilica are related to the life and teachings of Christ while that of Beḷūr is on life and teachings of Lord Kṛṣṇa. The outermost circles in both are about the various aspects of commoners and their lifestyles as can be seen in the pictures below.

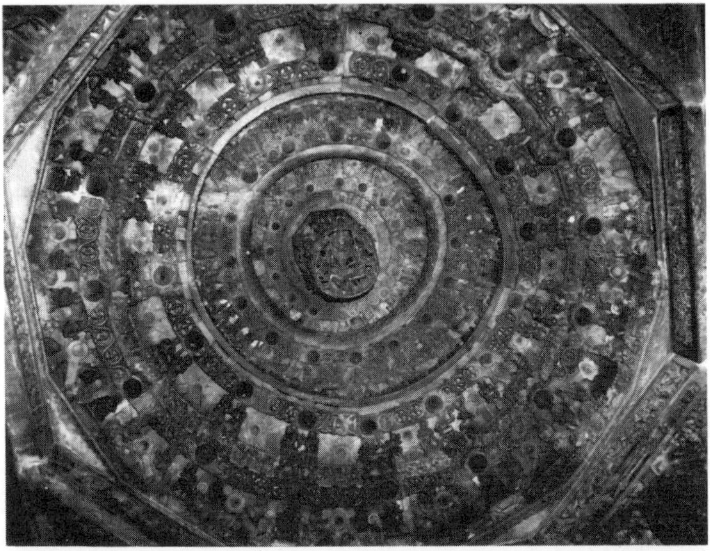

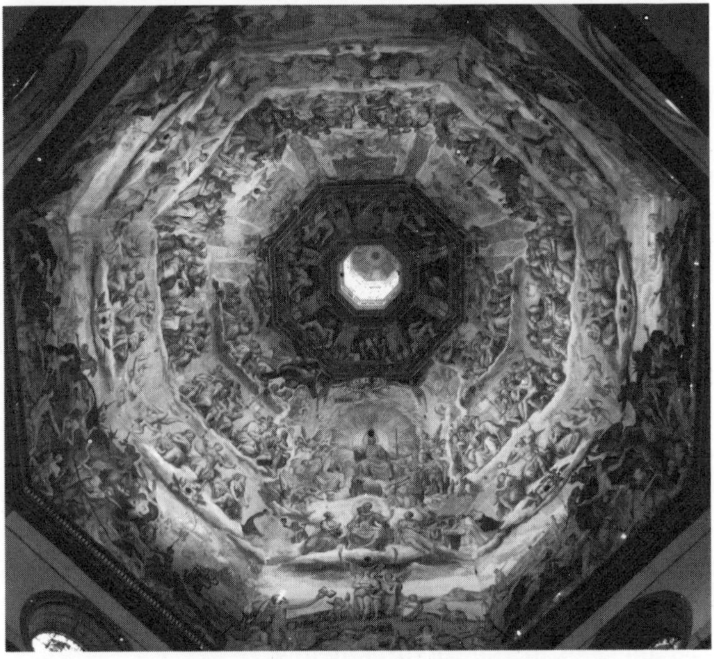

Pl. 23: The *maṇḍala* at Beḷūr temple,
the domical ceiling at the Basilica Santa Maria.

A SCIENTIFIC PERSPECTIVE OF THE MAṆḌALA AT BEḶŪR CENNAKEŚAVA TEMPLE

The *maṇḍala* at Beḷūr Cennakeśava temple is probably designed according to the specifications of *sudarśana yantra*, observing the sub-category of *jyotirmayī yantra*. The central deity, Lord Narasiṁha, who presides in a *sudarśana yantra* is conceived as the source of light (*agni*), luminous like the sun. The Eastern understanding of light in a spiritually advanced place like India is different from the scientific and material creation of light. Light also symbolises subjective visual image and a phenomenon accompanying inner illumination. Light is a physical entity governed by and conforming to the physical laws, but the light of knowledge is a transcendental perception. It is viewed as light, as the *maṇḍala* is related to the power and sense of sight. When a light wave hits an object, eyes send a message to the brain about the object. Upon reaching the brain, psychological responses occur; the brain deciphers the information about the object and interprets the meaning of the message. The principle of light is the very principle in the eye. If eyes were not there, light itself would have no meaning. At the same time, if the principle of light illuminates the objects of form, only then the eyes function. Knowledge is acquired by the sensations coming to us through sense organs, the most important of which is the sense of seeing. The photons of light end their journey when they fall on eyes, affecting the consciousness. This concept is used in *jyotirmayī sudarśana yantra*. An interesting feature is that even the structure of human eye is also maṇḍalic with the pupil centred in the iris. The structure of human eye seems to be an inspiration for the design of this *maṇḍala*, as the structure of *maṇḍala* roughly resembles the structure of human eye.

The beginning of light as well as knowledge remained as much a mystery as the beginning of space, universe and time.

The subject "light" attracted the attention of ancient Indian philosopher Gautama who in *Nyāya-Sūtra* (ibid. III.1.38-70) has discussed the physical nature of light and its importance on visual organs. He postulated that light rays emitted by the wick (deity) came in contact with the eyes and the objects — large or small — were visible. The subject was elaborated in *Vātsyāyana Bhāṣya*, in fourth century CE. According to Nyāya Vaiśeṣika, the *tejas* or the light of a burning lamp gradually spreads in increasing circles and illuminates the objects of various sizes. Further, the Mīmāṁsaka school of Kumārila Bhaṭṭa stated that vision and light go on expanding their range gradually, depending upon the extent of stretch, which terminates at the object. It was also discussed that flame is a collection of large quantity of light particles (photons) at the burning zone of the wick, and they travel in all directions like sound waves, at high speed.

The phenomenon of light and reflection, as understood in the twelfth-thirteenth century CE, is expressed in the *jyotirmayī sudarśana yantra,* and can be understood by studying this *maṇḍala.*

The whole structure of this *maṇḍala* can be correlated to the properties of light, the dispersal of light waves and their interaction with the material body. Wave theory speculates that light source emits light waves that spread in all directions at an unmatched speed. The source of light is conceived to be in the figure of Lord Narasiṁha (an *avatāra* of Viṣṇu) and the activities of Kṛṣṇa (another *avatāra* of Viṣṇu), is spread all over the body of the *maṇḍala*. The intention of giving the pictorial form of various activities of Lord Kṛṣṇa is to indicate that the psychological vibrations felt on mere visualisation of the central and surrounding deities, enhance positive vibrational motion in humans. According to the laws of light waves, when a light wave of a given frequency strikes a material with electrons having the same vibration frequencies, it absorbs the energy of light wave and transforms it to vibrational motion. The light emitted by the source is absorbed by our eyes, sending a signal to the brain. Light emitted by the source has profound effect on matter. Its interaction (of light with matter which is much faster as compared with sound vibrations) contributes to the colour appearance of our surrounding. The activities of Lord Kṛṣṇa, at various stages of his life, reflect the various colours of life. These pictorial representations may also be viewed as mirror surface, reflecting the glory of the source — for without light, there is no sight. The visual ability of humans is the result of complete interaction of light, eyes and brain. Hence, the pictorial form of deities is like luminous objects that enlighten the human brain. Light is like *jñāna,* which enables one to recognise and understand the manifestations of Lord Kṛṣṇa. Knowledge liberates the mind and the knowledge of the ultimate enables the eternal liberation. The light is the light of consciousness, which not only illumines, but imparts warmth in life.

E.C.G. Sudarshan, a renowned physicist, explains about the mathematics of wave pattern in an essay on man and the cosmos and says that waves spread out while moving from one localised region to another. This energy and motion also spread out over larger and larger distances, while their intensity correspondingly decreases. Max Planck postulated in 1901 that the energy of photon is inversely proportional to the wavelength. Photons have higher energy with shorter wavelength, near the source. In the *maṇḍala,* the dispersion of light is clearly indicated to be in expanding circles and probably the intensity, which decreases with distance, can be compared to the hierarchy of deities, semi-divine gods like *gandharva*s in the outer circles, royal families, and finally humans in the outermost panels.

The ripples of waves, which are designed as concentric circles of the *maṇḍala,* have the typical pattern of "transverse waves" which means the movement of the vibration is at right angles to advance of the wave motion. This complex phenomenon is explained in the *maṇḍala* by giving the small figures in each concentric circle progressing at right angles to the advance of the wave. The sight has to focus on each piece of sculpture in a circular pattern to understand the purpose of the *maṇḍala*.

Simultaneously the *maṇḍala* exhibits the wave particle duality of modern physics as propounded in de Broglie's theory of matter waves. According to this, light waves exhibit both particle and wave-like behaviour. Light interacts with matter as particle but propagates as waves. While the structure of the *maṇḍala* exhibits the ripple wave pattern, the individual sculptures and the fractal representations all over the body of the *maṇḍala* can be viewed as particles of photons. The light of spirituality in the centre is spread over through the particles, to activate the sense of sight of human eyes. The *maṇḍala* is a good example of the amalgamation between science and religion or physics and metaphysics that help the devotees to understand the divine artistry in the unfolding patterns of light.

Observing all the waves, playing on the surface of the ocean, manifesting and disappearing after a temporary existence, into the very waters from which they arose, one can conclude that ocean is source and rest house for the waves — the substratum from which the phenomenon arises, exists and merges into it. The whole picture of this *maṇḍala* signifies the importance of light and conveys a theme that it is central for all activities of living things in the universe. Waves are everywhere like sound waves, light waves, radio waves, etc. everything vibrating at molecular level, sending waves into the universe. The entire universe of perceptible form is comprised of vibrations which create waves of various frequencies or wavelengths. Understanding the physical world is incomplete, till we understand the properties, nature and behaviour of waves.

2.10. Maṇḍalas in Square Grids

Temples of all religions observe the basis of a square for their construction plans. According to ancient architectural traditions, Hindu temples are symbols of models of cosmos and the form represents cosmos symbolically. Square represents the terrestrial life, its absolute and mystical form. It is a geometric construction that gives precision, establishing proportions. It is indicative of the four cardinal points and a division of matter and space. The numerology associated with a square is 4. The square of 4 — 16, is a perfect number. Square is a fundamental figure that sets boundaries in the four directions of north, east, south and west. The element earth, that contains matter and that which comes in a definite shape with length, breadth and height is symbolically represented as a square or a cube and hence not represented as a circle or sphere, the shape in reality. Even the constituents of the human body like muscles and skeletal structures that have mass are considered as earth according to Hindu philosophy. Square is said to be the measure of man because a person with arms extended to the sides reaches out as wide as his body is tall.

Square is an artificed shape. It is the mark of order and finality to the expanding life and its forms. Hence, it is the symbolic shape in architectural forms. It is interesting to see the *maṇḍala*s in square shape, with smaller square grids around the periphery. Even the *vāstupuruṣa maṇḍala* is drawn in square grids, and the divisions' layout before carving a sculpture is designed in square grids. Square shape is called *sakala* in Sanskrit meaning complete or together with parts. The site of any space can be divided using *pada-vinyāsa*. It is a method whereby any site can be divided into specific number of square divisions called *pada*. The *maṇḍala* will be known by the number of divisions on each side.

Sakala is one single square called *ekapada*.

Pecaka is 4 squares corresponding to *dvipada* or two divisions.

Pīṭha (9 squares) corresponds to *tripada* or three divisions of a big square.

Mahāpīṭha is 16 squares, resulting from 4 divisions.

Upapīṭha is made of 25 squares, by 5 divisions . . . and so on.

The knowledge of Vāstu is classified into three groups like Vāstuśāstra, Śilpaśāstra and Citrasūtra. Vāstuśāstra is the ancient Indian design principle of the organisation of space that accords with the laws of universe. It deals with the *maṇḍala* with 64 or 81 square parts, which is used in the construction of buildings, forts, temples and the precise knowledge of finding the proper land, its purification, drawing the ground plan measurement of its components, etc. Even the town planning is drawn according to the *vāstu maṇḍala*. The second group of Śilpaśāstra deals with the measurement of the sculptures and icons, and the designs on the ceilings and pillars. The measurements of the body parts of a sculpture are drawn on a basic plan of square grids. The third group of Citrasūtra deals with the paintings that adorn the walls of the temple (refer details on *Pl.* 14, for a demonstration of the schemes used in *citrasūtra*).

The square shaped *maṇḍala* designs, often seen in Śaivite temples are categorised under the Śilpaśāstra. The most common square *maṇḍala* is the nine square grids, where the central block may come with an iconic representation, or all the nine blocks may be of equal size with a lotus design within. The main deity is positioned in the central block and the surrounding deities called the *āvaraṇa devatā*s are placed in the eight lotuses surrounding the main deity. The surrounding deities are positioned in the four cardinal and intermediate directions which may expand into many concentric patterns. The nine-square *maṇḍala* can be either a *navagraha maṇḍala* of heavenly bodies or the representation of the protectors of the eight directions as the *dikpālas*. The theme is read according to the central deity. Some Śaivite temples have the various forms of Lord Śiva, or his *tāṇḍava* aspects, artistically carved in dancing postures, within the square grids of the *maṇḍala*.

2.11. The Significance of the Aṣṭadikpāla Maṇḍala at Marale Siddheśvara Temple (*Pl.* 24)

Marale Siddheśvara temple has a ceiling in square shape in the *gūḍha maṇḍapa*. This very beautiful square *maṇḍala* has nine divisions; the central one is slightly bigger than the surrounding eight ones. In all the nine blocks, deities are carved in iconic form.

THE STRUCTURE OF THE MAṆḌALA

It is a combination of circle and square shapes. The *bhūpura* square courtyards are three-layered. The central deity, positioned in a circle, is enclosed in the inner square block, with the motif of lotus bud fractal design that is 16 in number. In between the inner and the second squares are the eight *āvaraṇa devatās*, all positioned in circular-shaped *maṇḍalas*. In between the circular designs are the four-petalled designs that run alternating with the deities. The second square is enclosed in an octagon and is laced with scrollwork design. The octagonal structure is further secured in a big *bhūpura* square block in the corners of which is the beautiful design of *kīrtimukhas* positioned inside the triangular corner part, symbolic of the four legs of the *siṁhāsana* (the pedestal). All the three squares and the octagon are decorated with the conical design, the fractal representation of the deity, which are 16 in the innermost square, 64 in the middle square, 72 in the octagonal frame. The iconographic characters of the deities reveal that it is an *aṣṭadikpāla maṇḍala* (the protecting deities of the eight directions). The central deity is a form of Lord Śiva, may be the Siddheśvara, to whom the

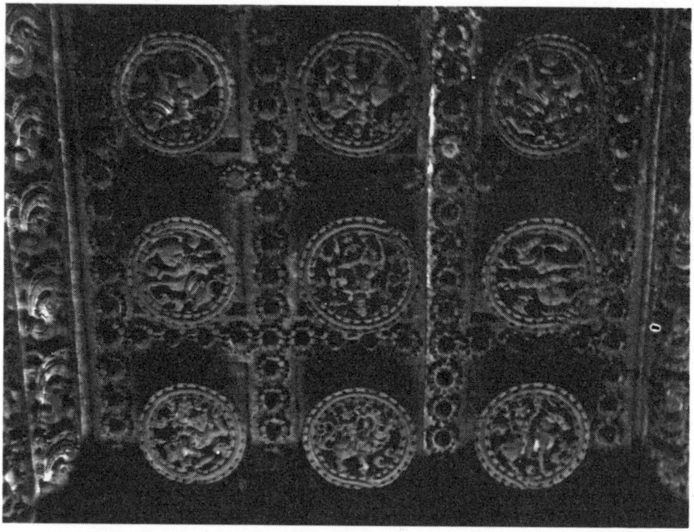

(a)

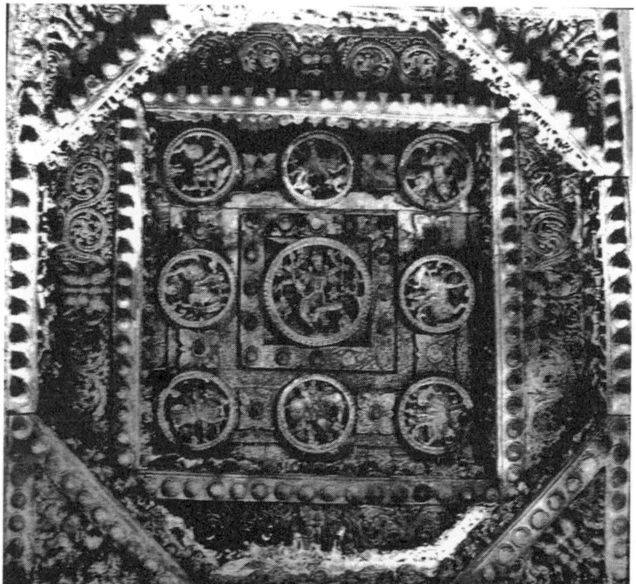

(b)

Pl. 24: *Aṣṭadikpāla Maṇḍala* at Marale Siddheśvara temple and a varied version of the Aṣṭadikpāla

temple is dedicated. The god is designed with multiple hands holding various *āyudhas* (the weapons) and is standing in a dancing posture. The Śaivite god of south Indian origin Siddheśvara is the representation of a superhuman being with eight supernatural powers like the power of becoming minute, light, great, control over passions, creating anything at will, irresistible will, supremacy over all and subjugation of all at will. This central deity has 16 fractal representations of conical design on the inner square boundary.

Aṣṭa in Sanskrit means the eight parts of the whole. On the four cardinal and intermedial directions are the figures of the eight directional deities with the specific representation of the attributes in their hands and mounted on the *vāhanas* — the assigned animals. They are:

	Gods	**Directions**	**Vāhanas**	**Attributes in their hands**
1.	Indra	East	Elephant	*Aṅkuśa* and *vajra*
2.	Agni	South-east	Ram or goat	Rosary and water vessel
3.	Yama	South	Buffalo	Noose, club
4.	Nirṛti	South-west	Shoulder of a man	Sword and shield
5.	Varuṇa	West	*Makara* (crocodile)	*Pāśa* (rope)
6.	Vāyu	North-west	Stag	Banner and staff
7.	Kubera	North	Horse or man-drawn chariot	*Varada* and *Abhaya*
8.	Īśāna	North-east	Bull	*Śūla* and *kapāla*

The Hindu concept of *aṣṭadikpālas* (the 8 guardians and protectors of the 8 quarters of the world collectively known as "Dikpālas") is very old, commanding sufficient iconographic notice. The early epic literature mentions them *devas* or the *loka-pālas*. The world is no doubt maintained and guided by the supreme through its various expressions. The *dikpālas* at the macrocosmic level are compared to the eight constituents of the human at the microcosmic level. Lord Kṛṣṇa explains in the 13th chapter (*śloka*s 1-9) of *Bhagavad-Gītā* about the *kṣetra* (the field) and the *kṣetrajña* (the knower). The field or the specified space of *dikpāla*s is compared with the matter — the body as *idam śarīram*, which is composed of the five elements at the gross level, called *tanmātras*. At the subtle level the *manas* (the unmanifest, the mind), *buddhi* (the intellect — deciding factor) and *ahaṁkāra* (the ego quotient of self-reference) are the constituent factors. The names of *dikpāla*s like Agni, Vāyu, Varuṇa, etc. clearly indicate the five elements.

The *aṣṭadikpāla*s are iconographically represented with their specific *vāhana*s (animals on which they are seated) and their attributes. Animals have always been the most immediate, important and powerful foundation for symbol systems in Hindu culture. No other source has provided such a varied range of iconography because there are few human qualities which find expression through animals. Psychology of particular animal behaviour has followed religion in attaching the various Hindu gods to animals, with the essential symbolism of the instinctual, the unconscious and the emotions. Reverence is also paid to animals by indicating the perception that they are more in touch with the unseen cosmic forces than humankind. Their superior sensory and physical abilities led to the belief that they possessed spiritual powers, hence the clans or the tribes adopted them as totems. For the same reason the animal skin, furs or feathers were worn to symbolise the magical alliances in which animals were the patrons of the wearers.

The significance of the animals as the *vāhana*s of *aṣṭadikpāla*s:

Ram — is symbolic of Agni (fire) an emblem of solar energy. The renewal of fertility and virility and the returning warmth of sun makes it the *vāhana* of Agni.

Crocodile — being an aquatic animal, *Makara* is the vehicle of Varuṇa, the god of element water. It is a creature of primordial and occult power over water, known for its destructive veracity.

Buffalo — a sacrificial animal, symbolises death. The much static quality is probably compared with the static quality of element earth. According to *Ṛgveda*, Yama was the first man to die, who reached the other world and led the path of the other world to the mortals and hence depicted as seated on a he buffalo — called the *mahiṣa*.

Stag — is known for its lightness and speed, supernatural power and grace, for which reason the element *vāyu* is depicted with deer or stag as his *vāhana*.

Bull — recognised for the vital energy. The horns of the bull which are in the shape of the crescent moon make it a lunar symbol. God of north-east — Īśāna is either shown as wearing a crescent moon or seated on a bull to indicate the association with the ethereal zone of *ākāśa*.

The above-mentioned are the gods relating to *pañcabhūta*s — the *sthūla śarīra* or the gross elements of matter — the body is composed of. The three protectors of the remaining directions are related to the subtle body — the *sūkṣma śarīra*.

Horse — an animal known for its vitality, velocity and beauty. The powers of horse are indicative of the force of life, speed of the wind and speed of the thought, for which a horse — the *aśva* symbolises the mind — the *manas* as it is called in Sanskrit. Kubera — the protector of north, rides on a horse. Some Āgamic texts also depict Kubera riding on a chariot.

Shoulder of a man — The regent Nir̥tti depicted to be mounted on the shoulders of a man is the emblem of the intellect (*buddhi*) the deciding factor, that can transmit physical and spiritual energy, a symbol of power, action strength and protection.

Airāvata — the white elephant is the vehicle of Indra — the regent of east symbolising power. Indra is the perceiver of ego.

Airāvata means pertaining of *aira* (matter). Indra on Airāvata is ego that is fascinated by matter (the body) — *ahaṁkāra* as it is called in Sanskrit.

A SCIENTIFIC PERSPECTIVE

The purpose of installing an *aṣṭadikpāla maṇḍala* in a temple is to pass on the knowledge of the cardinal directions, that is essential before undertaking any type of construction work, be it a house, a mansion, a temple, as well as city planning. The allocated land or the plot for construction or the map of the plot is first purified by performing the rituals. The eastern direction is first located using the science of geometry and the west is also located, which is joined by drawing a line called the *brahmasūtra*. Intersecting this line in the centre, is drawn the *yamasūtra* connecting the north and south points. The east point is called the Indra, west is Varuṇa. Likewise north point is Kubera and the south point becomes *Yama*. Intermediary lines are marked intersecting at the centre. The north-east line from centre is Īśāna, the line extending from centre to south-east is Āgneya, south-west is Nirṛti and north-west is Vāyavya. A square block thus encompassing the eight directional lines is called *sakala* (the total area) that is used for any construction. Hindus, when they plan to erect any edifice for religious purpose, first perform a simple geometric construction on the ground establishing east and west and constructing a square therefrom. Upon this diagram they lay out the entire building. After establishing the square, a circle called *nāgasūtra* is drawn that touches all the four cardinal directions as a symbol of the initiation of the path. Knowledge of the directions is essential to plan the entrance door, water, fire and storage aspects within the building before the construction.

The eight-sided octagon drawn on the symbolism of number eight is emblematic of renewal and the cardinal directions. Eight-sided form is to mediate between the symbolism of the square, representing earthly existence, and the circle standing for eternity. In the *maṇḍala* of Siddheśvara temple (see *Pl.* 25) the inside of the octagon has four *kīrtimukhas*, like the face of a lion on all the four cardinal directions, and four intermediary directions have *kīrtimukhas* outside the octagon. These faces are the dramatic means of projecting symbolism in religion, representing the supernatural force, of protection, and frightening the enemies or demons, providing a focus for worship. Animal face was also used to symbolise the baleful twin brother of the creator God. In Indian tradition, it is also symbolic of *māyā* and the mask of God. The *nāgasūtra*, a labyrinth of laced scrollwork filling the space between the second square boundary and the octagon, is a symbol used in ancient temples as the sacred initiation routes imitating the weaving paths of the Sun or the planets. Such intricate designs also represented the protective symbols, of frustrating the evil spirits with blockages.

The repeated conical bud-like motifs that decorate the square and octagonal boundaries are the common fractal representations of the centre of the *maṇḍala*, even though it is an iconic form in this *maṇḍala*. On each of the octagonal sides, there are nine representations. Number 9 is a powerful representation of Hindu tradition, symbolic of the planets or the eight directions with Śiva in the middle, and a triple synthesis of the mind, body and spirit of the three worlds. On the outer square boundaries, it is in the multiplication of nine.

2.12. Maṇḍala of Square Grids at Marale Siddheśvara Temple (*Pl.* 25)

Another type of square grid *maṇḍala* where lotuses are designed inside the square grids — a combination of squares and circles, with the iconic representation of the central deity in the central block is often seen in the Śaivite temples. If the central deity is with the iconographic representation of Sun, the *maṇḍala* is viewed as a *navagraha maṇḍala* of the nine planets. If the central deity is a form of Lord Īśvara, it is viewed as a *maṇḍala* of the Śaiva Siddhāntas with the subordinate deities of Vidyeśvaras and Mantreśvaras, or the eight forms of Lord Īśvara as the Mūrtyāṣṭaka.

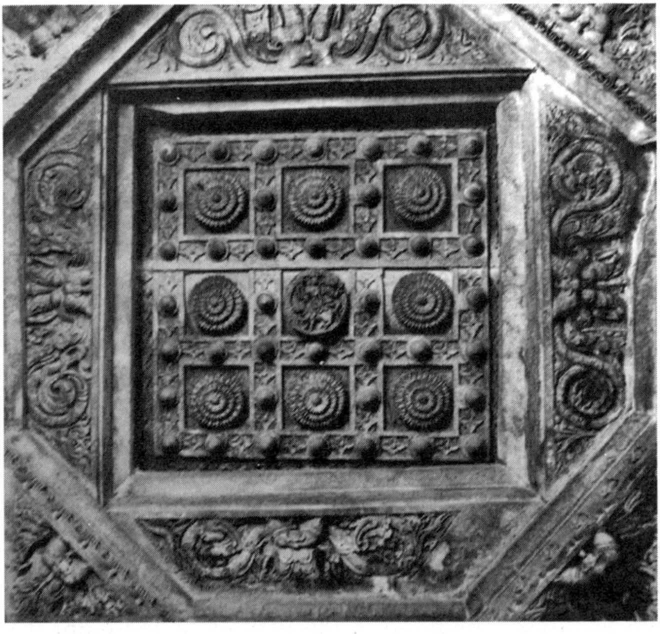

Pl. 25: *Maṇḍala* of square grids at the Marale Siddheśvara temple.

In the *maṇḍala* of Marale Siddheśvara temple, the central deity in iconic representation is the Maheśa Mūrti (a representation of the lord) as a *līlā mūrti* (the blissful sports or pastimes). The Śaiva Siddhāntins speak of three *tattva*s (Śiva, Sadāśiva and Maheśa), representing the *niṣkala* (subtle and formless, a state of Supreme Being with no beginning or end and boundary), *sakala niṣkala* (having body or form and at the same time formless, like multiple heads and hands) and *sakala* (with the concrete body of God).

The Sadāśiva or Mahāsadāśiva-mūrti of Śiva is supposed to illustrate in an esoteric or mysterious manner, the whole philosophy of Śuddha Śaiva school of Śaivism. The souls are believed to exist in pure regions which are pure in their nature, and those that live in impure region with impure nature need to be purified of impurities of dirt of action called the *mala-karma* and ignorance. The Vidyeśvaras, and next in the rank the Mantreśvaras are the troup of deities in pacific form, of pure region (the *śuddha bhuvana*s), created by Sadāśiva, who help the souls to be rid of *mala*, and the beings of lower order attain higher evolutionary stages. These groups of gods are represented in *maṇḍala*s as lotuses indicative of purity.

The Maheśa-mūrti of Lord Śiva in concrete form, is the fountainhead of all *līlā mūrti*s which may appear in *ugra* (the terrific), or the *soumya* (the calm state). It is the Maheśa-mūrti who manifests himself to the devotees in different forms performing sports (*līlā*s), and help to uplift the impure souls. He appears in 25 epithets, usually holding *mṛga, paraśu, khaḍga, vajra,* etc. seated on the animal, in a sitting posture or may be in dancing form also.

The iconic form of Maheśa-mūrti is seen in the centre of the *maṇḍala* and the eight Vidyeśvaras are in eight square grids as lotuses, and the lotus buds encircling each lotus may be the representations of Mantreśvaras who come next in ranking. It is a combination of the form and formless aspects of Śiva *tattva*s. The whole set-up is placed in a square boundary, which is enclosed further in an octagonal boundary, indicative of *aṣṭakoṇa* (symbolic of all the eight directions). *Kīrtimukhas* with the *nāgasūtra*s and scrollwork (the lines of initiation) can be seen on the four directions within the octagonal boundary. On the four corners are *kīrtimukha*s, enclosed in triangular corners, which symbolise the four legs of the *siṁhāsana,* the four-legged pedestal on which the gods are invoked. On the other cardinal directions are four more *kīrtimukhas*; the motif is with the extension of snake design on the inner octagonal boundary. (For details on *kīrtimukha*, see section 1.8.)

When all the square grids are in lotus designs, without iconic representations, they are read as Śiva and the eight forms of Śiva, namely Bhava, Sarva, Īśāna, Paśupati, Ugra, Rudra, Bhīma, and Mahādeva.

According to the description of *Viṣṇudharmottara Purāṇa* and *Aṁśumad-bhedāgama*, these deities are required to be present in sculpture or a set up in Śiva temples.

3

Golden Ratios in Maṇḍalas

And their Application in Hindu Divine Sculptures

3.1. Golden Ratios and Geometry in the Maṇḍala of Iṭṭagi Mahādeva Temple (*Pl.* 26)

HISTORICAL BACKGROUND

IṬṬAGI is situated in Yelburga taluk of Koppal district of Karnataka

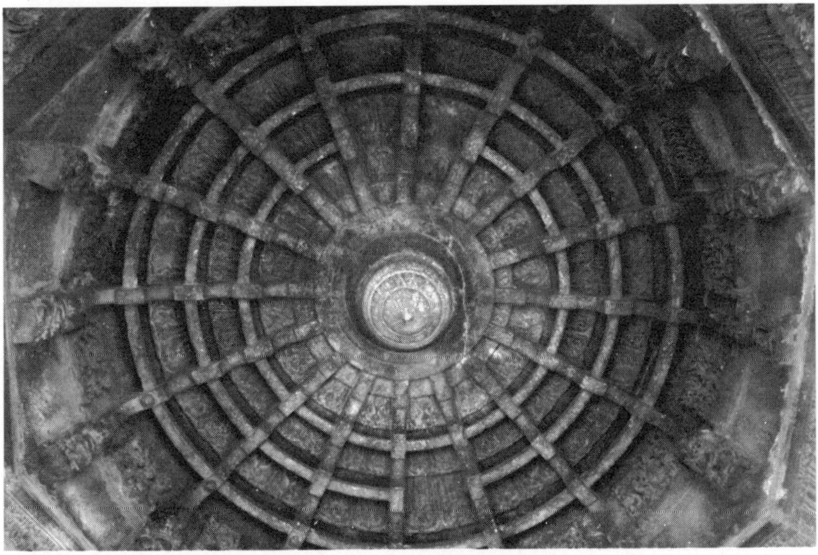

Pl. 26: *Maṇḍala* of Iṭṭagi Mahādeva temple.

state. This place is famous for the Mahādeva temple, which is one of the finest of the later Cāḷukyan temples. The temple was built in CE 1112 by a general named Mahādeva (a *daṇḍanāyaka* of the western Cāḷukya king Tribhuvanamalla Vikramāditya VI), and is dedicated to Lord Śiva. It is amongst the larger temples built by the western Cāḷukyas and perhaps the most famous one. One of the inscriptions of this temple praises this as *devālaya cakravartī* (emperor among temples). The temple is acclaimed to be one of the best in the country, both in magnificence of its architectural style, and decorative details.

The highlight of this temple is the *garbhagṛha* (the sanctum) with a *liṅga* (the phallic symbol of Lord Śiva) — surrounded by 13 minor shrines each with a *liṅga.* The shrine has a huge pillared hall with a total of 68 pillars both big and small, and 26 of them are big and support the roof. The temple has two other shrines dedicated to Mūrti Nārāyaṇa and Cāṇḍāleśvarī, the parents of the Cāḷukyan commander Mahādeva.

The domical ceiling, the *bhuvaneśvarī* of the *navaraṅga* hall of Mahādeva temple is very beautifully designed which looks like a spider web on a flat picture, but like an opened umbrella in its domical structure with a circular *maṇḍala*.

STRUCTURE

This *maṇḍala* looks like a spider web, which is beautifully designed with accuracy in its divisions. The central dot (*bindu*), the residence of the deity, is encircled by a *valaya* of five concentric circles in increasing order of its circumference like the ripples of a circular wave pattern and finally enclosed in an octagonal boundary. From the inner core are 16 spokes that radiate up to the biggest last circle. Each spoke ends with a rectangular block with a figure of the *abhimānī devatā.* The 16 divisions resulting by cutting the circle diametrically at eight points look like a superimposed design on a base structure of concentric circles (the *valaya*). All circles at base level have a squarish design with a carving of probably the *liṅga* (it is hard to trace the exact motif) in it which appears more like a unit of measurement. The centre point *bindu* hangs down like a pendant and the unique pattern of the *maṇḍala* is enclosed in an octagonal boundary. All the 16 intersecting points of the radii on the outer circle have fractal representations of the central deity, the conical bud that is visible. On the inner circles it is just a design with a central point.

PHILOSOPHICAL PERSPECTIVE

The *maṇḍala* gives a picture of the distribution of energy from the central power, the deity which is equal in all directions and that which expands in wave pattern. *Bṛhadāraṇyaka Upaniṣad* (2.1 and 19) mentions of the spider, sitting at the centre, issues threads in concentric circles, all held at one point and it also issues divergent lines in between, but all can be traced back to the central point of the web. *Śvetāśvatara Upaniṣad* (ch. 6.10) also explains that "the one God who is propelled by his own nature, spreads around himself like a spider in the manifestations of the primordial matter. May he grant an entrance to the world of *Brahman*."

This *maṇḍala* is a symbol reflecting the metaphysical concept of unfolding of energies. The concentric lines of the *maṇḍala* define its volume and create a rhythmic unit — the point of integration. The centre is the radiating source of energy that generates all forms. The spider's web is a simple metaphor, as it focuses on the Indian thought that all existence is governed by a single principle that is a reservoir of collective energy. The *maṇḍala* also hints about the cosmic unity underlying physical diversity. Such patterns with a geometric design often symbolic of the laws of the universe were used in Eastern religion as an aid to meditation as well as an instruction chart with revelatory symbols. The philosophical thoughts about the central power fit into a scheme of straight lines and perfect concentric circles in this *maṇḍala*.

SCIENTIFIC PERSPECTIVE

Mathematics was a specialised discipline of knowledge. A few persons with an exceptional interest in the subject and its application confined themselves to this specialised area. In ancient and medieval periods, study of mathematics was a pre-occupation of a few astronomers scattered all over the country. The intellectual efforts of Indians of ancient period in the development and application of mathematics in *maṇḍala*s is a unique feature.

Geometry is a part of mathematics concerning length, area, volume, etc. The perfect geometric pattern with circles and radiating divisions correlate with many geometric theorems and the *phi* ratios. A visual nature of these aspects through a *maṇḍala* made the subject more accessible than other branches of mathematics like algebra and arithmetic. Geometry was viewed as a practical science, which helped in computing the distances, heights of similar geometric figures or objects. Geometry was viewed as a practical science which helped in computing the distances, heights of similar geometrical figures or objects. Geometry was thus put into axiomatic form, to enlighten the viewers about the evident truths of the universe.

The *jijñāsus* (the seekers of scientific data) often wondered about the aspects of the earth like its huge mass, area, volume and capacity. To have a data, they had to calculate the area of a circle, in terms of its diameter, its circumference and then convert to the surface area of earth. The *maṇḍala* was used as a device where the art of measuring the area of a circle was demonstrated. It can be studied with four aspects:

1. The concentric circles,
2. The radiating lines making sectors on the concentric circles,
3. The motifs beneath the radiating lines, and

4. The skeletal frame for the construction of domical structures.

The *maṇḍala* has several concentric circles, the area and volume of which is divided by a polygonal structure of 16 radiating lines. The idea of volume and area gives a picture of geometry and mathematics. In post-Vedic period, mathematics developed, dealing with practical problems. Problems with geometric treatment were discussed under topics as *kṣetra* (plane figure), *khāta* (excavation or cubic figures), *citi* (piles of bricks), *krakaca* (cubic figures), *chāyā* (shadows dealing with similarities and proportions). This mode of knowledge continued up to the time of Bhāskara II, or even later. The typical mathematical problems that interested Indian mathematicians of ancient and medieval periods prompted them to the knowledge of astronomical calculations. Trigonometry, geometry, and calculus were all developed as an integral part of astronomy as discussed by P.C. Sen Gupta in an essay of the book *The Cultural Heritage of India* (vol. VI, p. 55 on calculus). This *maṇḍala* was also like a model chart to calculate the circumference of circles with different radii.

Calculus: Rudimentary ideas of integration and differentiations are found in the works of Brahmagupta and Bhāskara II (twelfth century CE) to determine the area and volume of a sphere by a method of summation analogous to integration. In the first method, the surface was divided into elementary annuli, by drawing a series of parallel circles about any point on the surface. The number of circles according to Bhāskara II can be as many as desired. The area of the sphere is given by the sum of areas of the annuli. This method might have been adopted to find the area of the circle other than using the *pi* constant.

Beneath every radiating and dividing line in the *maṇḍala* is the quadrilateral block pattern in the sectors of the concentric circles. This may be treated as block, or a unit of calculation. A sum of all these quadrilateral blocks gave the approximate surface area of a circle. It is a simple calculation like building blocks. These methods were probably laid to teach the students of astrology and geometry as temples were centres of education, culture and religion. Since the knowledge of cosmos was sacred, it was laid out as *maṇḍala*s.

On all the four concentric circles, the block design (probably the figure of a *liṅga*) is carved in varying geometric patterns like a trapezium, square and a rectangle, which are designed as units of measurement to calculate the area of a particular circle. The inner two smaller circles have the 16 blocks of trapezium. The area of the circle was calculated by finding the area of the given trapezium block and multiplying it by 16.

The third circle has the pattern of square blocks of two units in each sector that is divided by the radiating lines on the circle. The area of this particular circle was calculated by finding the area of each square block and multiplying by 32.

Similarly the fourth circle has the design carved in rectangular blocks of two units in each division and the area of the circle was determined by finding the area of each rectangular block and multiplying by 32.

The approximate area of the *maṇḍala* could be known by the sum of areas of the parallel circles. These calculations were required for the mathematical calculations, for example, the surface area of the wheel of the cart was essential to calculate the number of revolutions made by the wheel to cover a particular distance, as well as in architectural constructions.

To find the area of the circle, *maṇḍala* was divided into a large number of triangles, with their bases lying on the outermost octagonal side on the surface of the *maṇḍala* and their apices coinciding with the centre. The sum of the area of these triangles gave the area of the circle (ref. figure of cut triangles in *Pl.* 27).

Golden Ratios or the Fibonacci Sequence: A set of numbers observing a particular sequence, which can run up to infinity, is called Fibonacci sequence — named after the Italian mathematician, who lived in CE 1225. It is also called as "phi" ratio and in Indian architecture, it is called golden ratios (*deva pramāṇa*), because this ratio occurs in nature.

Numbers in this sequence are like — 1, 2, 3, 5, 8, 13, 21, 34, and so on.

The logic being when any number in the sequence is added to the previous number of the sequence, the sum is the third number, like,

0+1=1

1+1=2

1+2=3

2+3=5

3+5=8

5+8=13

8+13=21 and so on.

When a bigger number is divided by its previous number, the dividant is always a constant of 1.6, which is the golden value of "*phi*." Like 8/5, or 5/3, or 13/8, gives a constant value of 1.6, which is called "*phi*," the golden ratio, and the mathematics of this is closely connected with the Fibonacci sequences. The values are approximate when numbers are less than 5 and accurate for number 5 and above. Golden ratio, or the Fibonacci sequence is also applied in the rhythm patterns of Indian classical music which makes it pleasing to the ears. When the line segments of geometric figures observe the *phi* ratios — it was called golden ratios under sacred geometry, as the unique ratios are preferred by nature.

PHI OR THE GOLDEN TRIANGLES AND TRAPEZIUMS IN A CIRCLE (*Pl.* 27)

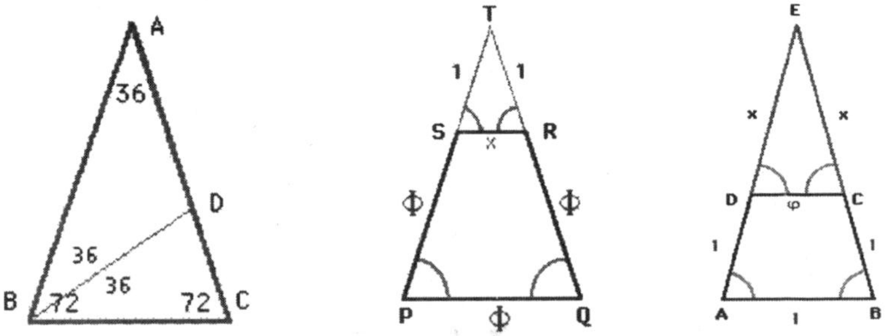

Fig. 2

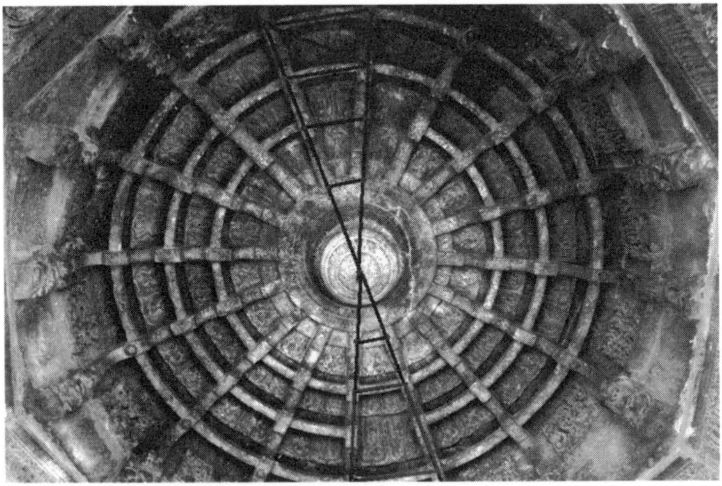

Pl. 27: Golden triangles and trapeziums.

Phi is an irrational number, an astonishing number, a constant value of 1.618 like the value of *pi* (3.141 or 22/7) and considered as the greatest treasure of geometry. The *maṇḍala* at Iṭṭagi Mahādeva temple gives the knowledge of the golden triangle and trapezium. The golden ratio of geometry which exists in nature was given a mathematical expression by the Italian mathematician Fibonacci and the golden ratio is also called by his name *phi* sections in geometry. It is amazing to observe that Indian architects used this in sculpturing temple designs and sculptures much before Fibonacci's time.

If *pi* is used in relation to circles, *phi* is the solution to quadratic equations. *Phi* like *pi* is a ratio defined by a geometric construction. In geometry, golden ratio results when a line is divided in a unique way. The ratio of the length of the entire line to the length of the larger line segment is the same as the ratio of the length of the larger line segment to the shorter one.

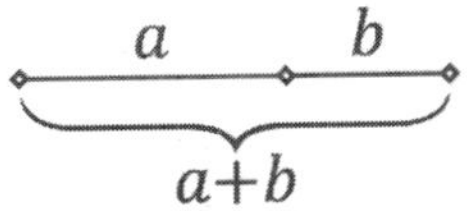

$a+b$ is to a as a is to b

The *phi*-based geometric shapes are used to create interesting *phi maṇḍalas*, embodying the *phi* proportions that are found throughout the creation. By the interaction of *phi* ratios, it is possible to create infinitely large and infinitely small patterns observing the same ratio of the original pattern, and hence called a golden ratio and divine proportion. Many geometrical shapes like triangle, rectangle, square, trapezium, and circle, when observing the golden ratio with the sides are categorised as golden triangle or rectangle and so on. *Phi* also appears in a number of geometric constructions using circles which produce *phi* relationships.

Triangles may be isoscelers or equilateral golden triangles, when inscribed in a circle. In isoscelers triangles, the ratio of the hypotenuse and the base lengths are in a golden ratio. The triangle can be cut into sections, each smaller triangle observes the golden ratios in their angles and can also be cut into trapeziums with golden sections.

Phi trapezium has the top and bottom sides parallel. All the three sides, except the top shorter one, are equal in length as seen in *fig.* 3 of *Pl.* 27, i.e. *AB*=*BC*=*AD*. The top and bottom sides are in golden ratio. That is side *AB*/*DC* = *phi*, i.e. 1.618.

When the sides of the golden trapezium are extended to form a triangle, two isosceles triangles result — a big one and a small triangle on top (ref. fig. 2 & 3 of *Pl.* 27). Both triangles measure 72° at the bottom two angles and 36 at the top angle. When the bigger side is divided by the base ratio of 1.6 it is golden.

In the *maṇḍala* of Iṭṭagi Mahādeva temple, all the triangles in the 16 sectors observe a golden ratio of *phi* (see fig. 2 of *Pl.* 27). When the conical bud-like fractal representations on the concentric circles are considered as points, and they are joined by lines to construct a triangle (in a two dimensional picture) the golden ratios can be traced. *Phi*-based geometric shapes are used here to create some interesting *phi maṇḍala*s embodying the golden ratios and proportions that are found throughout the creation and iterating into the infinitely small and infinitely large, much as the universe. Many of the sculptures of gods in temples are designed on the golden proportions of triangles (ref. *Pl.* 48 of Saranath Buddha) for which reason the elegance charms the devotees instantly.

SKELETAL STRUCTURE OF DOMES

The design of the *maṇḍala* bears a resemblance to the skeletal structure for the construction of domes that was evolved during fifteenth century CE. Even though the dome was considered as a conventional symbol of heaven in both the Eastern and the Western architectures, Indian architects did not master the art of constructing perfect domes of larger dimensions. The domical structure was used mostly in the domical ceiling — *bhuvaneśvarī*, of the *navaraṅga* hall of the temple, which was of much smaller dimension when compared to the size of domes seen in the cathedrals and basilica of European architecture or the Islamic mosque. However, Hindu architects had a clear picture of the technique of building domes, which is demonstrated not only in the *maṇḍala* of Iṭṭagi Mahādeva temple but in many other temples also. These domical ceilings in the temple did not meet the definition of a perfect dome as seen in the European architecture, but the frames of both bear striking resemblance and hence are compared here.

During fourteenth-fifteenth century CE European architecture witnessed the development and understanding of structural engineering of the domes. The aspiration of raising domes of colossal height came with its own problems. The stones of big size, at basal levels weighing several tons often got crushed under its own weight and the stones of many domes thrust outward by the pull energy called the "hoop stress" much like an inflated balloon bulges outward when compressed from above. This resulted in the domes getting into series of cracks especially where the dome curved inwards and the fabric of the dome stretched at its haunches around the circumference. After a series of trial and error methods, the Italian architect by name Filippo redesigned the architecture of domes by supporting the structure with a double-shelled skeletal frame in between the outer and inner surface of the domes to hold the masonry in place and the use of wooden centring or the scaffolding from the ground, that was incredibly expensive but in practice, got changed. Since the octagon was the skeletal frame of a circle, the double-shelled wall of the frame was transcribed in an octagonal or polygonal base on which the dome rested. The ascending order of rings in the building of the cupola served the vital function that was supported and bonded by the herring bone structure of bricks or beams on the outer edges. This octagon was further reinforced by the midribs which prevented the dome from collapsing. The outer wall looked octagonal but the inner shell of the dome was constructed and plastered in a circular shape. Because of the massive structure, the empty space in between the two walls was left open. One of the keys to raising the dome was the precise calculation and geometric measurement of each horizontal layer of brick or stone, as it was added in a gradually contracting sequence.

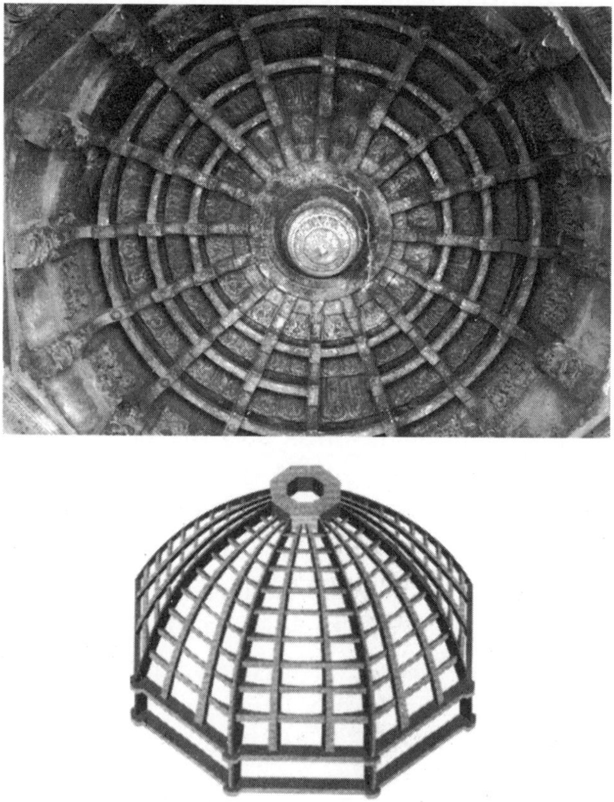

Pl. 28: Comparing the *maṇḍala* at the Iṭṭagi Mahādeva temple and the framework for a dome designed by Filippo Brunelleschi.

The structural parts are exposed outside in the case of domes and the inner surface was plastered smooth, whereas in the *maṇḍala* of Iṭṭagi temple, the structural beams are seen on the inner side and the smoother surface is concealed behind the beams. The central circular stone of the *maṇḍala* can be compared to the apex stone of the dome. The height of the dome from springing point to apex is 177 ft and the height of the basal drum is 108 ft. It represents a golden ratio cutting between the octagonal drum and the dome's height.

This ratio can also be observed in the Iṭṭagi Mahādeva temple.

The author has observed striking similarities between the structural elements and construction of the *maṇḍala* of Iṭṭagi Mahādeva temple of twelfth century and the skeletal structure frame that got evolved in fifteenth century in the Santa Maria dome in Florence, which is the biggest masonry dome constructed with brick and mortar.

3.2. Golden Ratios in the Maṇḍala of the Hoysaḷeśvara Temple at Halebiḍ

HISTORICAL BACKGROUND

Halebiḍ, as it is called now, flourished as the capital of Hoysaḷas during the twelfth and thirteenth centuries CE, and was called Dvārasamudra. It is a small village in Hassan district, situated 224 km from the city of Bengaluru, and 16 km away from the famous Hoysaḷa temple of Beḷūr. The temple was constructed by Ketamalla — the chief of the staff of the Hoysaḷa king Viṣṇuvardhana during CE 1121. It is a Śaivite temple bearing the deities as two *liṅga*s (the phallic symbol of Lord Śiva) and named after the Hoysaḷa king and queen — Hoysaḷeśvara and Santaleśvara.

The temple contains two different sanctums each with its vestibule, *navaraṅga* hall and the bull (*nandī*) *maṇḍapa*. The two temples, built symmetrically side by side with separate *navaraṅga* halls, are connected by a corridor. The south part of the hall is better designed with lathe-turned pillars and an elaborately carved flat ceiling with the *maṇḍala* of square and rectangular designs.

STRUCTURE OF THE MAṆḌALA

This *maṇḍala* at the Hoysaḷeśvara temple of Halebiḍ looks distinctly different. It is a rectangular *maṇḍala* with 9 divisions. The middle row has square blocks while the top and bottom rows have 3 rectangular blocks, all 9 blocks contain the icons of god within. The whole frame is enclosed in a rectangular frame with lotus motifs, which are also present in between the blocks. Outside the frame, the structure is different from the usual pattern of *maṇḍala* boundary. Lotus bud motifs can be seen only on either side of the width part of the big rectangle, which are not of the same number. The left side is better decorated with the *kīrtimukha* in between the motif of creepers, followed by the figures of humans in miniature form engaged in activities of fine arts like drawing and playing musical instruments. The other side of the width part of rectangle has *kīrtimukha* with scrollwork, which is smaller in size. The longer side of the rectangle looks plain with step-like decoration probably to give the effect of depth and architectural stability to the *maṇḍala.*

Vāstuśāstra in ancient Indian design principle has a category called *citra-sūtra* dealing with the organisation of space and proportions in pictures adorning the walls of the temples. The *maṇḍala* of Halebiḍ explains the details and schemes regarding this branch of art.

The uniqueness here is that the figures, carved in blocks, are arranged in a clockwise direction, starting from the bottom of the central deity, and the viewers have to move in clockwise direction to get the correct orientation of the figures that are inside each block.

The central deity is Lord Gaṇeśa as Nṛtta Gaṇapati in a dancing posture. He has eight hands holding the specific attributes like *pāśa, aṅkuśa,* etc. with the broken tusk — the *danta* in one of the right hands.

His right leg in raised to *kuñcita ekapāda*, indicative of a dancing posture. On either side are miniature figures of instrumentalists, playing music for the dance. On the upper two corners on either sides are the flying *gandharva*s with the *cāmara*.

To the left side of Gaṇeśa in another square block is the figure of Garuḍa, with the beak-like nose, outstretched wings and a pair of hands holding *vajra* and a branch of the tree, or may be the *kuśa* grass. He is in a sitting posture with one knee stretched backwards and carrying Viṣṇu and Lakṣmī on his shoulder.

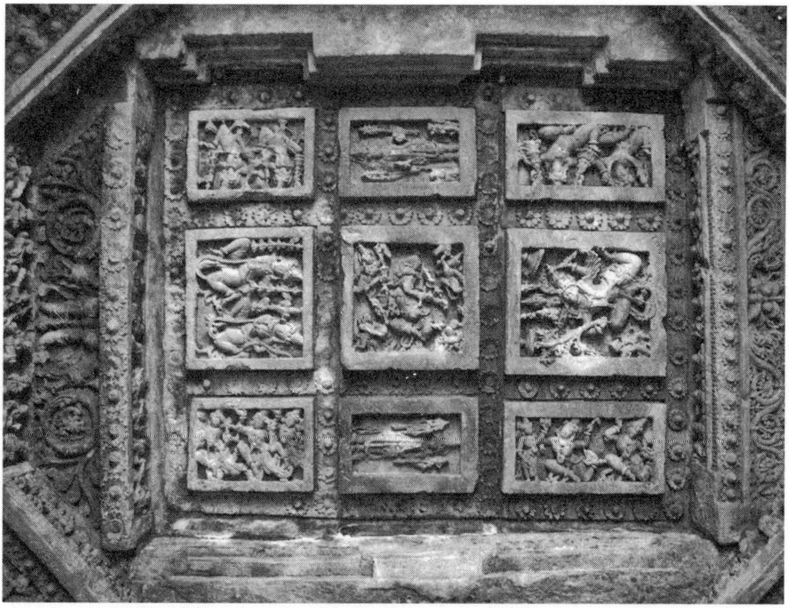

Pl. 29: *Maṇḍala* at the Hoysaḷeśvara temple, Halebiḍ.

The other square block is probably the figures of Rati and Manmatha (the God of love), as they are holding the bow and arrow, as well as flower bunches. Both of them are in the same leg postures as seen with the flying *gandharva*s.

The rectangular blocks on top and bottom of Gaṇeśa depict the figure of Viṣṇu in standing posture.

The figure in the bottom block has *śaṅkha* and *cakra* while the one on top holds *gadā, padma,* and with two attendants at the bottom.

Among the rectangular blocks in the corners, two blocks in the bottom row are with *gandharvas*, three in number, all look like they are singing and dancing, while the two blocks on top row has two figures of *gandharvas* holding flower garlands. It gives the picture of the celebration of celestial beings on the dance of Gaṇeśa. Every block is surrounded by lotus motifs.

THE SCIENTIFIC PERSPECTIVE

A careful study of this *maṇḍala* reveals that it is a frame containing a combination of square and rectangular frames with carvings, and has something to indicate about the divisions in each frame, as well as the total frame. Each square block has five small lotus motifs on each side which is indicative of the unit of measurement. Each rectangle frame has three lotuses on width and five lotuses on the length that means the ratio of sides is 3:5, that is a golden rectangle with Fibonacci ratio. An imaginary line connecting the two lotuses on either side of the frame gives a mathematical division of the picture, which hints that lotus designs are the scales of measurement in this *maṇḍala.*

GOLDEN RECTANGLE

When this ratio of 1:1.6, is applied to a geometric form of a rectangle, that is when the sides of the rectangle are in this ratio of 3 units in width and 5 units in length, it becomes a golden rectangle. If the length of the rectangle is 3+2=5 units, the point of 3 units on 5 is called the golden point. When a square with 3 units side is cut off from this rectangle, the remaining part is again a golden rectangle. Again a square is cut off from this smaller rectangle, a smaller golden rectangle results. Like this one can cut smaller and smaller golden rectangles, the ratios of which are used by architects and artists to make mathematical divisions in their working frames to create the perfect

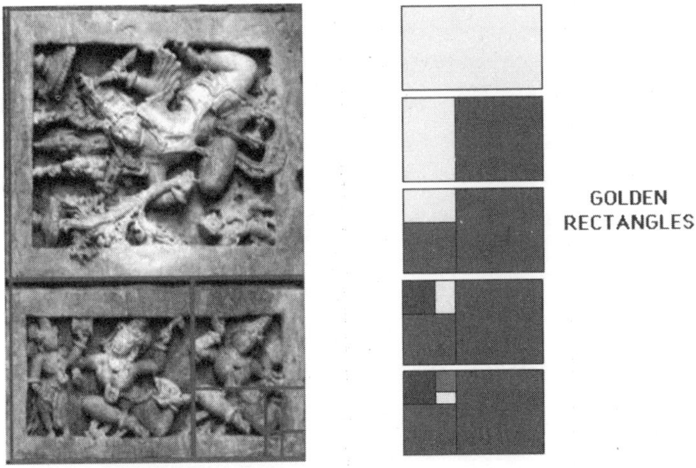

Pl. 30: A demonstration for the application of golden ratios and golden rectangles in the *bhuvaneśvarī* ceiling of Halebiḍ temple.

proportions that are pleasing to the eyes. Golden section is a unique ratio preferred by nature as the best geometry.

GOLDEN SQUARES: THE FIBONACCI SQUARES

With Fibonacci sequence, when the opposite process is applied in a rectangle, that means when a square is added to another

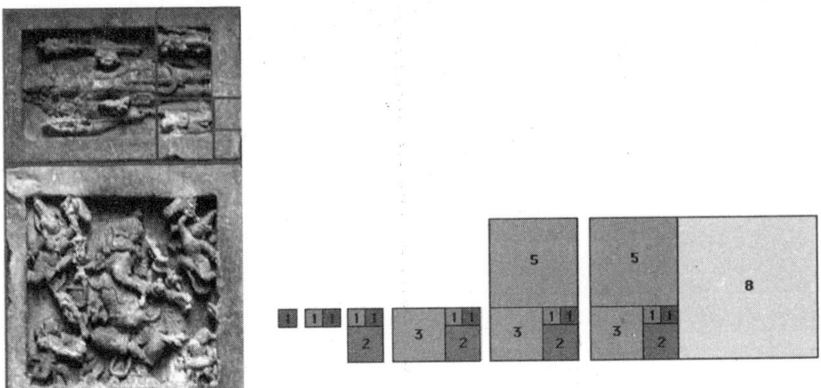

Pl. 31: A demonstration of the application of golden squares.

square of the same size to form a rectangle and new big square is added to the longer side of this rectangle, it results in a golden rectangle with *phi* ratio. Squares can be added on the longer side of the golden rectangle infinitely and the proportions of the picture are planned on these blocks to create a perfect design.

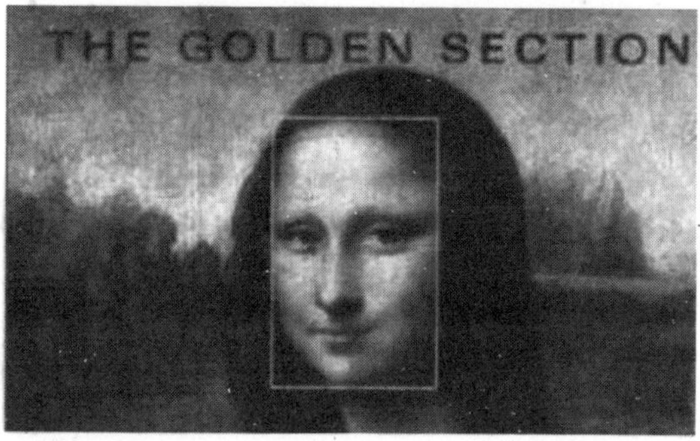

Pl. 32: Golden rectangle in the painting of *Mona Lisa*.

Leonardo da Vinci's painting, *The Last Supper*, is proportioned in the style of golden sections for the distance of the disciples to Jesus, which is in the *phi* ratio, so also the facial proportions of the figure of Mona Lisa based on golden squares for which reason they have a universal appeal. Fibonacci ratios, like fractals, occur in nature. The famous philosopher of fifth century BCE, Pythagoras considered it as the key to the physics of cosmos. Things in nature like the branching of trees, turning of the waves of the sea, spiral sea shells are all based on *phi* ratio as it was the best geometry for growth, energy conservation, elegance and bearing some fundamental relationship to the platonic solids. Even the skeletal proportions of the human arm, hand and finger joints are in Fibonacci ratios. This aspect of Fibonacci ratio that is present in humans harmonises with the Fibonacci proportions of golden rectangles, for which reason golden rectangles are extensively used in sculptures and paintings.

The *maṇḍala* of Halebiḍ gives a very clear picture of the Fibonacci ratio. It is like a guide chart for artists, giving the knowledge of how to plan the main figure, dwarf figures and multiple figures in one frame. The frame with lotus design, adjoining the scrollwork in the outermost boundary indicates the Fibonacci ratio to be 21 lotus on one side and 13 on the other side, which indicates that lotus designs are the units of measurement. The inner squares are 5/5 units in measurement and rectangles are 5/3 units, indicated by the number of lotuses, which make it a golden rectangle. When a square and the adjoining rectangle are joined, it becomes a bigger golden rectangle, with the measurement of 5:8, which gives a *phi* ratio of 1:1.6.

The figure on *Pl.* 30 gives a picture of how divisions are to be made, if three *gandharva* figures are made in one rectangular frame. First, a line is drawn cutting the frame into a square and a smaller rectangle in *phi* ratio. Two figures are drawn on the square piece and one figure in the rectangle. This one figure area is further cut into a square, where the upper part of the body is drawn and a smaller rectangle to draw the lower part of the body. The rectangle is further cut into a square and a rectangle to draw the thigh and ankle part of the legs of *gandharva*. This scheme adds aesthetic beauty to the picture with perfection in the body proportions of the figure.

The two rectangles in the bottom row of the *maṇḍala* are with three *gandharva* figures and the top two rectangles in top row are with two figures.

The middle frame of the *maṇḍala* with the figure of Lord Viṣṇu in *Pl.* 31 indicates how a line is drawn, observing the *phi* ratio to plan the upper part of the body with the attributes in the bigger square part, and leg part with the dwarf attendants in the smaller rectangular part, all in the scheme of Fibonacci squares.

Hoysaḷa architects have adopted the golden ratios even in the long rows of animal panels in the lower friezes of temple walls, for which reason they look very proportionate even in small frames.

The central figure of dancing Gaṇeśa also provides details as to how geometry can be used to compose paintings or sculptures. On the square platform *ABCD*, midpoint on each side is marked forming smaller square *EFGH*. The four corners are right-angled triangles, and are used to draw small figures of flying *gandharva*s on top and instrumentalists at the bottom. In the central square, the figure of Gaṇeśa is drawn, fixing the point of forehead in between the eyebrows and the navel point on the diagonal axis *EG*. The diagram given below comes as a variation by Grail geometry, an ancient proof of Plato's theorem.

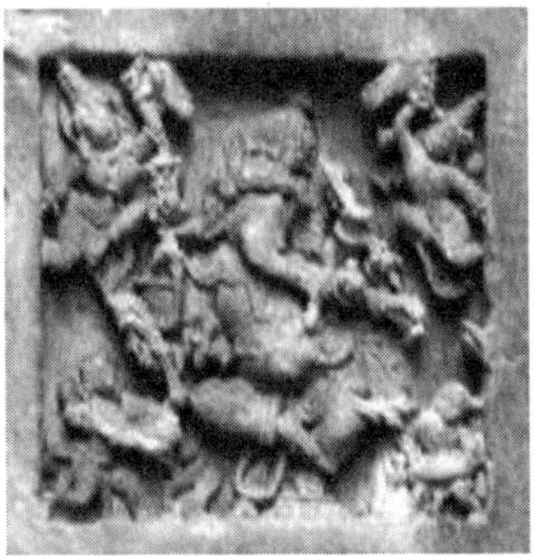

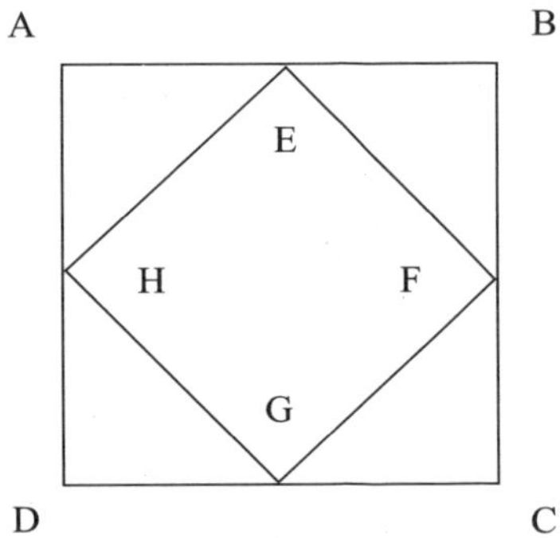

Grail geometry

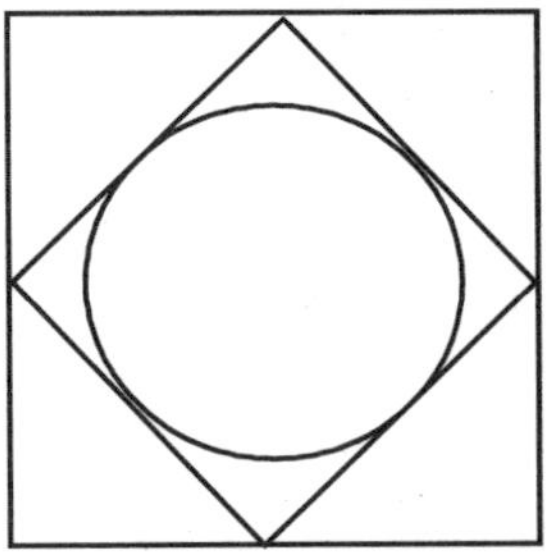

Templar variation

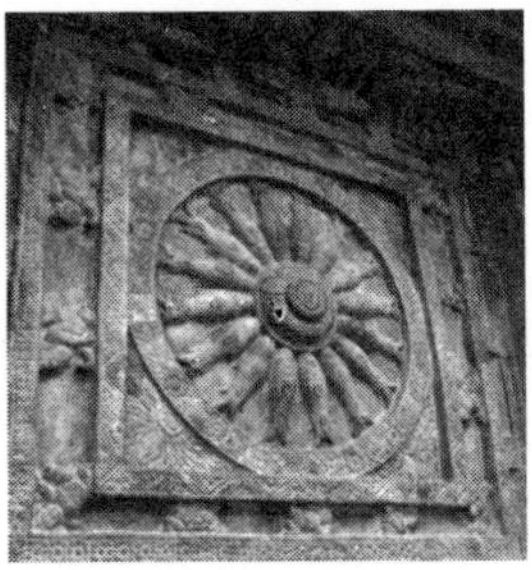

Maṇḍala in Bādāmi Cave

Pl. 33: Geometry of the Gaṇeśa panel.

Another variation of this, the Templar variation of Plato's theorem, can be seen where a circle is inscribed within the smaller square, so as to be tangent to all sides. The circle may be used to draw the circular *maṇḍala*s (as we can see in *Pl.* 13, the *maṇḍala* in the Bādāmi cave).

Another interesting information about the geometry for composing the frame before carving the sculptures or drawing a painting is also seen in this *maṇḍala.*

If a rectangle is drawn which has the golden ratio of 1 unit high and 2.236 units long, it can be cut into a square in the centre with 1 unit side and on either side results a golden rectangle with *phi* ratios. Thus the golden rectangles can easily be subdivided for laying the proportions of the required figure.

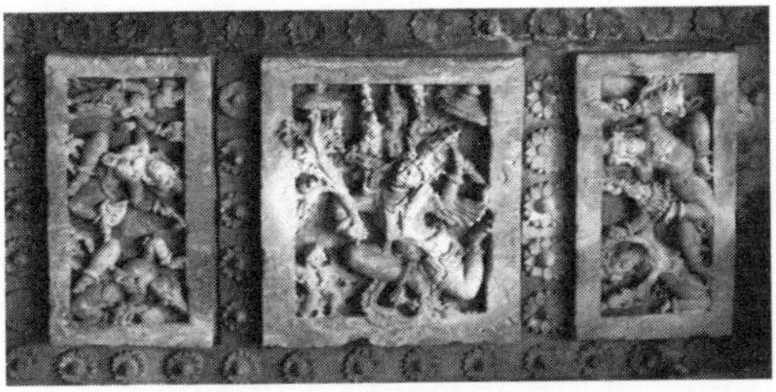

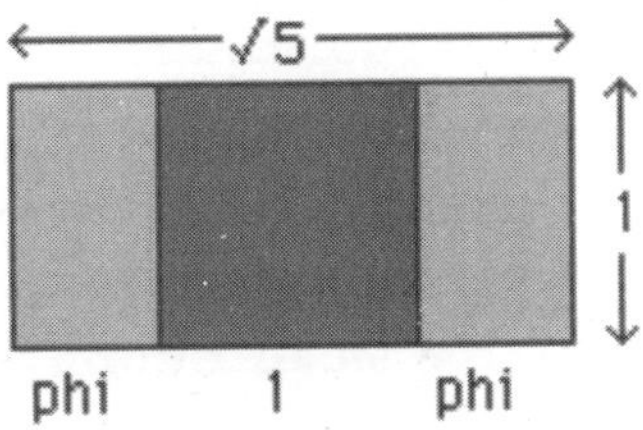

Pl 34: Golden square and rectangles.

In the author's opinion, if the square block in the centre of the model figure is indicative of five unit measurement (five is a golden sequence number) it can be assumed as *pañcatala* as it is called that is always used to carve the figure of Lord Gaṇeśa. One smaller rectangle, with three unit measurement (3 is again a golden sequence number) attached to this, makes it a golden rectangle with sides of 8/5 units of measurement.

These ratios were used to produce a pleasing rectangular frame much like golden rectangle. A demonstration of this is given in the ceiling design of Halebiḍ Hoysaḷeśvara temple, where the central square with the figure of dancing Gaṇeśa or the adjoining Garuḍa figure is planned with two golden rectangles on either side. The unit of measurement is given through the lotus design which is 3:5, a *phi* ratio for the smaller rectangle. The longer side of the rectangle has 5 lotuses. The smaller side has 3 of them. The breadth and length in the borders rows depict 13 and 21 flowers which is a *phi* ratio. One rectangle and the central square show 8 flowers. The depiction of 3, 5, 8, 13, 21 is a representation of golden ratios.

There is another demonstration of how an L-shape can be cut from the square, as seen in the square with Garuḍa figure. The well-known geometrician Nick Lord found the ratio in which a small square can be cut on one side from a big square, and balance the L-shape to draw the smaller figures. The ratio was again a golden *phi* ratio between big square side and the removed square side. The L-shape had the balance point in the midpoint, which has been used in the figure of Garuḍa to fix the forehead point between the eyebrows, when the L-shape was planned on top side. The length of L-shape was used to draw the small figure of Lakṣmī and Nārāyaṇa on Garuḍa's shoulder as well as the umbrella of royal insignia on his head.

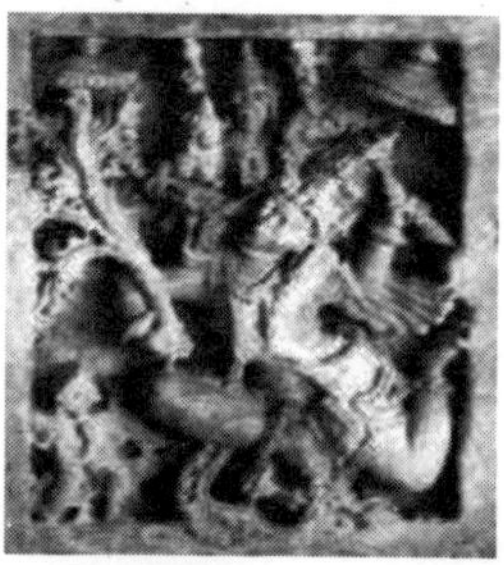

Pl. 35: Location of balance point in a square frame.

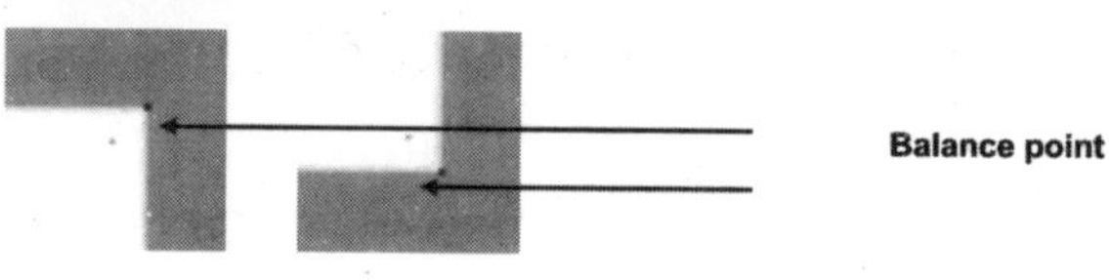

When the L-shape was planned on the bottom Navel side, the balance point of L-shape has been used to fix the navel point of Garuḍa. The left knee and the navel point are on the diagonal line. These ratios gave a perfect balancing between the big and smaller figures in one frame and the body proportions of the main figure as well as the dwarf figures.

The adjoining square on the left side of dancing Gaṇeśa (see *Pl.* 29) demonstrates how a square can be cut into two parts to fix two figures of *gandharva*s in one square block.

The Hoysaḷa sculptors used these ratios and proportions earlier to Phibonacci discovering it in 1225 CE to carve the panels and sculptures all over the temple which made the art of proportions easy and aesthetically beautiful.

3.3. Application of Golden Rectangles in the Hindu Divine Sculpture of Tirupati Veṅkaṭeśvara

The sculpture of Lord Veṅkaṭeśvara at Tirumala in Tirupati hills, situated in the state of Andhra Pradesh in the southern part of India, has been chosen by the author as one of the figures for analysis as it is a sacred and the most popular sculpture attracting millions of people. To attract huge crowds, a divine sculpture or a temple calls for certain aspects like:

1. A proper place where the elements of nature are in harmony;
2. Situated above a hill which is considered to be the abode of gods; and
3. In a forest or on a river bed, where the *abhimānī devatā*s — the troop of benevolent gods who are believed to be present in such places — act as promoters of peace and joy, enhancing the beauty of the main deity.

Apart from the location, religious beliefs, Purāṇic and mythological backgrounds, one of the main reasons for the

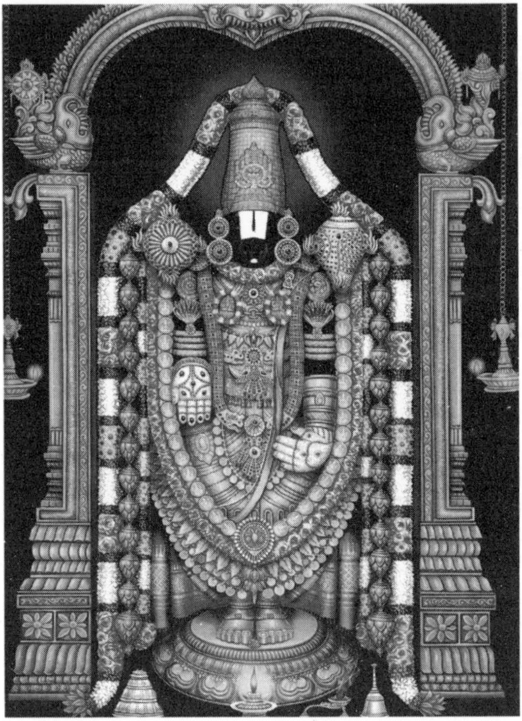

Pl. 36: Figure of Lord Veṅkaṭeśvara at Tirupati.

popularity is probably the golden ratio that is observed in the proportions of the sculpture which gives a spontaneous admiration and acceptance of the grace and majesty involved. Even though observing mere golden ratios will not make a sculpture divine, it is no doubt an essential ingredient. Golden ratios in sculptures give a perfect frame to the figure. Installing compassion, beauty, and expression is in the sculptor or the artist's capacity which can be compared to infusing soul to a figure. Golden ratio is a mathematical perfection in nature, containing the ground principle of all formatives, striving for beauty and completeness.

For the purpose of analysing the sculpture from the perspective of the golden ratios, a two-dimensional picture of the image (ignoring the decoration like garlands) is considered. The figure of Veṅkaṭeśvara has two shoulders, which, according to the Bhāgavata tradition, is called Ādi Vāsudeva and is considered in this book for analysis. It is called Para Vāsudeva when he is depicted with four shoulders. For the benefit of the readers, and to understand how the golden sections are used in the sculptures a construction method is provided by the author. Enthusiasts may try it out to understand the geometric ratios in the figure of the deity.

THE FRAME OF THE FIGURE

The figure, when analysed according to the golden sections, can be constrained within the frame of two golden rectangles as width is the deciding factor in the golden rectangle. The two rectangles share a common side at the navel region. The figure has *mahāpuruṣa lakṣana* — the special features, adopted for Hindu divine sculptures (for details refer *Pl.* 44), where the width across the shoulder is in the same measurement as from the top of the skull to navel point (which is usually in a golden ratio in an ideal human figure) and the ears are longer. The lower earlobe is drawn up to the chin point in the sculpture which is up to the lip section in humans. The sacred marks of *padma* appear on the palms and feet. In human body, the distance between the navel and foot, to its total height is a *phi* — the golden ratio — and the genital point is the midpoint of the body. In the figure of Lord Veṅkaṭeśvara, navel point becomes the midpoint of the total height, when crown is included for the total height, for which reason the figure can be divided into two rectangles, sharing the same side at the navel region *A–B*.

The divisions in the construction method of the top rectangle are marked with alphabets in capitals while that of the bottom rectangle has alphabet markings in small letters.

The top rectangle *ABEF* defines the crown part, the face and the chest region with the consorts Śrīdevī and Bhūdevī. The bottom rectangle *ABgh* defines the palms, legs and feet. The analysis shows a methodology in the geometrical construction of the figure.

Draw two golden rectangles *ABEF* and *ABgh* of any width but having sides in golden ratios. It is easier if the sides measure in *phi* sequence like, 1, 2, 3, 5, 8, 13, 21 and so on. If the choice is a non-*phi* number, the golden ratio will have to be derived by dividing the longer side by 1.618 which is the *phi* constant. For example, if the longer side is 10 units divide it by 1.618 to get the length of smaller side, which is 6.2 units.

Locate the midpoint *P* from the centre of top side *EF* and *p* at the bottom line *gh*. Draw the line *P–p* to divide the rectangle *ABEF* and *ABgh* vertically into two halves to be able to draw the facial features and the limbs symmetrically.

The position of the *cakras* which is adorned by varieties of ornaments can be located on the figure see *Pl.* 37 marked as following:

The point *O* on the midline locates the mid-part of the head and the position of *sahasrāra cakra*.

The point *Q* indicates the throat and the position of *viśuddha cakra*, that is always decorated by a garland of flowers in the figure.

The *padma*, the wheel pendant, that can be seen in the midpoint of *Q* and *R* and also in between the two consorts embedded in the chest indicates the position of *anāhata cakra*. The point *R* marks the *maṇipūra cakra*, indicated by the waistband and a snake motif above the *padma* in the navel region.

Below this can be seen the moon pendant across the *gaṇḍa bheruṇḍa* pendant — which depicts the bird with two heads, marks the position of *svādhiṣṭhāna cakra* (see *Pl.* 39).

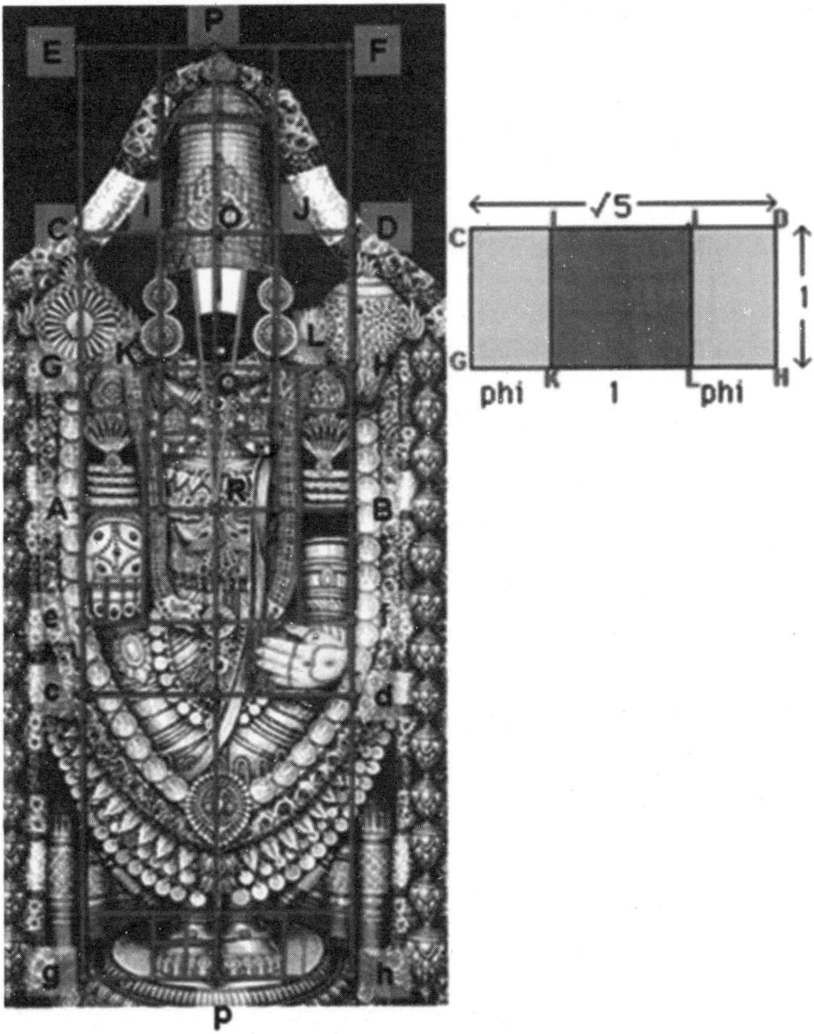

Pl. 37: Golden ratios in the figure of Lord Veṅkaṭeśvara.

The point *q* in the lower rectangle that is in line with the finger tips of the right hand indicates the position of *mūlādhāra cakra*. This can be located above the head of the lower pendant of *gaṇḍa bheruṇḍa* — depicting the bird with two heads and marked by the wheel motif.

THE TOP RECTANGLE (*Pl.* 38)

Construct a golden rectangle *ABEF*.

Cut a line *CD* at the golden section of the longer side *AE* to get a square *ABCD* and a rectangle *ECDF.*

Divide the square *ABCD* into four equal parts by bisecting lines, call it *GH* and *OR*. Mark the midpoint as *Q*.

The top two squares give the details of the face, earrings and the attributes *śaṅkha* and *cakra* while the bottom two squares give the details of upper arms, and chest region with icons of Śrīdevī and Bhūdevī — the consorts of Lord Veṅkaṭeśvara.

Measure the golden ratio of the side of the small square *CG* (divide the length by *phi* constant 1.6) and call it Golden Ratio–1.

Similarly, measure the golden ratio of the smaller side *CE* of the top rectangle *ECDF* (divide it by 1.6) and call it Golden Ratio–2. Golden ratios 1 and 2 are required often to define the face and hand sections and the white mark of the face.

For an easier calculation in *Pl.* 37 of the frame, the measurement of ec = Golden Ratio–1 (also equal to JD of face dimension)

The measurement of *Ae* = Golden Ratio–2 (also equal to IJ of face dimension).

For those who wish to try out the construction method, the procedure becomes easier if the Golden Ratios 1 and 2 are measured and kept ready.

TO DRAW THE FACIAL DIMENSIONS (ref. *Pl.* 38)

From the points *C* and *D* bisect the Golden Ratio–1 towards the point *O* — the mid-part of the skull and mark them as points *I* and *J* respectively.

Repeat the bisection Golden Ratio–1 from points *G* and *H* towards *Q* — the chin point on the midline and mark the points as *K* and *L*. The resulting square *IJKL* is for the face dimensions.

From the chin point *Q*, draw an arc 3-4-5 with the dimension IJ, the Golden Ratio–2 across the vertical lines *IK* and *JL*, which defines the arc of forehead in line with the crown. This is the height of the face, also equal to the hand measurement which is called *tala* in Indian ichnometry, as the unit of measurement.

From point *O* mark the nose point with Golden Ratio–1 and mark it as 7.

From point *O* mark the mouth line with Golden Ratio–2 and mark it as 8.

Measure the length 7-*Q*. With this as the radius, draw an arc from the nose point–7 towards *Q* from ear to ear which defines the chin, cheek and lower are part of the face.

Measure the length *O*–4, with this as radius draw a semicircle from point 4 above the arc of 3-4-5 to define the skull part.

DESIGN OF THE TIRU NĀMA

The white mark on the forehead called the *nāma*, with an upward line in its centre, is an identification mark of the Vaiṣṇavite religious sect — the followers of Lord Viṣṇu as the supreme God. It is very prominent, covering a large part of the forehead. It is in a geometric shape of a golden trapezium.

Measure the line 8-*Q* (the line from mouth to the tip of the chin) from points 3 and 5 of the face arc 3-4-5, mark the two points 3*a*, 5*a* with dimension 8-*Q* which defines the top points of forehead mark called *Tirunāma* that is always white in colour.

Measure the distance of points 3*a*–5*a* and draw a small arc from the chin point *Q*, to locate the lower seam line of *nāma*.

Now join the line with points *3a*, and *5a* to the navel point *R* which gives an isosceles triangle. Mark the lower points of the *nāma* at *3b* and *5b*, where the arc cuts the lines of the triangle. The shape of the *nāma* appears with 3a, 3b, 5a and 5b which is a trapezium (the sides *3a*-*5a* = *3a*-*3b* = *5a*-*5b* and *3a*-*5a* runs parallel to *3b*-*5b*). Extend the mouth section point line up to the legs of the triangle to define the width of the lips.

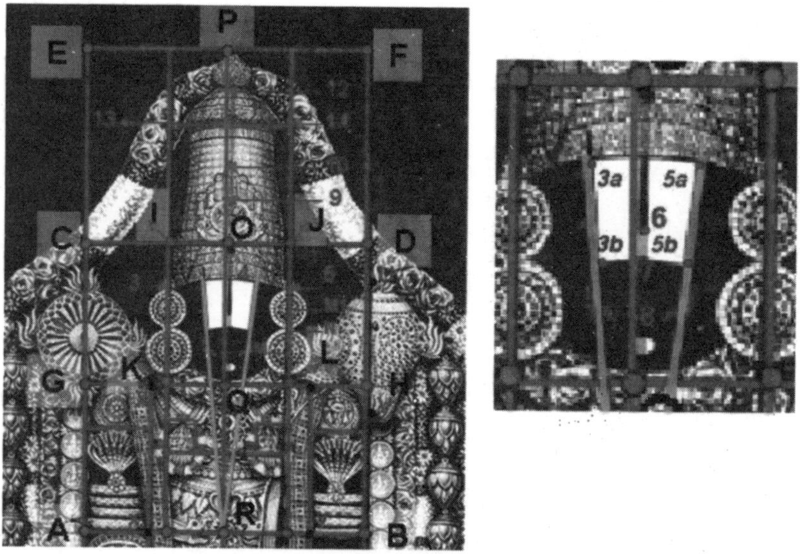

Pl. 38: The top rectangle and *Tiru Nāma*.

Locate the midpoint of *OQ*, call it point-6, which is the base point of the black line mark (*kastūrī tilaka*) and join it to point 4.

Eyes are drawn on either side of the *nāma* from the line of point 6, which is also the midpoint of *OQ*.

Measure Golden Ratio–1 and from the nose point 7, draw an arc parallel to the lower part of face curve, which defines the height of neck, as well as the width and curve of the flower garland around the neck.

Measure the length 3–*k*, and draw the arc of eyebrows on either side of *nāma* from point *Q*.

TO DRAW THE EARRINGS

The ears are decorated by two earrings of different sizes. To locate the size and position of the lower earring:

From point *J*, cut Golden Ratio–2 (also equal to *IJ*) on the line *JL* and mark it as *M*.

Cut a point again from point *J* on the line *JL*, with Golden Ratio–1, (also equal to *JD*) and mark it as *N*. With *MN* as radius draw a circle from point *M* to define the lower earring.

To define the upper earring: Measure the midpoint of the line *JL* and mark it as *M1* with *M1*-N as radius draw a circle from point *M1* to define the upper earring. The diameter of the lower and top earrings is also same as the bottom and top length of the white *nāma* mark. Point *M1*, eyes and point 6 all appear to be on the same line in a two-dimensional picture.

Repeat the same procedure for earrings on the other side.

CAKRA (THE WHEEL)

CGKI is a golden rectangle. Measure the width of GK, and cut it on the line *GC* from point *G*, which is the diameter of the *cakra*. Locate the midpoint, mark it as *S*, and draw the circle of *cakra* with *GS* as the diameter. Half part of *cakra* comes within the frame line and the other half is outside the frame line. Mark the fire motifs on the four cardinal points. The radius of the inner circle of the *cakra* is in a golden ratio to the radius *S-G* of the outer circle.

ŚAṄKHA (THE CONCH)

Repeat the circle of *cakra* on the left side also. Mark the upper point of intersection on the line *HD* as *U* and *HU* is the diameter. Conch is offset in structure and not symmetrical like *cakra*. Only one-third of the circle comes within the frame line and two-thirds come outside the frame. Measure the radius (also equal to *GS* of *cakra*) and cut a point from H on the line *HB*, and mark it as point *V*. Join the point *V* to the horizontal diameter of the circle and shape the angles at *V* into a smooth curve to give the shape of a conch. Mark the fire motifs on both the horizontal and the vertical points.

The height of the *cakra* is same as chin to forehead that is Q-4.

The height of the *śaṅkha* is same as chin to skull point that is Q-O.

TO DRAW THE UPPER ARMS (ref. *Pl.* 38)

The two lower small squares *AGQR* and *BHQR* on either side of the midline *QR* define the upper arms with the motif of the snake, the *cakra* shoulder seal, and consorts in chest region.

Cut Golden Ratio–1 from the point *Q* on *QG* and *QH* and mark it *X* and *Y*. Repeat the procedure from point *R* and mark *x* and *y*. Draw the line by joining the points from *Xx* and *Yy*. The rectangles *AGXx* and *BHYy* define the snake and the shoulder motifs.

The rectangle of arm band can further be bisected into two rectangles in golden ratio. The lower one holds the 3 coils of the snake's body in its square section and the hood with 5 heads in the rectangle section. The upper rectangle holds the *cakra* seal of the shoulder.

The same procedure is repeated on the left side but in shoulder rectangle a *śaṅkha* seal is drawn in the tangent circle.

POSITION OF THE CONSORTS

The figures of the consorts Śrīdevī and Bhūdevī in a sitting posture, are embedded in the chest region of the sculpture. They hold lotus flowers in their hands and wear the crown.

From point *R*, cut two points with Golden Ratio–1, and Golden Ratio–2 on the line *RQ*.

Draw a bisecting line across the line *QR* horizontally. The difference in their heights defines the height of the icons of the consorts, on either side of the midline.

Extend the lines *IK* and *JL* downwards, which cut to give the left and right width of the squares. Complete the square shape on both sides, in which the figures of Śrīdevī and Bhūdevī are drawn respectively.

Each of these squares can further be divided into four parts. The top two squares hold the crown, face, chest and lotus in the two hands of the goddess, while the lower two squares are used to draw the legs in seated posture, the abdominal region and the two arms.

CROWN DIVISIONS

Measure the height of the line *O*–4, and from point *O* cut four divisions consecutively on midline *OP* and mark it as points 9, 10, 11, and 12 respectively.

Extend the lines *KI* and *LJ* upwards up to the line *EF* to mark the rectangle for the crown.

O–4 is the base of the crown from the forehead line to the top of the skull.

The height of *O*–9 is used to draw the lion faced *kīrtimukha*, drawn in a small circle with diameter *O*–9.

At the base of the circle, on both sides are drawn the motif of *yāḷī* — which is a hybrid representation of parrot's body with elephant's head and the teeth of a crocodile. This motif can also be seen on the big frame around the deity on both sides.

The distance between the points 9–10 is used to draw what looks like a fractal representation of the *vimāna* of the temple in the centre and three supporting pillar-like structures on either side, totally making it seven divisions.

Point 11 marks the height of the long part of the crown. This is also the Golden Ratio–2, from *O* to point 11. Draw an arc with Golden Ratio–2 from point *O*, cutting the frame line extensions *IK* and *JL* that defines the canopy line of the crown.

Cut the width of Golden Ratio–1 on this arc, mark it as points 13 and 14, which defines the width and narrowing shape of the crown.

Join the points *I* to 13 and *J* to 14.

Join point 12 to the points on the arc of lower line–13, and 14, and shape the triangle into a curvy, semi-circular shape which is the canopy of the crown. The upper part from point *P*–12 marks the length of the feathery decorative motif.

THE BOTTOM RECTANGLE

Both the top and the bottom rectangles share the common side *AB*. The bottom rectangle has markings in small alphabets, but for *AB* and *R*, which are common to both.

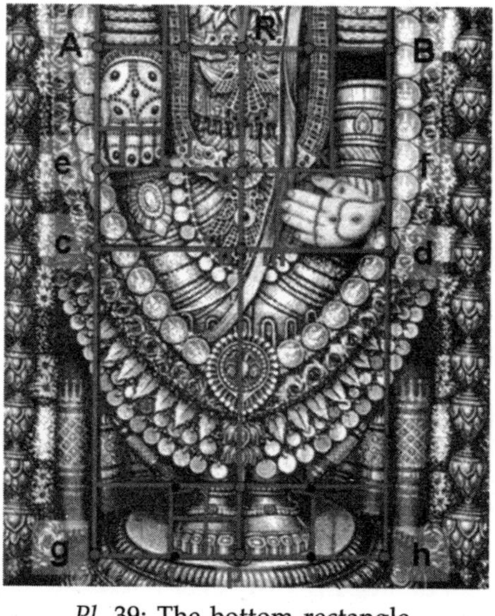

Pl. 39: The bottom rectangle.

Draw a golden rectangle *ABgh* with the same dimension as *ABEF*. Cut the golden section line *cd* from the bottom line points *g* and *h*, to result in a square *ghdc* at the bottom and a golden rectangle *ABdc* on top of it.

Draw a midline *Rp*, from point *R* up to the bottom point to cut the rectangle into two halves.

The rectangle *ABdc* gives the details of the right hand, left arm from elbow downwards and the left hand. The midpoint *R*, of *AB* is located as the navel point.

TO DRAW THE RIGHT HAND

From point *R*, mark the Golden Ratio–1 on both side *RA* and *RB* and mark it as points *x* and and *y* respectively.

Draw the line *ef* with Golden Ratio–2 from points *A* on line *Ac*, and *B* on line *Bd*. Join the line *ef*, and mark the midpoint as *q*, which is the genital point.

Extend a vertical line from *x* and *y* downwards, up to the line *ef*, and mark it as points *j* and *k*. The golden rectangle *Aejx* defines the contour of the right hand from wrist in downward direction, which is called *varada-mudrā*.

The golden rectangle can further be cut 2-3 times to rectangles and squares. The first section, of square, marks the tip of the thumb and the palm. The fingers occupy the rectangle. In the second section of the rectangle, the three fingers are in the square section while the index finger comes in the rectangle. This small golden rectangle can further be cut to the square holding the two joints of the index finger and the last joint in the rectangle as demonstrated in the figure.

The corresponding rectangle *Bfky* on the left side defines the lower arm band from elbow to wrist.

THE LEFT HAND

From the point *f* and *d*, cut Golden Ratio–2, towards the mid-line mark it as points *l* and *m*, and complete the golden rectangle *flmd*, that defines the left hand in a turned position called *kaṭyāvalambita-mudrā*. The rectangle can be cut into a square section to hold the palm part and the thumb while the four fingers are on the rectangle. In the second section, the three fingers are in the square and the index finger in the rectangle.

Feet: Mark the Golden Ratio–1 on the bottom line *pg*, *ph*, and midline *po*, and call it as *u*, *v*, and o respectively. With *p–u* as the side, complete the square *puso*. Likewise complete the square *pvto*, on the other side with the length *pv* as side. These two squares define the dimension of the feet of Lord.

Each square can further be cut into four equal parts. The bifurcating line comes on the anklet that adorns the feet, dividing the toes in one part and the heel in the other part, as demonstrated in the figure.

The ratios as found in the picture of the highly decorated statue are very close to the *phi* (the golden ratios). Errors are bound to occur in photograph and further translating it to the computer. When the measurements are taken on the bare sculpture, the accuracy in golden sections may coincide very precisely. The beauty of the sculpture is such that it conforms to the golden ratios for the body frame, and is extended from limbs to the smallest finger joint.

3.4. Golden Ratios in the Naṭarāja Sculpture of Cidambaram

The cult of Naṭarāja is one of the most prominent manifestations of Śaivism. As such it has to be understood against the background of the religious thoughts, conceptions, and visions that underline Śaivism. Śaivism has a long history of going back to hoary antiquity of Chalcolithic Age and is perhaps the oldest living faith in the world. The ancient and authoritative religious scriptures of Hinduism like the Vedas, Upaniṣads, *Rāmāyaṇa, Mahābhārata,* Āgamas, and Purāṇas give a clear picture of the insight and a gradual deepening of the evolution in understanding "Śiva," obtained by the ancient sages through their spiritual practices and disciplines and its culmination when Śiva was contemplated upon as the Ultimate Lord of the universe.

In the Vedic hymns, Lord Śiva was represented as Paśupati. A glimpse of this can be seen in the seals of Indus Valley Civilization, where Śiva is sitting as a sage with wild animals. In Vedic hymns he was also associated with fire (*agni*) as the annihilator, moon (Soma) as the bestower of joy and happiness, Śaṅkara — the curer of diseases and as the divine doctor. As Rudra, he was visualised as the sole destroyer. Death was understood to be a definite occurrence with all living forms, whatever is the apparent cause of death. The agent of death, the fierce one, the real destroyer was conceived as the anger of Rudra — the terrible one. As Mahādeva, Śiva was the most pre-eminent among the gods. He is an object of worship for millions of people throughout the country.

In Upaniṣadic period, the earlier conceptions about Śiva's godhead got elevated from religious beliefs to deeper thoughts of spiritual vision, assimilating the cream of spiritual truth. The search for the ultimate truth — "Śiva" reached fulfilment with the discovery of *ātman* — the supreme power who was both the creator and annihilator. This divine power was understood to lie hidden mysteriously in the multitude of creations as the *antaryāmī* — that, ruling the entire world.

When the dwelling power was contemplated as the creative force, homage was paid to the Supreme Lord Īśāna — who assumed a twofold form of male and female forces joined together eternally, to bring the whole creation in its diversity and multiplicity. The concept of Śiva as the soul, and Śakti as the body, was worshipped in the concrete symbol of *liṅga* and the *yoni*, and the anthropomorphic representation of it got expressed as Ardhanārīśvara (the androgynous form of Śiva). Universal Life force energy was not seen as an abstract power but as the source of all life. The reality was translated to the sperm and the ovum as the seed and the ground of life in tāntric practices.

Lord Kṛṣṇa has said in *Bhagavad-Gītā*:

> those who worship the eternal, unmanifest and unthinkable lord who is firm and motionless, but pervades all with the senses, obtain me ultimately.

But the path of the unmanifest was treated with greater difficulty by human beings. Men with ordinary capacities required something which they could grasp with their senses especially with eyes to meditate upon, so that "that something," which is boundless was visualised in the form of an image with indescribable beauty, serenity and power which would ultimately lead them to the supreme. It is here that sages realised in their hearts as to what that apt symbol or the image of the supreme could be reaching their original vision with devotion and ecstasy. The qualities and values of the supreme soul were laid out in a symbolic and geometric form which was termed a *maṇḍala*. The Āgama Śāstras (the scriptures) considered the images of deities seen in states of *yoga* — an exalted thought and vision came out with the *dhyāna ślokas* — the prescriptions for making such a divine figure in visible form to be a true representation of the supreme. This leads to the conclusion that God did not create humankind in his image but, humankind created God according to their vision.

While thinking about the mysteries and multitude of the

variety in creation at the physical level, the ancient philosophers categorised the process of creation into three groups:

1. *Saṅkarṣaṇa* — meaning the act of drawing together, and contracting. All the five elements (the earth, water, fire, air and space) were understood to be the essential components of all living forms (got incorporated with divine figures also) which was the most fundamental act in creation.
2. *Pradyumna* — The root word *dyumna* means splendour, energy, wealth and inspiration. *Pra* — is the prefix to the verb meaning forward. The life force created by the five elements got divided into two principles that were equal but opposite forces of nature, recognised as the static and the dynamic forces or the male and female forces. The multitude of forms were created by the union of the male and female forces.
3. *Aniruddha* — meaning eternal and free, which manifest in living forms that are created by the union of the male and female principles giving birth to the multitude of living things in this universe and the process is an eternal one. In mythological connection, Aniruddha is the son of Pradyumna.

In the figure of Naṭarāja, the aspect of Saṅkarṣaṇa (the assimilation of the five elements) is indicated through the iconographic representation of the five elements. The element *pṛthvī* (the earth) is shown in the body with muscles and bones. The element water is depicted either as the face of river Gaṅgā in his *jaṭā* (hair tied into a bun in the middle part of the head), or as fountain of water flowing from his head. The element fire is indicated in actual form held in the back left hand in the *agnipātra* (a small container to hold fire). The element air is indicated as the flying robes and the locks of hair, which agrees with the iconographic representation of air (depicted as flying objects or the flying *gandharvas*). The element ether (the space) is indicated in having half moon in his hair decorations, as ethereal aspects of sun, moon or stars are the iconographic representation of space. The figure of Naṭarāja is a pictorial allegory of the five elemental forces through which the whole universe is created, sustained and ultimately destroyed.

The aspect of Pradyumna is indicated in the *patra-kuṇḍala* a feminine ear ornament in round shape in the left earlobe and the *makara-kuṇḍala* the crocodile shaped one, in the right earlobe that is worn by men. Some philosophers also observe this unity in the body where the posture is firm and with masculine majesty but the flow of muscles is soft. (The feminine aspect of *Śakti* force is always embedded in the chest region of the sculpture of Lord Viṣṇu.)

The aspect of Aniruddha is hinted in the vibrations of *ḍamaru*, as sound vibrations are proved to be the source of creation.

Considering the values and qualities conceived to be the pre-requisite to depict the supreme power, a logical geometric figure was formed, called the *ṣāḍguṇaya yantra* which indicated the six great qualities, viz. *jñāna, tejas, aiśvarya, bala, śakti,* and *vīrya,* that were visualised to be present in the supreme power. The structure of this frame was drawn by interlacing two equilateral triangles — symbolising the cosmic male and the female principles, resulting with a hexagon in the middle, the perfect figure of nature representing the element air and its quality of movement, and six small equilateral triangles at the points. Each of the small triangles represented one great quality.

Figure of Ṣāḍguṇaya Yantra

It is essential to understand the interpretation of *ṣāḍguṇaya yantra* as the figure of Naṭarāja is based on this diagram. The six qualities are:

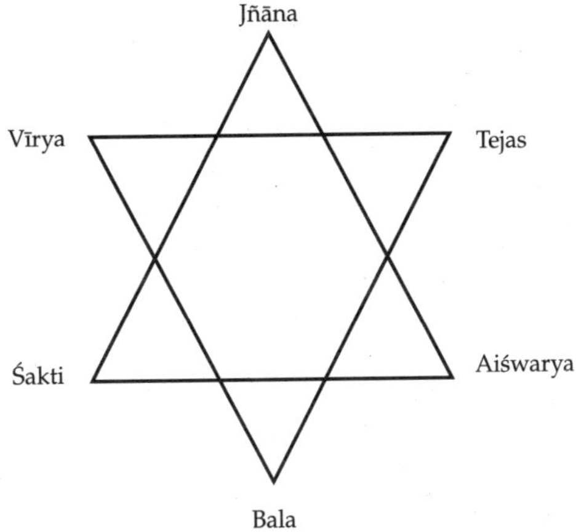

1. *Jñāna*: The power of knowledge, iconographically indicated by the spread of seven hoods, the ultimate realisation of the *kuṇḍalinī sahasrāra cakra,* indicating enlightenment in the top triangle.
2. *Tejas*: meaning sharpness, heat, brilliance and bright appearance of human body. The iconographic representation of heat and light is in the form of the element fire and symbolic of the power that drives away the darkness of ignorance.
3. *Aiśvarya*: The majestic power, supremacy, sovereignty backed up by wealth and affluence. The divine faculties of omnipotence is symbolically represented by the flying silk robes — a garment befitting the Supreme Being.
4. *Bala*: symbolically represented by the firmly placed right foot (right side is again with reference to the *piṅgalā nāḍī,* associated with intellect). *Bala* means the strength, virtue, figure comparable to an army of forces. The demon of darkness is firmly deactivated by the pressure of strength of virtues. The reinforcement of added pressure is indicated by the bent posture of the leg, which is a natural posture while stamping on something with force.

5. *Śakti*: The ability, capacity, strength, the power of active self and positive energy of a deity (comparable to a kind of missile). The eternal and perpetual flow of the dynamic energy of the central force of supreme power is represented in the free movement of the left leg (the left side also refers to the *iḍā nāḍī* — the emotional quotient of mind, which is for ever moving freely irrespective of gender, time and space zones). Since mind plays a powerful role in human body, intellect depends on the power of mind for its functioning and there has to be a harmony between the mind and spirit. Hence *śakti* is depicted as merged with the *puruṣa*.
6. *Vīrya*: meaning heroism, prowess, the perpetual energy that regenerates, power of potency. This is indicated through the vibrations of sound of the small percussion instrument (the *ḍamaru*). A percussion instrument indicates the aspect of rhythm — the rhythmic cycles of birth, growth and death and the restart of life through the vibrations which is the quality of life force in the universe.

The two actions of God were conceived to be protection and elevation to spiritual path. *Abhaya-hasta* — the hand gesture that is held by the front right hand symbolises protection and also preservation. The stretched left hand across the chest points to the raised left leg. In philosophical terms, left side is associated to the aspect of emotions, movement related to mind — the *iḍā nāḍī* while the right side refers to the firmness of the intellectual aspect called the *piṅgalā nāḍī*. When the *māyā* is destroyed by the intellect (indicated by the right leg stamping the demon of ignorance), the mind which resides in the body elevates from mundane to the spiritual path. This is symbolically and artistically depicted in the upward movement of the left leg to which the left hand is pointing.

The figure of Naṭarāja is visualised as the "Divine dancer" because of the association of movements and vibrations, which are the fundamental characteristics of the art of dance. The "cosmic dance" of Śiva is both a symbol and reality. The aspect of rhythmic movement is compared to the rhythm of triad — the creation, preservation and dissolution that is taking place in the universe, with each one of us and within every atom of the universe, running as a mathematical law of the universe. Naṭarāja personifies the elemental force through which the whole universe is created, the eternal process of creation by the cosmic bi-unity, the rhythm of birth, growth and death, that has established an equilibrium, balance and bliss in the universe. Each living being, made up of the five elements, merges with the five elements ultimately. It is for this reason of rhythm of birth, growth and death, that Lord Naṭarāja is presented as a dancer. The art of dance exhibits a unified form, where a dancer cannot be separated from the dance, which is the end product of the creative art of dance. A piece of painting or sculpture remains separated from its creator because the medium of expression is through a material. But dance cannot be separated from the dancer because the medium of expression in dance is the body itself. The creation is not different from the creator. His rhythmic dance is called *ānanda tāṇḍava* (the blissful dance). In Indian art, the aspect of rhythm is indicated by the percussion instrument and the aspect of melody or movement is indicated by a melody instrument like a flute or a *vīṇā*. *Tāṇḍava* is the vigorous mode of presentation in the art of dance, which can be compared to the kinetic aspect of vigour that is maintained by the renewal of birth — as "Aniruddha."

Art has played a very important part in the life of Indian subcontinent. Works of art were meant to convey the truth, as experienced by the artist. Indic deities were personifications of concepts and qualities. The figure of the dancing Naṭarāja was brought to us in art, to awaken the divine qualities that are present in every human at the microcosmic level. The early art of India is thus a valuable record of the Indic vision coming from the Upaniṣads of seeing the material world as *māyā* apprehended by the limited perceptions of sense organs. Early Indian art embodied the deep philosophical concepts of clearing the veils of *māyā* and seeing the eternal, which is beyond the material forms of the world.

Looking and meditating upon a deity helps one to find godly qualities grow and fill the thoughts so that there is no space left for base desires and pain. The aesthetic experience is considered of great value in the Indian thought. The experience of beauty when we respond to a work of art is a moment akin to *Brahmānanda* — the final ecstasy of salvation itself, when we perceive the grace that underlies the whole of creation.

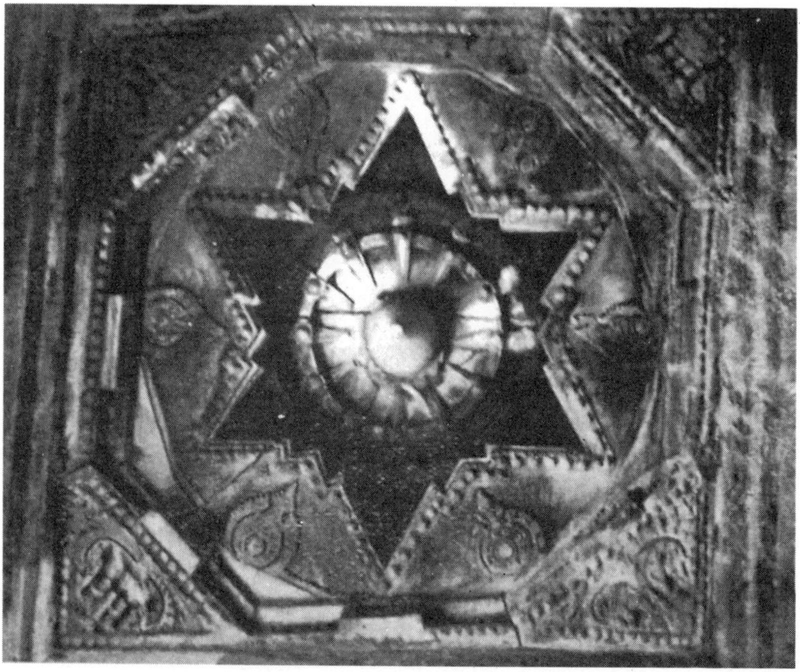

Pl. 40: Hullekere Cennakeśava temple ceiling.

The *bhuvaneśvarī* of Hullekere Cennakeśava temple has a ceiling which can be compared to the *ṣāḍguṇaya yantra*. The two big equilateral triangles are interlaced and embedded, tangent to the sides of an octagon (octagon is the nearest comparison to a circle). The star figure is compared to the star of David figure. The angles of the star indicate small triangles, representing the six great qualities, and the maṇḍalic design by the side of each angle is probably the baleful representation of the twin aspect of the devine quality. The central conical figure, a symbolic representation of the deity has 12 spokes around ending with the smaller cones on the inner circle — a fractal representation of the central deity. Six spokes bisect the angles of the triangles, marking the midpoints of the lines of the bigger triangles. The alternate spokes when extended mark the golden sections of the sides of the bigger triangles.

GOLDEN RATIOS IN THE CONSTRUCTION OF THE FIGURE OF NAṬARĀJA

The golden section is a well-known concept since classical Hellenistic period. It dates back to the period of ancient Egypt and is used in architecture and fine arts.

The idol of Naṭarāja, with four arms is accepted all over the world as the perfect figure with physical, metaphysical and spiritual thoughts. The body proportions in the idol meticulously observe the golden ratios, for which reason it looks beautiful. The frame of the figure, based on *ṣāḍguṇaya yantra* can be studied in the following unique construction method developed by the author. Before drawing or sculpturing the figure, the frame, which is called *vyūha* (the plan needs to be drawn). The plan of the figure of Naṭarāja is based on two interlaced equilateral golden triangles. On any circle with the centre as *S*, six equally spaced points — *ABCDEF* are marked with the dimension of radius, without altering the compasses. Every alternate points is used to make equilateral

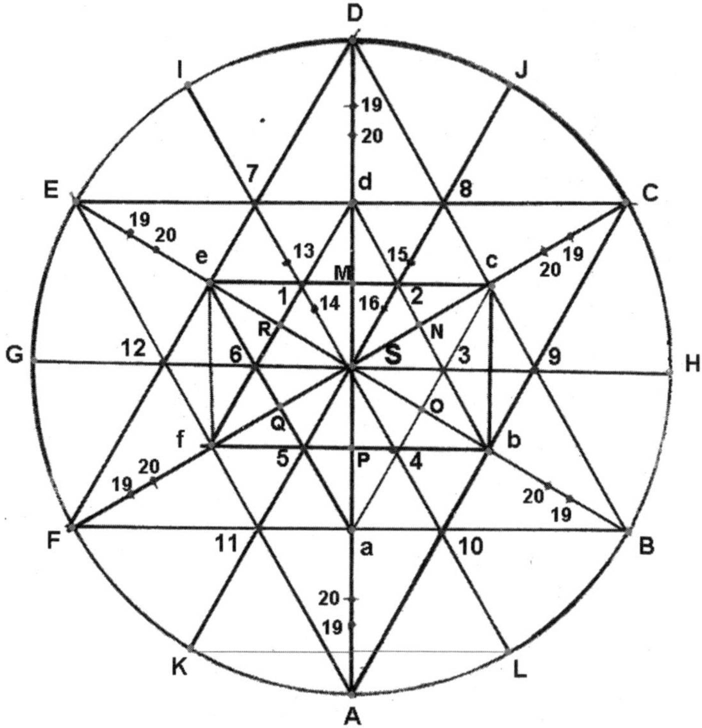

Pl. 41: Frame of Naṭarāja sculpture.

triangles. The intersection of sides gives many golden sections and smaller equilateral triangles. When the midpoints of the sides of the triangles are joined, they result in many golden sections. The point of intersection between any side of the inner triangle and the outer one, also divides the sides according to golden section. Each partition of a golden hexagon into two triangles allows a homology from one triangle to another. This means all pairs of triangles are in "Desarguesion" position — conversely all hexagons with this property are golden.

Construction of the frame:

1. Draw a circle with centre marked as *S*.

2. Draw the horizontal diameter, call it *GH* and the vertical diameter as *AD*.
3. From (top or) bottom point, cut six arcs in progression, with the dimension of radius, and mark the points as *ABCDEF.* Join the alternate points to construct two interlaced equilateral triangles — *DFB* with the apex upwards and triangle *AEC* as the downward triangle with the base point at *A*. This is called the Star of David with six small equilateral triangles on all the six points and a hexagon on the inner side. Mark the points of the angles of the hexagon as 7, 8, 9, 10, 11, 12.
4. Draw the bifurcating diameters *AD, EB, FC* from the angles of the big triangles, which cuts the sides of the triangles at midpoints. Also draw the two diagonal diameters and mark them as *IL* and *JK* respectively as shown in the diagram (ref. *Pl.* 41).
5. Locate the midpoints of the sides of the hexagon and mark them as *abcdef*. Join the alternate points to construct two interlaced equilateral triangles, *aec*, and *dfb*, and locate the inner Star of David.
6. Note the six smaller equilateral triangles and the inner hexagon. Mark the sides of the inner hexagon as 1, 2, 3, 4, 5, 6 and their midpoints as *M, N, O, P, Q, R* — as demonstrated in the figure of the frame.
7. Join the points ef, and cb, which gives a golden rectangle.
8. Note the six triangles on points A,B,C,D,E,F. Measure the golden section of the height or the axis of triangles, like *A–a*, or *F–f*. (To get it, divide the measurement by 1.618 which is the *phi* or golden constant. It is also equal to half of the base of the triangle like 10–11–A) With this measurement of golden sections (a-10 or a-11) mark two points on the midline from points, like *A* and *a*, and mark these points as 19 (towards the apex) and 20 — towards

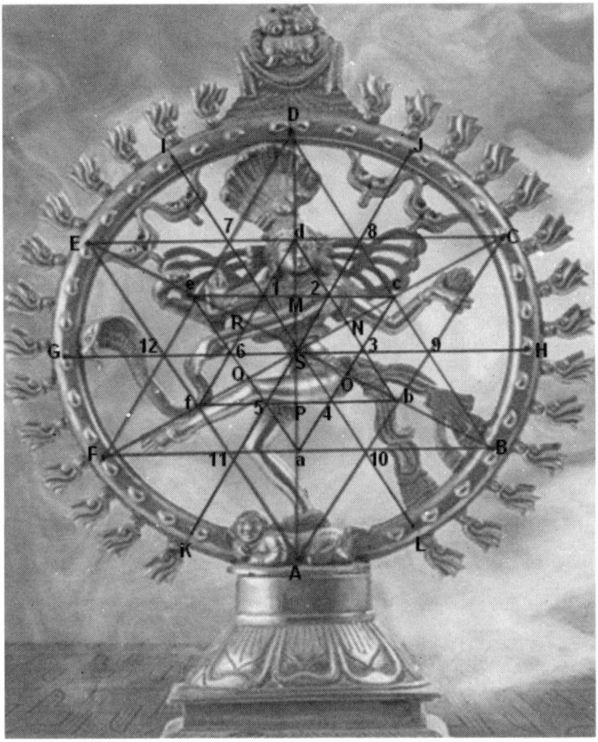

Pl. 42: The sculpture of Naṭarāja with the frame superimposed.

the base, in all the six triangles. (These as referred as point 19 of triangle at *F*, or point 20 of triangle at *D*, etc.)

The midpoint of the circle *S* is the navel point. The divisions below the diameter *GH*, cover the legs of the sculpture, the flying robes and the left hand part, while the upper half of the circle covers three hands with the accessories, face, the seven hoods of the crown and the snake around the navel point.

TO DRAW THE LEFT LEG : THE TRIANGLE AT F,
INDICATIVE OF THE QUALITY OF "ŚAKTI"
(To be drawn on frame of *Pl.* 41)

1. Join the points *Q–O*, which marks the upper line of the thigh. Locate Q on the line FS. The line between 5 and 4

marks the lower line of the thigh. Join the points *o* and 4 in a semicircle to give the shape of left hip.

2. Locate the midpoint of *f*–11 and join it to point *F*, which gives the dimension for the width of the foot from point 19 up to the line. Draw the toes from point 19 on the line *F*–*f*, so that the second finger falls on the line *F*–*f*. Point 20 marks the midpoint of the foot on which the anklet is drawn around. Draw the heel beyond point 20, which is indicated and covered by the anklet.
3. Join point 5 to point 20 of the triangle at *F*, which marks the lower line of the leg and knee point at point 5. Draw a curve from point 5 on both sides to give the shape of the bent and slanted knee. (mark the midpoint of 5–*P* and an equal distance on 5–*f* to draw the curve of the inner knee).
4. The line of points 20–*Q* mark the upper line of the leg from knee point at point *Q*.

TO DRAW THE RIGHT LEG : THE TRIANGLE AT A, INDICATIVE OF THE QUALITY OF "BALA"

1. Measure the axis *P*–*a* and cut it on the side 5–11 from point 5 of the triangle 5–11–*a*, which marks the outer knee point. The same dimension from point *a* on the line a-11, marks the inner point of the knee.
2. Join the outer knee point to point 19 of the triangle at *A*.
3. Locate the midpoints of 11–*a*, and *P*–4, and draw a line connecting these two points to define the length of the inner thigh up to the inner knee point. Draw the breeches from midpoint of *P*–4 on the left thigh. The seam of the right leg breeches can be drawn from the midpoint of 5–*a*.
4. Draw the line *K*–*L* on which the foot rests above the point *A*.
5. Join the inner knee point to point 20 of the triangle at *A* and extend it till it intersects the line *K*–*L*, that marks the

heel point. Shape the slight curve of the calf muscles.

6. The point of intersection between *11–A* and *K–L* marks the position of joints of the toes. Extend the dimension between the angles on the line *K–L* to mark the tip of the toes. Join point 19 of triangle at *A* to the toe tip point.
7. Shape the heel and toes of the foot as shown in the diagram. (ref. *Pl.* 43)

TO DRAW THE FRONT LEFT ARM

To draw the arm, the shoulder, elbow, wrist point, hand and the gesticulation called the *mudrā*, the angles of folding at wrist and elbow are to be considered. Shoulder points of the two front arms can be located on the lines *S*–7 and *S*–8. The dimension from armhole to shoulder (15–16) is the measurement of the width, *M*-1 or *M*-2.

1. Measure the midpoint of *M*–1 or *M*–2 and with this dimension, cut two points on either side of point 2 on the line *S*–8 and mark them as points 15 and 16 which mark the upper shoulder and armhole dimensions of the left arm.
2. Repeat the same procedure on the right side, on both sides of point 1 on the line *S*–7 and mark them as points 13 and 14.
3. The imaginary line connecting points 13–15 and intersecting across the line *d–M* gives the throat point and the imaginary line joining points 14–16 across the line *M–S* locates the chest point. The upper arm passes through point *M*.
4. Join points 15 to 16 in a curve to get the shape of the left shoulder.
5. To draw the upper arm line, connect the point 15 to *M*–14–*R*–12 successively. The extension up to point 12 is

only to locate the shape of the wrist as the diagonal line *e*–6 cuts at the wrist section.

6. To draw the lower arm line, connect point 16 to the midpoint of the line 12–6, that defines the lower arm length. Line *e*–6 cuts at the lower part of the wrist section.
7. The midpoint of the line 12–6, is centre of the palm of the hand that continues with the middle finger joint diagonally.
8. Draw the finger tips within the midpoint of the line 12–*f*.
9. Draw the arm band below the point *M* and the bracelet at the wrist point on the line *e*–6.

TO DRAW THE BACK LEFT ARM

1. Draw the axis of the small triangle *c*–3–9 (the line 3–9 can be located on the diameter *G*–*H*).
2. Measure the length 16–2 (or 19–20) and cut it on the axis from both the top and bottom points. This defines the upper and the lower points of the elbow.
3. To define the upper arm, join the lower elbow point to point 16 of the shoulder, and the upper elbow point to point 15 of the shoulder.
4. Extend the line *M*–*C*. Cut a point from C on this line with the dimension of *M*–2, which is the inner wrist point. Cut another point from point *C* with the dimension of *C*–20, which is the outer wrist point.
5. Join the upper elbow point and the lower elbow point to the inner and the outer wrist points respectively. This defines the shape of the arm that narrows down from elbow to wrist.
6. The wristband is drawn at this wrist point. The curve of the palm that is bent at 90° to the lower arm at the wrist starts above this cutting.

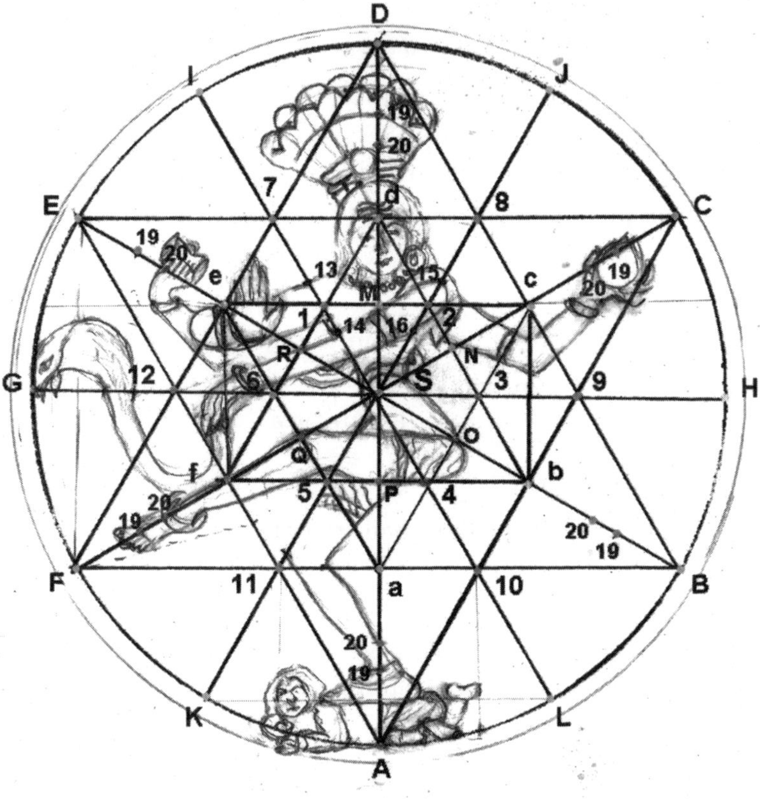

Pl. 43: A trial figure of Naṭarāja drawn on the frame.

7. Drawing the hand needs the skill of drawing. The thumb goes up to point 20. Draw the palm/hand holding the element fire, so that the upper apex of fire is near the point 19.
8. Draw the arm band above the elbow, the body of the snake is wound around the shoulder region at 15–2–16.

TO DRAW THE FRONT RIGHT ARM

1. Locate the right shoulder points 13–1 and 14. Join point 13 to point *e* to draw the upper part of the arm.
2. Measure the length *M*–1 and cut it on the axis of the

triangle *e*–12–6 from the midpoint on the line 12–6, which defines the point of the elbow section. Join it to the midpoint of 1–14, to define the lower arm line to the armhole.

3. Shape the curve of elbow by joining it to point *e* in a semicircle outside the point *e*, as shown in the *Pl.* 43.
4. To draw the dimensions of the hand which is in *abhaya mudrā* — the hand of protection near the point *e*:

   The extension of line from 16–14 marks the base of the thumb.

   The extension of line 2–1 marks the upper part of the palm.

   The extension of the line 15–13 marks the middle joints of the fingers.

   The base of the palm should be drawn between the angle of *e*–6 and *e*–*R*.

   Cut the dimension *M*–1 from the point *e* on the line *e*–7 to mark the height of the middle finger. The fingers are drawn up to this point which is also in line with the chin part of the face.
5. The hand indicates a 90° bend at wrist. Draw the bracelet at wrist point.

TO DRAW THE BACK RIGHT ARM

1. Extend the line *M*–*e*, cut two points with the dimension of *M*–1 and *e*–20 (the golden ratio of the axis *E*–*e*) on this line from point *e* which defines the outer and the inner wrist points of the back arm. Draw a line from this inner wrist point towards point *e* and connect it to the upper elbow point of the front arm.
2. Cut the measurement *M*–1 on the line *e*–12 from point *e*. Draw a line connecting this point to the outer wrist point,

which gives the shape of the back lower arm. The upper part of this hand is concealed behind the front arm.

3. Draw the curve of the palm from the two wrist points, the outer one passing through point 20. Parallel to this is drawn the inner curve of the palm up to the axis *E–e*.
4. Draw the fingers holding the small percussion instrument on the other side of line *E–e*, as shown in the figure.
5. Draw the bracelet at the wrist joint.

TO DRAW THE FACE AND THE NECK

The Naṭarāja figure of Cidambaram is designed with a tilt in the angle of head. Hence the bodyline of the centre does not pass through the nose. The deviation which is small at the nose region grows wider in the snake hood crown part. There are many variations in the figures of Naṭarāja. Such of those which do not show a tilt of the head have the bodyline and the snake's hood passing through the midline *D–A*. The face part of the Naṭarāja of Cidambaram observes half of the deviation in the angle of the side leg *b–d* to midline *d–p* of the triangle *d–f–b*.

1. *To draw the face*: Measure *d*–19 (or *d*–8) and from point 20, cut the point of nose on the line *d–M*. From this nose point draw the circle of the face with the radius of 19–20.
2. Extend the line *b–d* of the triangle *d–f–b*, which helps to identify the angle of the deviation of the neck from the centre.
3. From the point d with M-2 as radius draw the semicircle of the skull, which gives the total height of the head and mark the point of intersection on the extended line b-d as point *T*.
4. From the point *d*, cut an arc with the dimension of *d*–20 to locate the height of the three coils of the seven-hooded

snake. The face of river Gaṅgā fits into the angle between the central and the extended line.

5. From the point *T*, draw an arc with the radius of *d*–20, to get the lower line of the snake's hood. From the point *T* again cut the second arc with the radius of *d*–19 to get the upper arc of the opened up hoods of the snake.
6. The extended line of *d*–*b* passes through the third hood. With the measurement of 19–20 cut the width of the other heads of the snake from the 3rd hood four to the left side and two to the right side that completes the structure of the seven hooded snake, which is positioned as the crown above his head. The left end of snake's head comes near the intersection of the extension of the line *1*–*d* and 8–*D*. The total width of the seven hoods is the same dimension as the axis *D*–*d*, of the triangle at *D*.
7. This representation of the seven-hooded *kuṇḍalinī* snake, as a crown above the centre of the head is symbolic of the enlightenment at *sahasrāra cakra* — the ultimate level of spiritual awareness, which is an indication of divine status in Hindu iconography. The number 7 is indicative of surpassing the seven levels of awareness called as *cakra*s.
8. Regarding the dimension of facial features:

   Mouth is drawn in the mid-position of nose point and the chin arc between the lines *M*–*d* and 2–*d*.

   Eyes are drawn in the mid-position from nose point to the forehead arc and eyebrows above the eyes. The bridge of the nose appears to continue with the left eyebrow because of the tilt of the face to left side. The third eye (the eye of *ājñā cakra*) is located between the eyebrows.

   The ear decorations start from the eyebrow level on top and is drawn up to the chin line. On left side is the circular earring called the *patra-kuṇḍala* and on the right side is the earring called *makara kuṇḍala*.

The area of forehead is decorated with the three horizontal lines of white coloured *vibhūti* which is the distinctive Śaivite mark.

Locks of hair fall from the head covering the top of the ears. The *jaṭā* — locks of hair are depicted flying in an artistic and stylised way that extends up to the point 20 on the line *E–e* on right side. On the left side they are drawn up to point *c* (and drawn up to the extension of the line 3–*c*).

TO DRAW THE NECK

Connect the line 13–15. The point of intersection on the line *d–M* defines the throat point. From the nose point, draw the arc of the neck with the dimension of *M*–2 till it cuts the lines *d*–1 and *d*–2. Join point *M* to these two points which give the arc of the neck. Locate the midpoints from point *M* and the intersecting points on either side and join it to the lower part of face on both sides to define the height of the neck.

METHOD TO DRAW THE TORSO,
SNAKE AND THE FIRE MOTIFS

1. Locate the upper thigh point on the right leg where the line *Q–O* intersects the line *S–P*.
2. Draw a curve of the right torso from this point, proceeding by the side of the navel point *S*, and connect to point 14 which is the under arm point.
3. Cut the dimension of *M*–1 on the line *S–N* from the point *N*, to define the curve point of the left side of the waist. Connect point *O* (the hip point of left leg) to this waist curve point and further connect it to point 16, which is the armhole point of left side.
4. A hip band and the silk robe are tied below the navel point. The silk robes are depicted as flying, in harmony

with the movement of the leg and the waist. The two ends of the robe are centred at the triangle at *B*. The two ends can be located between the lower five fire motifs on the left side of the frame.

5. A huge serpent with opened hood is depicted curling around the navel region to indicate the opening up of the *maṇipūra cakra*. The head part of the snake comes above the diameter *G–H*. Cut the measurement of *d*–19 on the line *G*–12 from the points *G* and *d*–20, from the point 12, which defines the width of the hood. The mouth and eyes of it can be seen between the line *E–F* and the circular frame of the sculpture. The body of the snake flows along the stretched left hand, curls around the left shoulder and is wound around the navel part.
6. The dwarf demon Muyaḷagan, who is stamped firmly by the left foot of the deity measures the length of the line 11–10. An axis drawn down from the points 11 and 10 on the line *K–L*, defines the width of the demon in lying down posture. The body of the demon is in line with the width of the circular frame and only the face part above the eyebrows falls inside the frame probably to indicate the aspect of *tamas*.
7. The frame has distinctive marks of ovalish design (see *Pl.* 42) which appear like drops of water in shape. For a given volume, the surface area of sphere is minimum. For any system to be in equilibrium the potential energy must be minimum. This is possible if surface area is minimum for liquids. Therefore liquid drops are seen spherical. These designs of droplets all over the frame symbolise the aspect of equilibrium and harmony between the elements of nature. They are also used here as the units of measurement to cut the sides of the Star of David. The symbol of burning fire comes in between

these marks all around the frame outside, excluding the space occupied by the dwarf figure. An interesting feature of the fire motif is that all of them have the golden spiral design in them (for details on golden spirals, see (see *Pl.* 46) the last part of the text on Gommaṭeśvara). The base of the fire motifs is placed exactly at one *tala* space measurement — which is equal to the hand measurement of *abhaya-hasta* or the height of the face or the measurement of *d*–20. The ovalish designs also have the same spacing but they are placed in between the fire motifs.

8. A lion-faced *kīrtimukha* (see *Pl.* 42) a symbol of the baleful twin representation of the deity that wards off all negativity (see section 1.9, for details on *kīrtimukha*) is carved on the top part of the frame along the mid bodyline. The width and height of this is same as the dimension of *S–d*.

9. The sculpture is mounted on a pedestal with eight petals.

   The figure of Naṭarāja has the motif of element fire all round the frame. The symbol of this element, which always moves upwards is symbolically represented in Indian art as a triangle with the apex upwards. So also *puruṣa* the static and the male force is symbolised with the representation of upward triangle (while *prakṛti* the dynamic female force is represented as a downward triangle) according to the sacred geometrical figures. Meditating upon Śiva (Naṭarāja) the ultimate truth, elevates the devotees upwards in their spiritual and awareness levels is probably indicated by fire motifs all round.

The above construction method is associated with the two-dimensional aspect of golden section. To carve a sculpture, it is required to consider the three-dimensional ratio of the measurements.

3.5 Divine Proportions (Golden Ratios) in the Sculpture of Gommaṭeśvara at Śravaṇabeḷgoḷā

The colossal statue of Gommaṭeśvara, standing erect from the summit of a large hill, is acclaimed as the biggest monolithic statue in the world. It is situated in a small place called Śravaṇabeḷgoḷā, in the Cennarāyapattana taluk of Hassan district, Karnataka state of southern India. The place lies picturesquely between two rocky hills that are covered by huge boulders. The image was made by Cāmuṇḍa Rāya, the minister of the Gaṅga king Rājamalla Satyavākya, who reigned between CE 974–84, obviously a follower of Jain tradition.

The traditional account is given in the several inscriptions around this place which mentions that Gommaṭa also named as Bāhubali, and Mahāvīra, the younger son of Purudeva, fought a fierce battle with his elder brother Bharata for the empire, won, and later generously handed over the kingdom of earth to the defeated elder brother, and retired from the world for penance. He thus became a "Jina" (conqueror) and attained enlightenment by his victory over self. Jainism was created by Mahāvīra, who was also the first *tīrthaṁkara* (a saint) of Jain religion, which is prior to Buddhism in period. Mahāvīra believed in a realistic and pluralistic world and not in the existence of any Supreme God as the creator of the world. He preached on morality in general and the right conduct, right knowledge and right action in particular. Stress was laid on the freedom from all passions. He was more a reformer of ancient ascetic cult. Jainism was spread by the followers like Candragupta Maurya (the founder of Maurya dynasty), took it to regions of Karnataka in the later part of his life and built *basadī*s (the monastic establishments for the spread of Jainism).

Body is the definition of who you are in Indian architecture. The perfect body symbolises the aspect of perfection of God.

The nudity of the image indicates spirit of absolute renunciation and the stiff and erect posture suggests perfect self-control.

The colossal and astonishing image, carved in light grey, fine grained sandstone, measures around 59 ft in height, and faces north direction.

The monolithic sculpture has withstood the test of time, standing undisturbed to the furies of nature, which prompts one to think how such a huge sculpture was designed with perfect body proportions and serene expression. The statue is supported up to the thigh region by the monolithic rock, which is designed like anthills, with snakes and creepers. The creepers are carved to be growing from the base up to the upper arm of the figure. The pedestal at the feet is in the form of a huge lotus flower.

The author has tried to compare the dimensions that are carved according to Indian ichnometry to the golden ratios, popularly known as Fibonacci ratios, a constant in ratios of the length to its breadth, that occurs in nature. The height of the figure from toe to head measures 59-60 ft, and the width across the shoulders, the widest part is between 22-23 ft approximately, which means that the measurement of the monolithic rock measured 60/24 ft minimum. The total height can be cut into two geometric figures of a golden rectangle and a golden square, that share a common side at the navel region.

THE FRAME OF THE SCULPTURE

The monolithic rock, a rectangular cube, was probably marked for the height, width and depth. Viewing the sculpture as a two-dimensional picture, the calculations for the plan of measurements can be enclosed in a rectangular figure *AA–BB*. The figure is symmetrical on the left and right sides.

The rectangle *AA–BB*, can be cut into a smaller golden

rectangle at the base *DD–BB*, that involves the body below the navel, the arms below the elbow, and a square, *AA–DD* on the upper side, which covers the head, shoulder and the upper arm. The midline section of the total height passes through the nose, navel and middle of the genital organ.

The golden rectangle *DD–BB* can further be cut into a square *DD–HH*, and a smaller golden rectangle *HH–BB*. The line *HH* cuts through the lower part of the knee region which is again marked by the joining of the tendril wound on the inner thigh part. The line *JJ* at the wrist point, which is the golden section from point *H*, of the side of the square *DH*, and also the points *KK* on the line *JJ*, mark the pelvic region, the widest part in the lower body. This is also marked by the upper end points of the tendrils wound on the thigh region, which continues on the wrist section.

The golden rectangle *HH–BB* covers the shin and the feet part. The tendrils on either side of the anthill depiction curve exactly on the line *HH*, which is also an artistic way of marking the location of the lower line of knee part on the uncut boulder. The ankle point location *GG* is again a golden section of the side *HB*, cut from the point *H*.

On the square above the navel region *AA–DD*, a golden section on the side *AD*, cut from point *D*, and mark it as *FF*. This cuts the base of the head at the chin point and is in line with the lower tip of the ears. The head is in a square shape, the measurement from ear to ear is same as the height of the head (from top up to the chin point). Considering the dimensions of the face in the statue, the golden measurement of *AF* which is the height of head from the chin the line in golden section of *AF* drawn from point *F*, cuts through the eyes and marks the upper tip of the ears. Mid point of *AF* is the nose point. The same measurement, if cut from the top of the head from point *A*, marks the position of the section at the base of the nose and the mouth which is marked as *OO*.

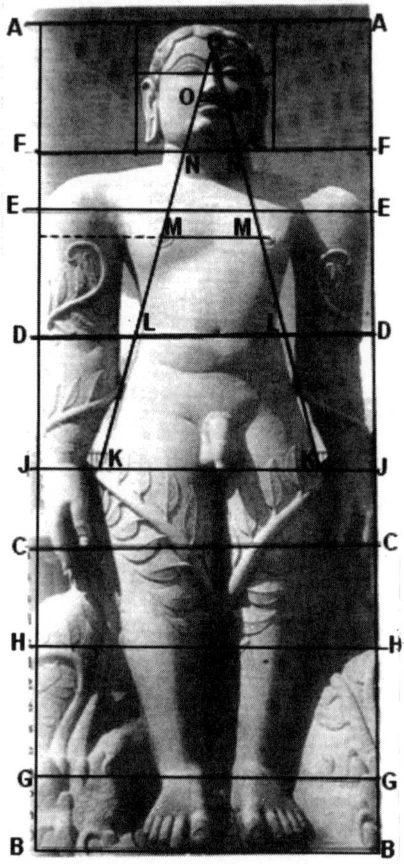

Pl. 44: Golden sections of Gommaṭeśvara.

The height of the face = length of the hand from the wrist = 1 *tala* unit measurement.

The width of the waist marked *LL* on the line *DD* is approximately the golden section of the pelvic width *KK*.

If an imaginary triangle is drawn from pelvic points *KK* to the *bhrū-madhya* point — the centre of eyebrows marked *Q*, it becomes a golden isosceles triangle, where the two legs are of equal length, the angles are 72, 72 and 36. The triangle can be cut into many sections creating smaller triangles with the same property and trapeziums. Each golden trapezium will have three sides equal in length, the top and bottom sides are parallel and in a golden ratio. The figure of Iṭṭagi Mahādeva temple (refer *Pl.* 16, *figs* 1, 2, 3 and 4) gives a clear picture of these geometric divisions, which is adopted in Hindu sculptural art.

In the sculpture of Gommaṭeśvara the following trapezium ratios are interesting:

1. In the trapezium *LL–KK*, the width of the waist marked *LL* = *LK* on the right side = *LK* on the left side. *LL* is parallel to the side *KK* and is in a golden ratio.
2. In the trapezium *LL–MM* = The height on right *LM* = the height on the left side *LM*. *LL* and *MM* are in golden ratio.
3. In the trapezium *NNOO*, the base *NN* = height *NO* on the right = the height *NO* on the left. *OO* and *ON* are in a golden ratio.
4. In the trapezium *KK–MM*, side *KM* on right = *KM* on the left = *KK*. Point *L* is the golden section of *MK*.
5. Similarly in the trapezium *MM NN*, *MM* = *MN* = *MN* and are in golden ratios.
6. The top triangle *QOO* has the angles of 72-72-36, defines the nose dimensions and the midpoint of the eyebrows. The angles are same at any section of the golden isosceles triangle *QKK*.

A comparative picture of the golden ratios in the human body, and the figure of Gommaṭeśvara is given for easy understanding of the proportions of the statue. There is a scale engraved near the left foot of Gommaṭa measuring "3' 4"." This scale gives the clue for the measurement of the statue.

According to the calculations of golden ratios, it is the basic and smallest unit used in the figure, which is the dimension from *bhrū-madhya*. The dimensions of the face, width of the shoulder, the navel section, and the total height of the sculpture can be calculated on the basis of 3' 4". The following calculations based on 3' 4" as the smallest unit are interesting.

This scale of 3' 4" in author's opinion is the measurement of forehead to the crown part, a basic unit for the measurements in a two-dimensional calculation.

When 3' 4" multiplied by the golden ratio constant (*phi* constant rounded off to a single decimal) 1.6 = 5' 4", which is the dimension from the centre of the eyebrow up to the chin.

The total height of the face *A–F* (refer *Pl.* 44) is 3.4 + 5.4 = 8.8 feet.

Since *AF* is the golden measurement of *A–D* from point *D*, the measurement of *F–D* = *AF* × 1.6 (8.8 × 1.6) = 14.0.

The total measurement of *A–D* = 8.8 + 14 = 22.8 ft (from crown to navel).

The measurement of *A–D* is also the width of the shoulder as *AA–DD* is a square.

The golden rectangle of *DD–BB* can be calculated by multiplying the side of the square and the golden constant, 22.8 × 1.6 = 36.48.

The measurement of the figure below the navel is 36.4 ft.

When these two dimensions are added, the total height of the figure can be estimated.

AD + *DB* = 22.8 + 36.4 = 59.2.

The total height of the Gommaṭeśvara is 59.2 ft when the scale of the inscription 3.4 ft is considered as the small unit of measurement.

The ratio between the dimension of the face (called *tala* in Indian iconometry, which is also equal to the measurement of the hand from wrist) is 8.8:59.2 = 6.77. The figure is approximately 6.77 *tala* measurement.

An interesting observation is, 3.4 is also the height of the neck.

Cut an arc with the dimension of *AF* from the centre of head *AA*, on the midline, which cuts the arc of the face below chin.

With the same dimension cut another arc on midline from the centre of the eyebrow point, which gives the height of the neck.

The sequence of golden ratio numbers are 3, 5, 8, 13, 21, 34, 55 and so on.

The ratio is very close to the measurements of Gommaṭa which starts from 3.4, 5.4, 8.8, 14, 22.8, 36.2, 59.2

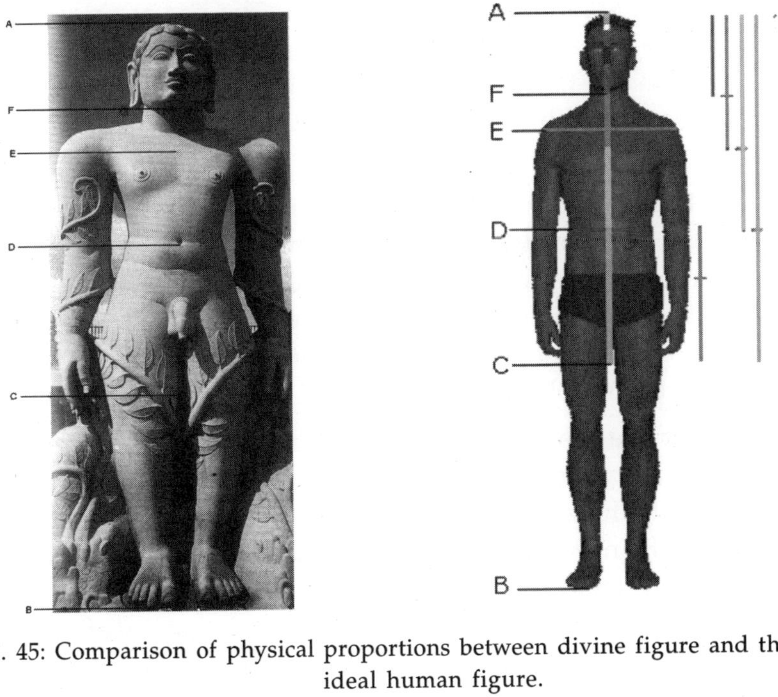

Pl. 45: Comparison of physical proportions between divine figure and the ideal human figure.

Department of Archaeology, Karnataka, quotes the total height of the image as 58 feet. The measurements taken by the Institute of Indian Art History, Karnataka University, Dharwad, using the theodilite instrument, indicate the height of the colossus is 58' 8". It is interesting to note that the height obtained by using golden ratios is accurate to an extent of 1 per cent.

Mahāpuruṣa Lakṣaṇas in Divine Figures: The special features of the Hindu divine sculptures.

The divine figures have slightly modified body proportions than the ideal human figures like longer hands, broader shoulders, longer ears, the engraved *padma* motifs on the body, etc. These special features are called *mahāpuruṣa lakṣana* that helps to identify the superhuman or the true divinities.

1. The measurement of hands will be slightly longer when *mahāpuruṣa lakṣaṇa*s are observed. The line at *C* (which is also a golden section of the total height when measured from the top point *A*) marks the point of the finger tips in an ideal human figure, whereas in the divine sculpture they become the thumb point.
2. The length of the arm from shoulder to finger tips is in the same measurement as the mid-section (from head to the genital position) of the body in the divine figures. The same measurement is given even in the figure of Veṅkaṭeśvara also. But in human figures, it measures up to the navel point.
3. For the same reason the shoulders are also broader. The width across the shoulders at *E* is equal in measurement to the height *AD*, which means the length of top of head to the navel region and the width of shoulders are in the same measurement (the same ratio is observed in the figure of Veṅkaṭeśvara also). But in an ideal human figure, the width across the shoulders are in golden ratio to the height of *AD*.

4. The ears, which are up to the lip level in a two-dimensional figure of human, are drawn longer up to chin level in the sculpture of Gommaṭeśvara.
5. The mid-section of the total height remains the same in both, cutting at the genital position.

The Motif of Tendrils: The tendrils or the creepers wound on the limbs of the figure from the base to legs and on hands are also indicative of the units of divisions of the bodyline, apart from the philosophical interpretations that are associated. One set of creepers appear from the base on either side, and curve at the knee position, outside the legs of the sculpture. The other set of creepers are depicted passing behind the legs and bifurcate symmetrically at the inner knee position on the line *HH*. They ascend up to the pelvic line *JJ*, and also indicate the wrist section of the hand. On the hands, they start in line with the midpoint of the body and the first loop is in line with the positions of the *mūlādhāra* and *svādhiṣṭhāna cakra* indicated below the fold on the lower abdomen. The continuation of the tendril on the upper arm is designed to be indicative of the line of *maṇipūra cakra* and the *anāhata cakra* that is from navel to the heart line.

GOLDEN SPIRAL

From the earliest times the spirals of nature have been a common artistic representation of the dynamic symbol of life force. The spirals carved on stone suggest a labyrinthine journey to after-life. By adding a wheeling momentum to a spiral it is interpreted as the eternal movement of the aspect of "time." The open and flowing line of spiral as seen in the sculpture of Gommaṭeśvara indicates extension, uninterruption, evolution and continuity much like the breathing and life. Ancient tribal cultures of South Pacific and Maori depict spiral motifs painted or tattooed on their body hinting at the same association. Golden spiral is a clear indication of the capacity of creating the infinitely small and infinitely large patterns observing the same ratio wherever they are drawn.

One interesting consequence of the golden ratio is that a golden rectangle (where the two sides, the longer and smaller sides, are in golden ratios) can be divided into a square and a smaller golden rectangle. The process of cutting can go on at *infinitum* and the function of fractally recurring golden rectangles is known as logarithmic golden spiral sections. This can also be used where the size of the revolutions grow with the golden ratio as seen in the spiral divisions of the sea shells. The power of *phi* (the constant ratio of 1.618 with the two segments) increases with the progress or increase in the size of sections. Golden spirals exist in nature like plants, climbers, flowers, etc. that is symbolic of growth from infinitely small to infinitely large sections.

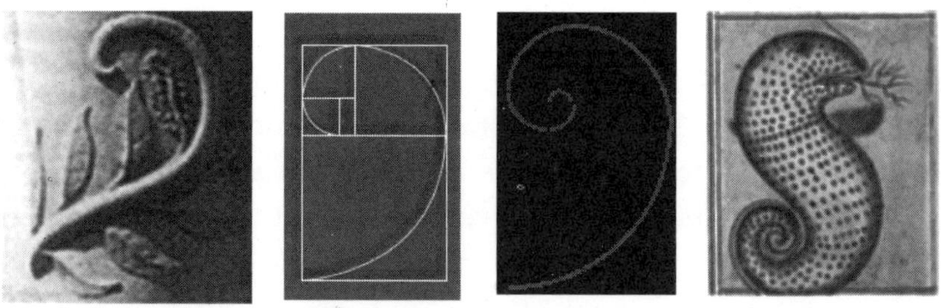

Pl. 46: Golden spirals.

In the figure of Gommaṭeśvara, the upper arm has the design of spiral-shaped tendril winding from the base of the arm and becomes bigger at the base on the legs. The top part exhibits golden spiral section. The height of the tendril is up to the golden section of the height from *D* to *E*, which is in line with the armhole cutting as well as the breast point. The spiral is also probably the mark of divisions of the chest region. Golden spiral is also made use of to represent the infinite power of the snake symbolism in *kuṇḍalinī* power. Even the trunk of Hindu God Gaṇeśa, the tail of Lord Hanumān are shaped like a golden spiral.

The symbol *AUṀ* also has the golden spiral in it but the association is in relation to the infinite sound vibrations the sacred *mantra* can produce.

3.6. Golden Ratios in the Buddha Image at Sārnāth

Sārnāth is a place 5 km away from the district of Varanasi, in the state of Uttar Pradesh. The place has many ancient monuments of Buddhist architecture, several *stūpa*s and sculptures of Buddha, dating from fourth-twelfth century CE. Sārnāth is one of the four sacred pilgrim centres of Buddhist religion and the place where Lord Buddha preached his first sermon.

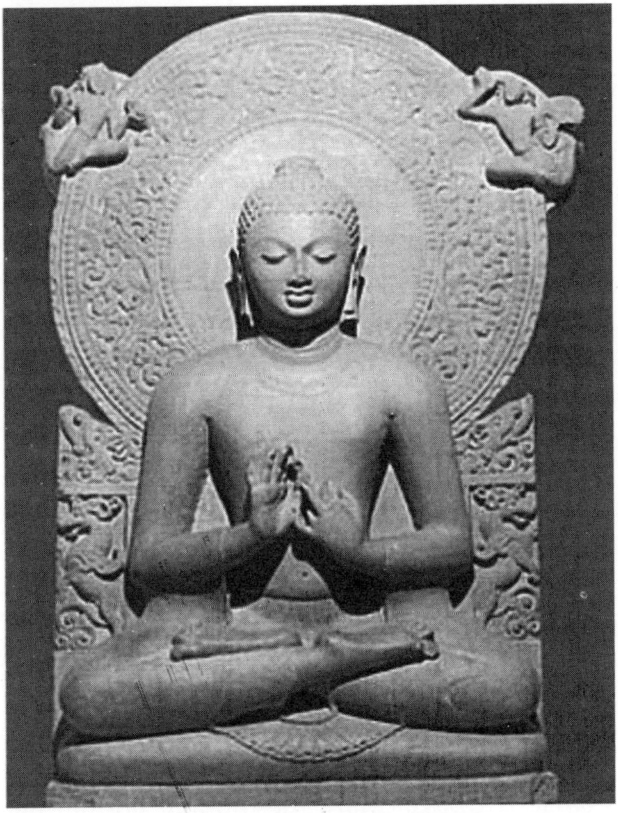

Pl. 47: Dhyānī Buddha at Sārnāth.

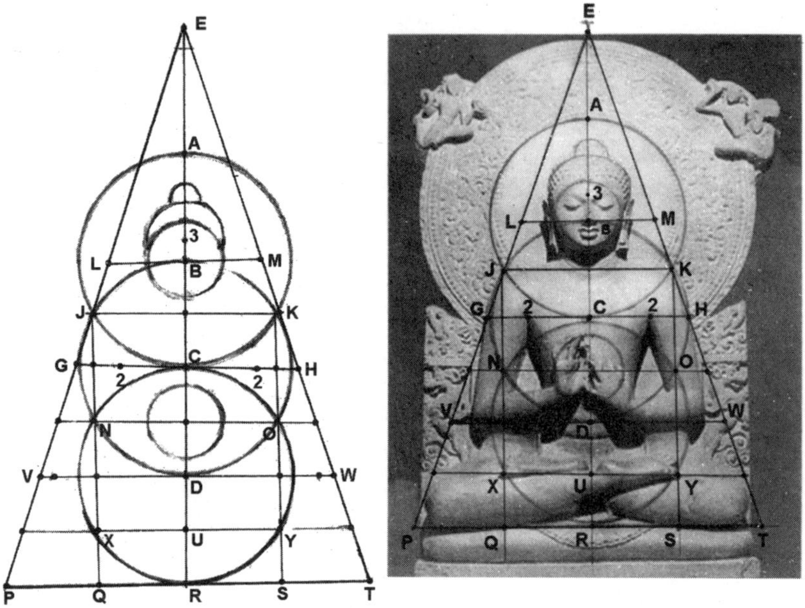

Pl. 48: Framework of the Buddha sculpture and its implementation.

The art of Gupta period can be seen at its best in Sārnāth. The Dhyānī Buddha image is acclaimed as one of the most graceful figures of Buddha.

The assessments of the golden ratios in the structure of the figure have been attempted by the author.

The framework of Buddha at Sārnāth is based on the combination of overlapping circles and isosceles triangles, drawn with golden ratios. The methodology in using golden ratios to arrive at the dimensions is an enabler for perfect shapes in two-dimensional plane.

The construction method is as follows:

1. Draw a verticle midline. The radius of the circle is chosen, preferably in golden number sequence. With *C* as centre, a circle is drawn. Mark the top and bottom intersecting points with the line as *B* and *D*.

2. With *B* as centre, draw a circle with the same radius and mark the top intersecting point as *A*. Draw another arc from point *A* with the dimension of radius, to mark the top intersection point and call it as *E*.
3. With *D* as centre, draw another circle and mark the lower intersecting point as *R*. The three circles with centre *C*, *B* and *D* are the overlapping circles. Draw a perpendicular line to the midline passing through the bottom point *R*, which is the base of the triangle.
4. Mark the intersecting points of the circles with centre *C* and *B* as *JK* (which are the midpoints of the sides of the triangle), and the intersecting points of circles with *C* and *D* as centre to be *N* and *O*.
5. To draw the isosceles triangle, connect the top point *E* to the circle intersecting points *J–K* and extend it up to the bottom line at *R*. Mark the base points of the triangle as *P* and *T*. Triangle *ETP* is a golden isosceles triangle with four overlapping circles in it. The base *PT* bears a golden ratio with the side *ET*. Half the base *RT* = 1 + *phi* of *TK*, which is also the midpoint of the *ET*.
6. Draw the horizontal line passing through *B* up to the sides of the triangle and mark the intersecting points as *L* and *M*.
7. Connect the circle intersecting points *J* to *N* and *K* to *O*. Extend it down till it cuts the baseline *PT* and mark the cutting points as *Q* and *S*.
8. Mark the points where the circle of *D* cuts the verticle lines *JQ* and *KS* as *X* and *Y*. Extend the line *XY* up to the legs of the triangle. The line *XY* bisects the midline *DR* and mark the midpoint as *U*.
9. Draw a line through the point *C* horizontally to cut the legs of the triangle and mark it as *GH*.

10. Draw a line through the point *D* horizontally up to the sides of the triangle and mark them as *V* and *W*.

With this construction the points in position on the sculpture are as follows:

C	=	Chest point.
B	=	Nose point.
D	=	Navel point.
R	=	The point below the right ankle, which is in line with the small fold of the garment.
A	=	Top point of the first halo.
E	=	The top point of the second halo.

1. The line *GH* cuts through the chest line, and the line *JK* defines the shoulder points. The arc of the circle of *C* between *JG* and *KH*, are the curves of the right and the left shoulders.

2. Line *XY* cuts across the line *DR* and the point *U* marks the lower point of the heels. The circle of *D* passes through the toes on either sides at *X* and *Y*. The upper part of the heels is measured as the golden section of *DR* from the point *R*. The line across this point horizontally defines the width of the foot at the little finger joint. The length of the foot from heel to the finger joints = the height of the face = the measurement of the hand from wrist to the finger tip = one *tala* according to the Indian iconometry.

3. Measure the dimension of *QS* or *JK*, and cut an arc from point *D* on the angles of the triangle at *P* and *T*. This defines the curve of the knee in sitting position. The extension of the line *XY* defines the height of the knee/thigh folding.

4. Cut the golden dimension of CG the radius of the circle

from the point C, on either side and mark it as 2-2. The dimension of 2-2 is cut at different places in the frame of the structure. It is the point of armhole to armhole.

5. Cut an arc with the dimension of 2-2, from the point C towards R on the line *DR*, which defines the arc of the lower abdomen where the garment is tied. Cut the dimension of the golden ratio of the length C-2 on this arc, equidistant from the centre, D which defines the width of the abdomen.

6. Join armhole point 2 to the abdominal points at both sides to define the shape of the torso.

7. To draw the shape of the thighs, join the upper points of the knee (extension of the line *XY*) to the abdomen points on both sides and make it into a gentle curve.

   Draw the curve of the knee in the angle of *STW* and *QPV*. Join point *Q* to *Y* and *S* to *X* in diagonal lines to get the shape of the legs below the knee.

8. The line *VW* through the point *D* marks the line of the elbow and lower arm.

9. To draw the arms, cut the dimension of 2-2 from point *D* on both sides *DW* and *DV*. Join this point to the circle intersection point near the points *G* and *H*, which defines the shape of the outer arm up to the elbow section at *W*. Join point 2 to the point where line *KS* and *JQ* intersects the line *DV–DW* to define the shape of the inner arm. Locate the point where the circle at C cuts the inner arm line to know the folding width of the elbow.

10. Draw a circle with the radius of the golden ratio of ½ *DC*, from the midpoint of *DC*. (Alternatively, to know the midpoint join the line *NO* which bisects the line *DC*, passing through the mid palm of right hand as well as the upper palm of the left hand). This inner circle

accommodates the cut of the wrist, the palm of the hands, and the length of the fingers.

11. The right hand holds *cin-mudrā* — the gesture of the hand for peace and concentration at meditation, where the index finger touches the thumb. The left hand is also in a similar *mudrā,* but the middle finger touches the thumb of the right hand, together it is called *dharmacakra-mudrā.*

TO DRAW THE FACE

1. Measure the dimension of 2-2, and cut it on the midline from point *C*, which marks the point of the *bhrū-madhya* the centre of eyebrows. And mark it as 3.
2. Cut the dimension of 2–2 from point *A*, which defines the point of the chin.
3. Cut the dimension of *C*–2 from point *A*, to mark the point of forehead.
4. Note the diameter of forehead line to chin which is equal to the smaller circle of hands between *D* and *C*. Measure the radius of this circle and draw the circle of face from the nose point *B*. The midpoint of point *B* to chin is the line of mouth.
5. With the same radius, draw the upper semicircle from the point 3 — the centre of eyebrow which defines the shape of the head. The *śikhā* (hair bun) is again a semicircle from the centre of the head with the radius of ½ of points *B* to 3, or 3 to forehead.
6. To mark the neckline, draw a line through *JK* cut the dimension of ½ of *C*–2 from the midline to know the width of the neck. Draw the curve of the neck (from the line across the mouth up to the line of neck).
7. Eyebrows and curve of the closed eyes emerge on either side from the point 3. The upper part of the ears begins from the end of the eyebrows. The lower part of the ear

is extended up to the chin line. The line *L–B–M* passes through the mid part of the ears.

8. Join the shoulder points *J* and *K* to the sides of the neck in a gentle curve.
9. The second and bigger halo is a circle drawn from the nose point *B* with the radius of *Q–S* or *J–K*.

The figure is adorned with a thin cloth, which can be seen draped from the elbows and on the legs which is the artistic ingenuity of the sculptor to make the drape thin-textured even in the medium of stone. This construction method gives a clear picture of the golden geometry involved in the structure of the sculpture.

Epilogue

EVER since the basic needs of food and shelter were met, man started to think about the creator as his contacts in life were with creations. The multiplicity and variety of creations was infinite with its execution in perfect order. The capacity of the unseen power got visualised into an idea of God. When man thought of giving a concrete form of God, he was at a loss probably because it was almost impossible for him to express the infinite and eternal power in one figure. He made a plan diagram of the concept and qualities of God before giving an expression of its manifestation into a figure. *Maṇḍala* was thus a power diagram where he used sacred geometry and numerology as the important ingredients.

Three aspects need to be considered for the study of a *maṇḍala* like the structure, philosophical and spiritual parts. When the body of the structure is analysed it becomes a scientific approach as the technology of graphic designs becomes valuable. Applications of the values of thoughts need a body much like the physical structure of the deity, where values, faith and divine qualities get infused. As said by the physicist Max Planck, science cannot solve the ultimate mystery of nature. Every advance in knowledge brings us face to face with the mystery of our own being. Science concerns with the nature of physical universe. But in its quest for finding the ultimate reality, physical sciences cross the barriers of physics and enter into metaphysics. Like a mathematical abstraction, the knower and the knowable mingle together in a wave of pure consciousness. Science ultimately emerges as the science of consciousness in tune with the essence of spirituality.

When philosophical aspects are considered, philosophy is the field of study that includes diverse subjects like aesthetics, ethics, logic, epistemology and metaphysics in which people ask questions whether God exists and, if so, what is the nature of reality. The fundamental method of philosophy is the use of reasoning to evaluate the arguments concerning these questions. Man concocted his values and psychological comfort zone in an attempt to visualise the idea of God.

The core part of the *maṇḍala*, the central dot or *bindu* associated with spirituality aspect did not undergo any change because God is still a mystery, yet to be explored as it is beyond the capacity of the five senses. The central dot — the *bindu* of *maṇḍala* refers to pure consciousness. The transcendental aspect of pure consciousness exists as a logical necessity, for there must be condition beyond which further analysis cannot go and the logical fallacy of "infinitum," can be evaded. The ultimate reality is projected to contain all things in their fullness. The technical term *caitanya* used to denote the universal intelligence or spirit, was expressed in the changeless and boundless central core point — that is without parts (*niṣkala*), and that which is unproduced and hence indestructible is all symbolised in the dot. Hence it does not come under the subject of knowledge. It is a principle of pure experience, realised only by the ecstasy of spiritual illumination. The *bindu* was just repeated as a fractal motif in the body and boundary of *maṇḍala*s, indicating the omniscience and the omnipotence of the central power.

The birth and longevity of the world was the second question that bothered the humans. The scientists and philosophers from ancient times to this day are yet to draw conclusions for this. Many such speculations are projected in the *maṇḍala*s also. The various aspects of cosmos and the scientific thoughts of how the world worked underwent a refraction when it was projected in a *maṇḍala* because the supreme power "God" was conceived to be the creator and controller of everything in the universe. Exploration into the mystery of the universe was like a spiritual passion. Scientists of ancient India believed that only gods knew the secrets of nature, and the development in science was based mostly on the rational observation of the world. All aspects of science were discussed with an overtone of philosophy in *maṇḍalas*. Thus science and technology came in parallel with the advance of rational philosophy in India.

It also hinted about the ultimate truth that at the substratum of all waves in an ocean is water, in other words, waves are manifestation of water, which is born out of it and ends in it. This universal truth is conveyed in every *maṇḍala*. Whether the theme of *maṇḍala* is on scientific data or a philosophical or the psychological aspect, it is perceived as a manifestation of the centre and they all ultimately involute into it.

Maṇḍala is created as a parallel to the idol of God. The symmetry, sacred geometry, golden ratios and divine proportions are seen in both the *maṇḍala*s as well as in the anthropomorphic forms of *maṇḍala*s as idols of God. At this juncture, *yantra*s and *maṇḍala*s can be treated as the basic plan design of God before its manifestation into an anthropomorphic form. A geometric form that is perfect in proportions or a figure that has sound physical structure infused with the serene expression of supreme bliss, elevates a sculpture to divine beatitude. Such figures are charged with vibrations related to religious faith and practices, transmit the blissful expression of the idol's face as blissful experience in the minds of the devotees. The perfect face and body of the divine idol have to have features in golden proportions — the ratios chosen by nature, or else it fails to cast the required impression in the devotees.

*Maṇḍala*s and divine figures are created so that we can relate to the universe with humility, awe, celebration, and reverence, with a deeper understanding. Interpretation of the primordial symbolism of the *maṇḍala* can lead not only to greater awareness, but ultimately to a transformation of the very ways in which a man responds to the world in all its impulses.

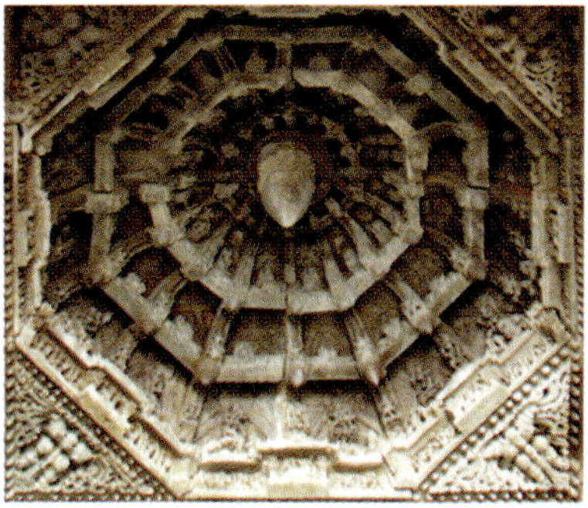

(a)

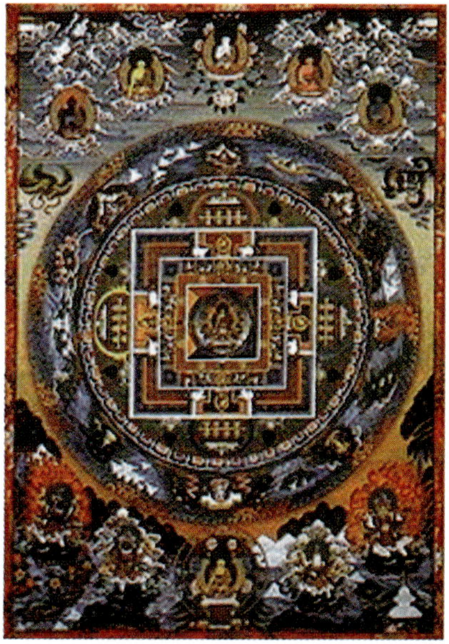

(b)

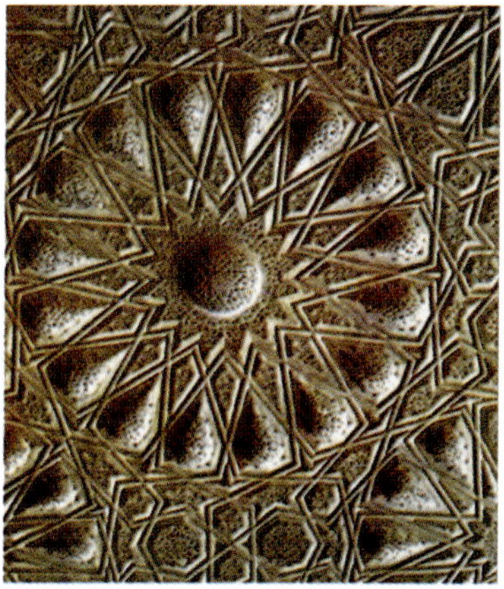

(c)

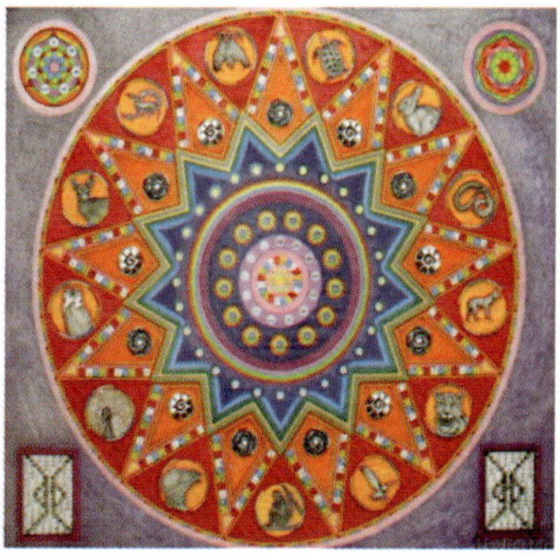

(d)

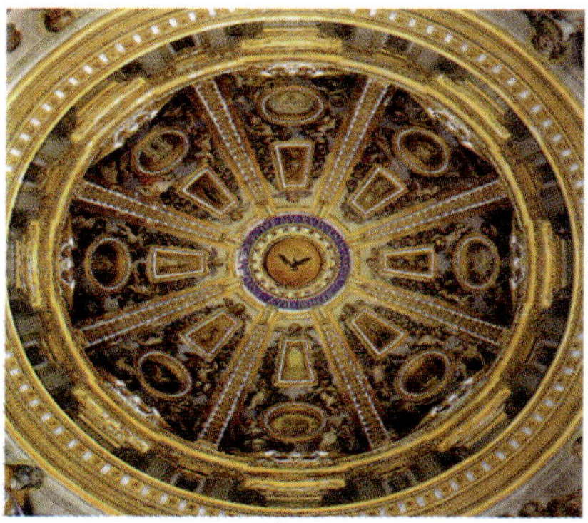

(e)

Pl. 1: Figure of Hindu, Buddhist, American, Islamic, European *maṇḍala*s.

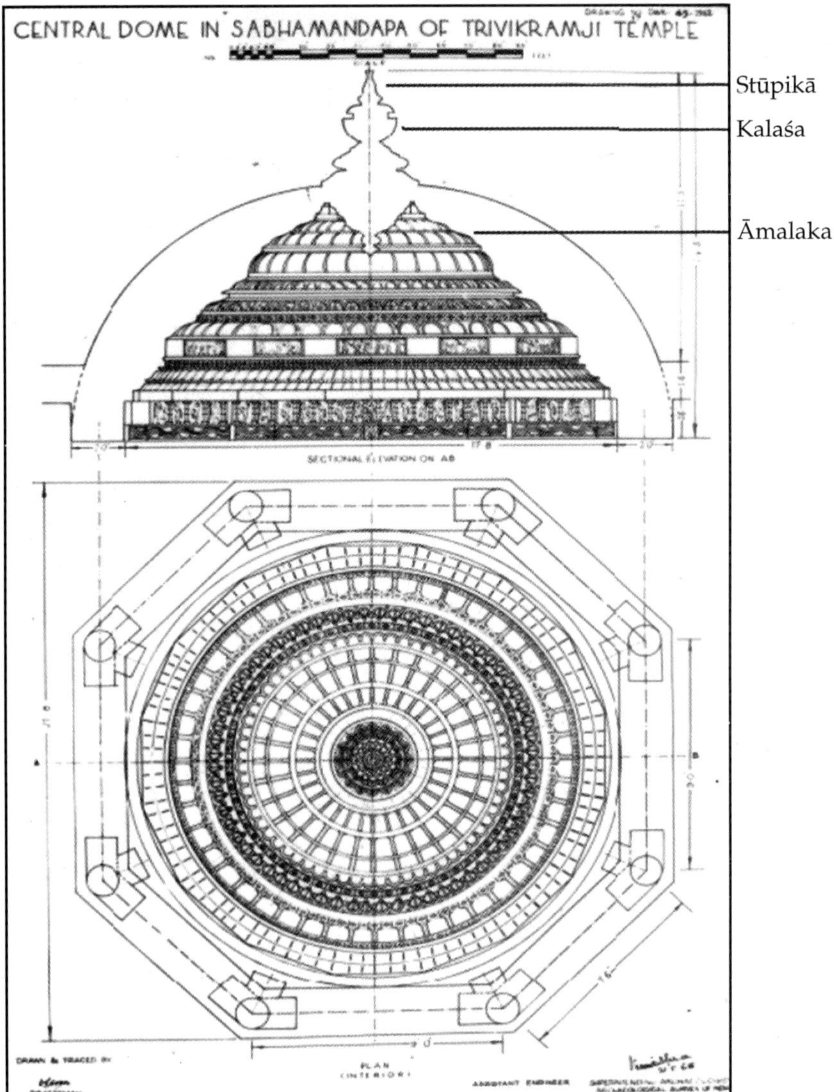

Pl. 2: Figure of the plan and cross-section of the *śikhara,* with *stūpikā.*

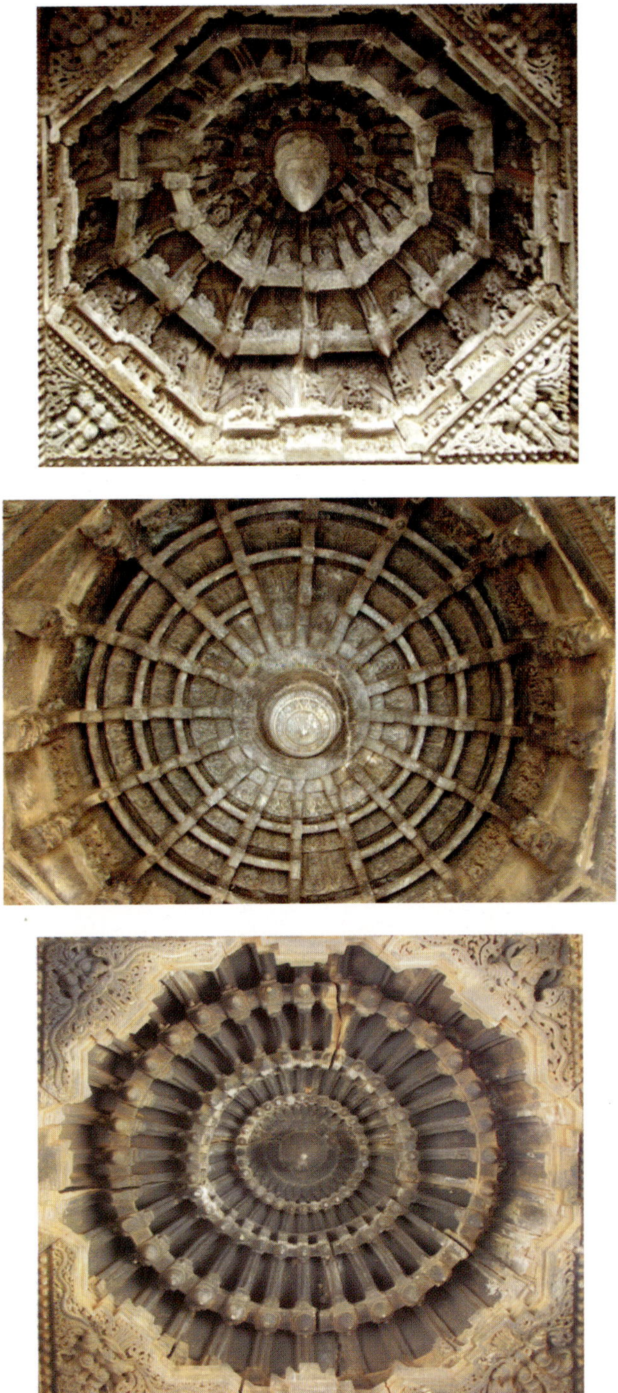

Pl. 3: Wave pattern in the *maṇḍala*s.

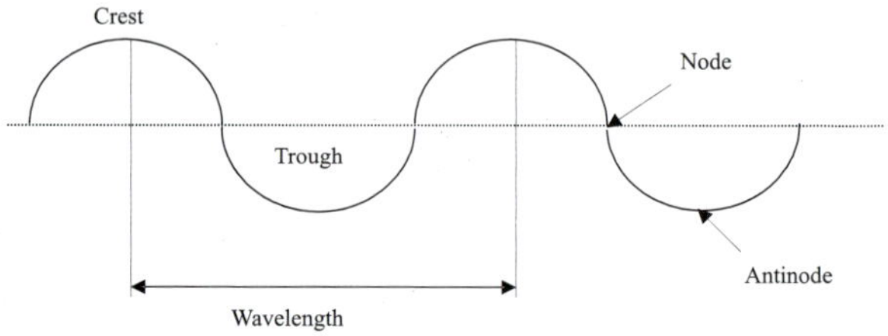

Pl. 4: Figure of crest, trough and wavelength in a wave.

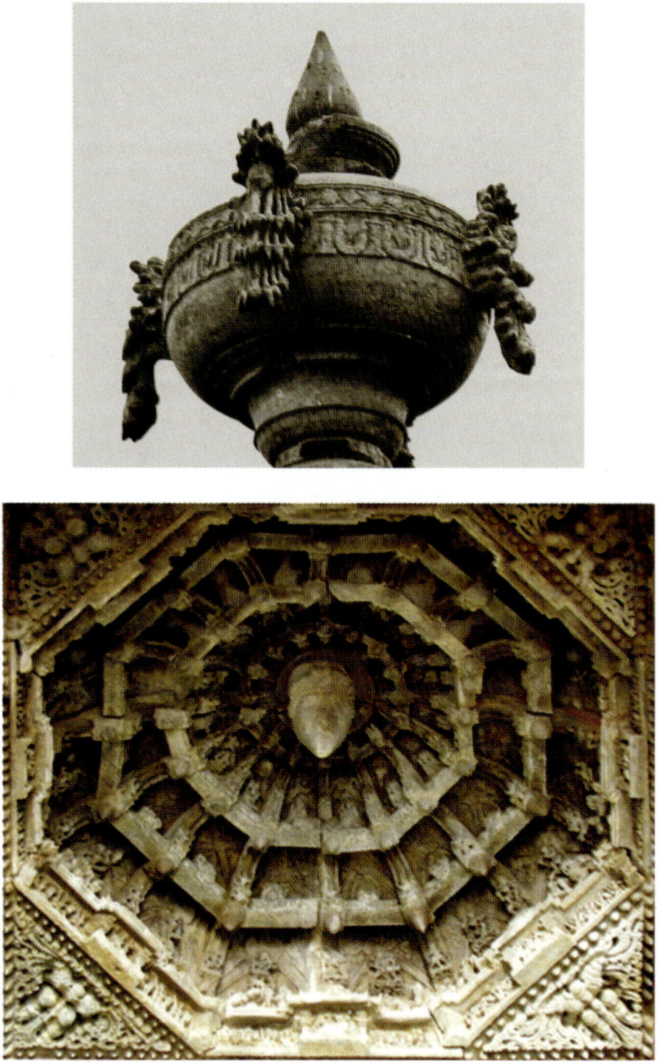

Pl. 5: A comparative picture of the lotus bud
in the *stūpikā* and the *maṇḍala* of the *bhuvaneśvarī*.

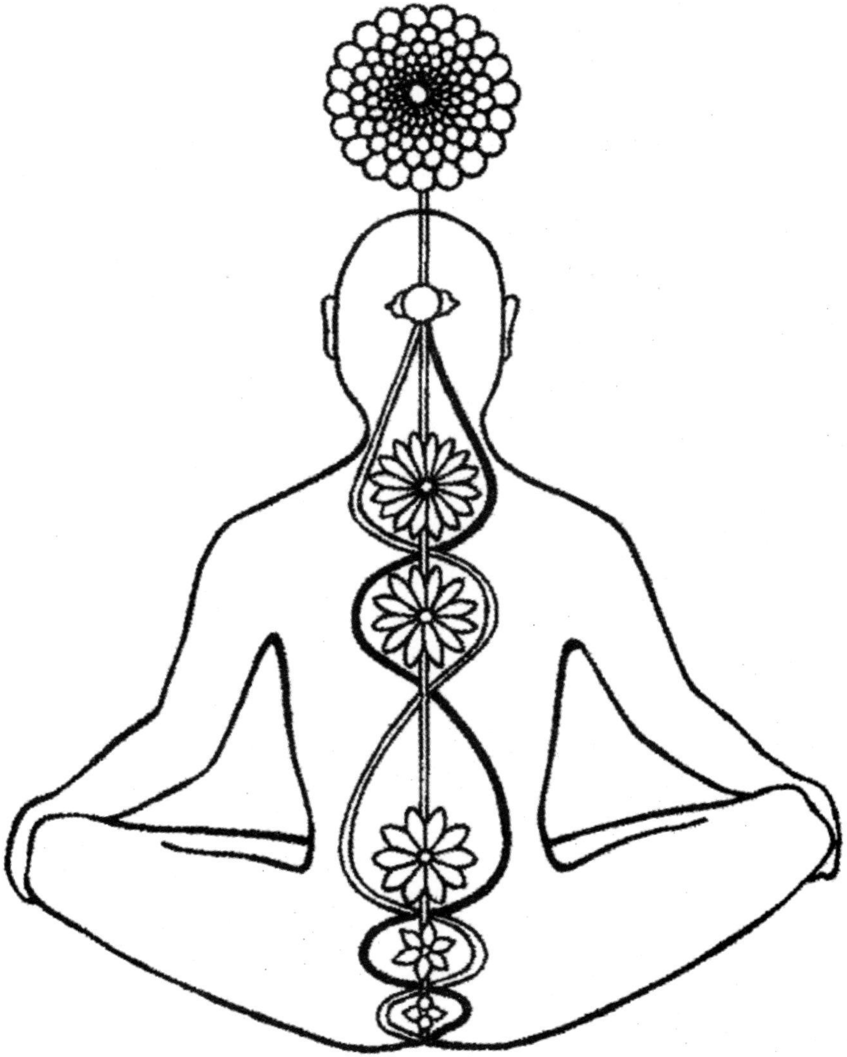

Pl. 6: Figure of the levels of awareness
in *cakra* representation of single-layered lotus.

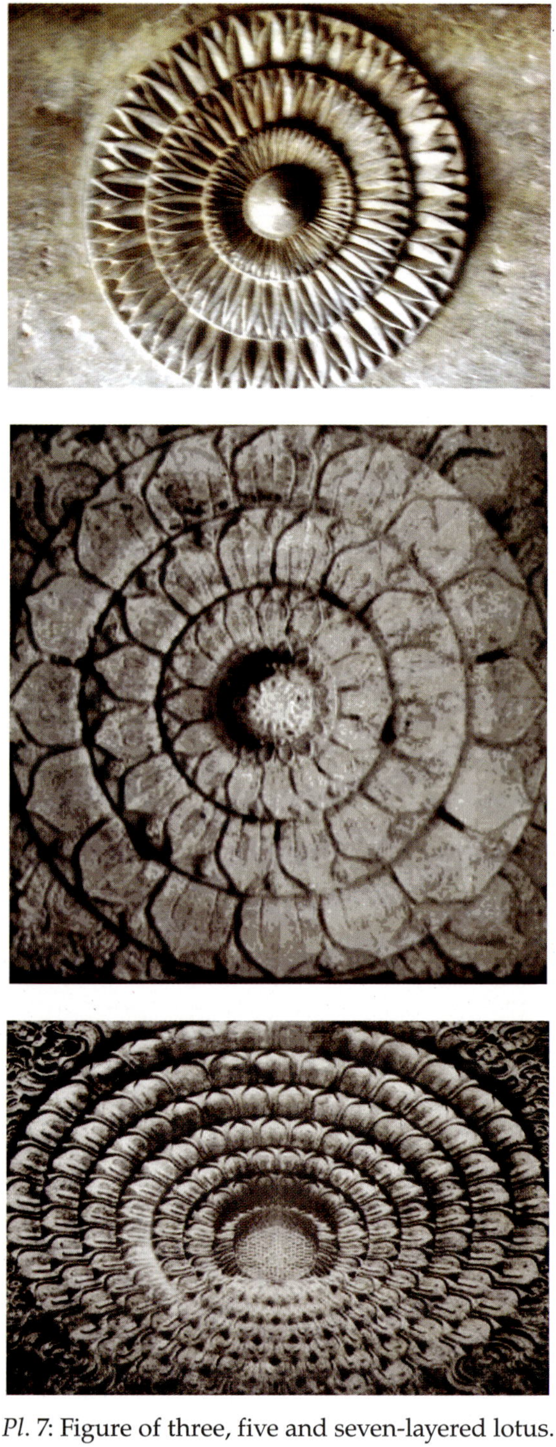

Pl. 7: Figure of three, five and seven-layered lotus.

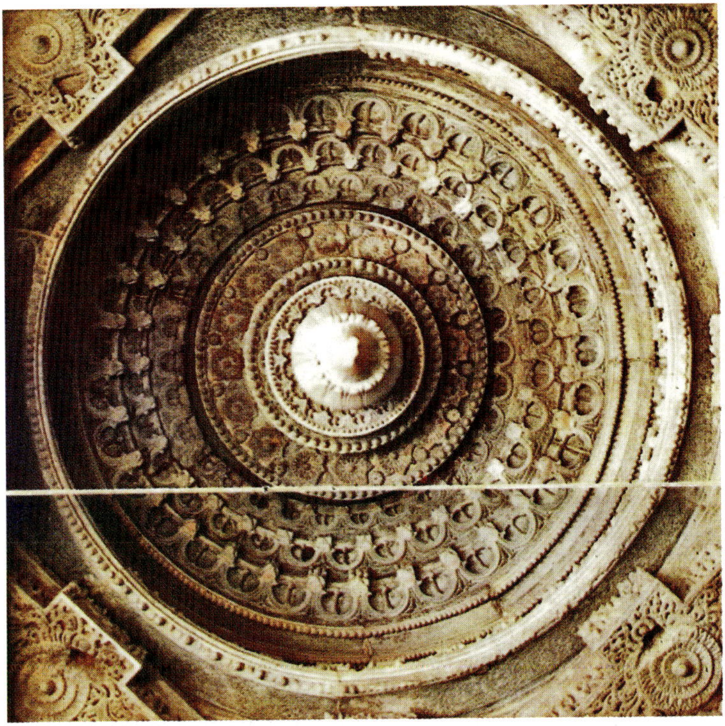

Pl. 8: Figure of five lotus design of *pañcāyatana*, where the central lotus is bigger than the ones in the four corners.

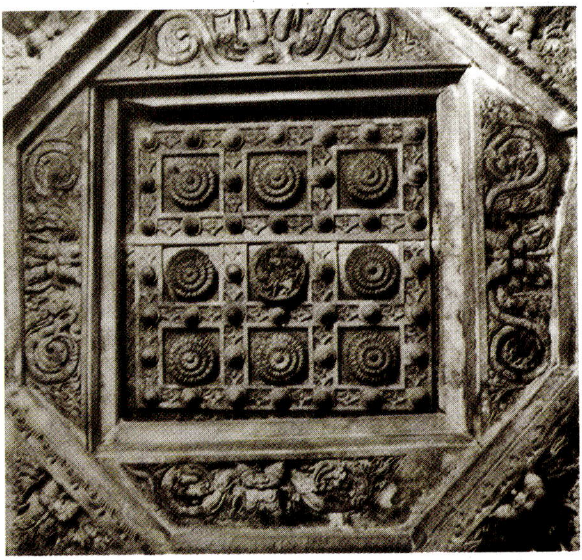

Pl. 9: Figure of nine square grids with three-layered lotuses with the *kīrtimukha* and *nāgasūtra* on the four sides.

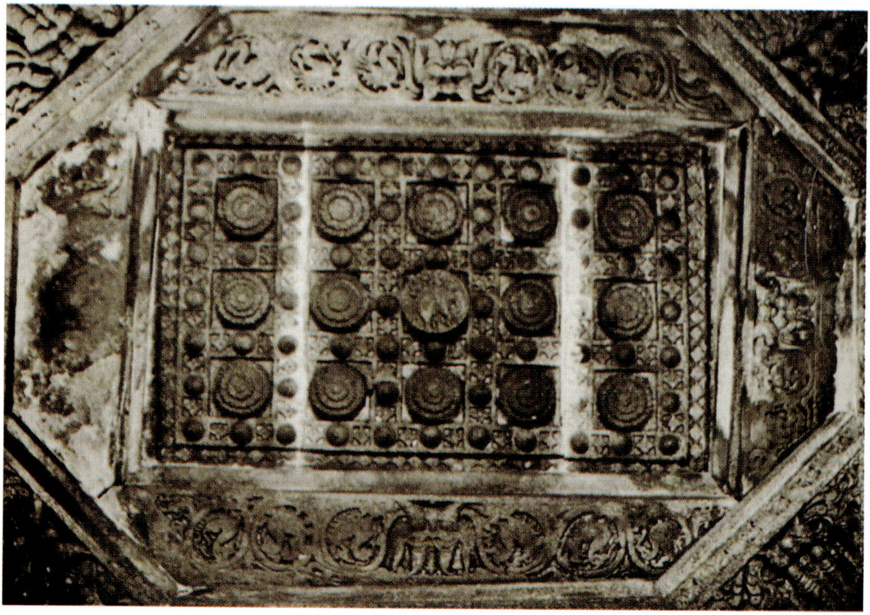

Pl. 10: Figure of fifteen square grids lotus *maṇḍala*.

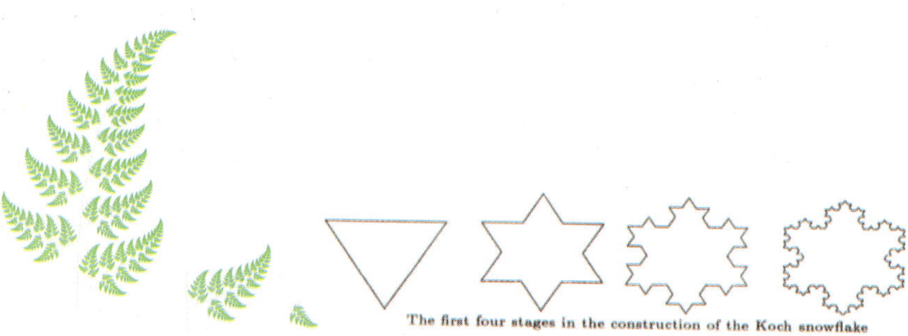

Pl. 11: Fractals in the leaf of the fern plant and in the structure of snowflakes.

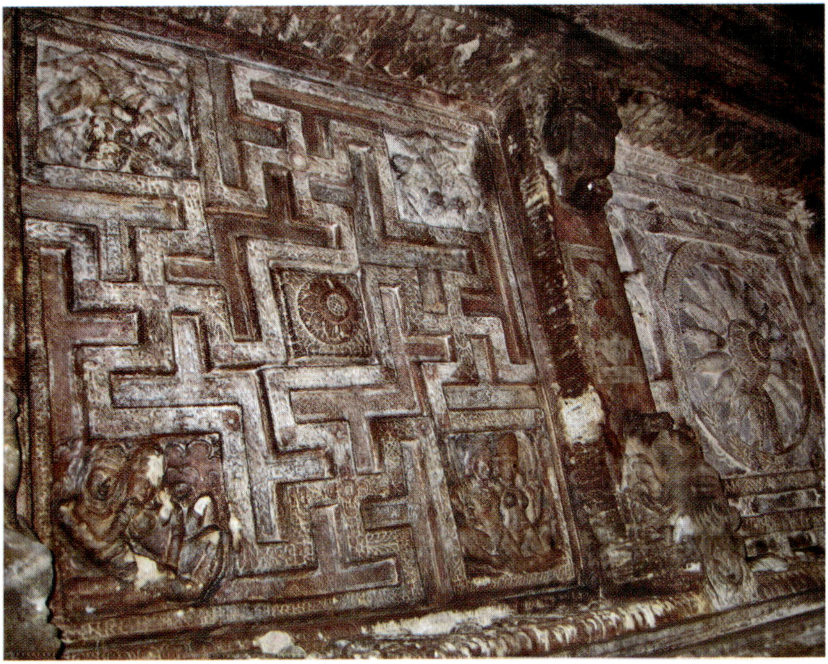

Pl. 12: *Maṇḍala* at the Bādāmi cave temple.

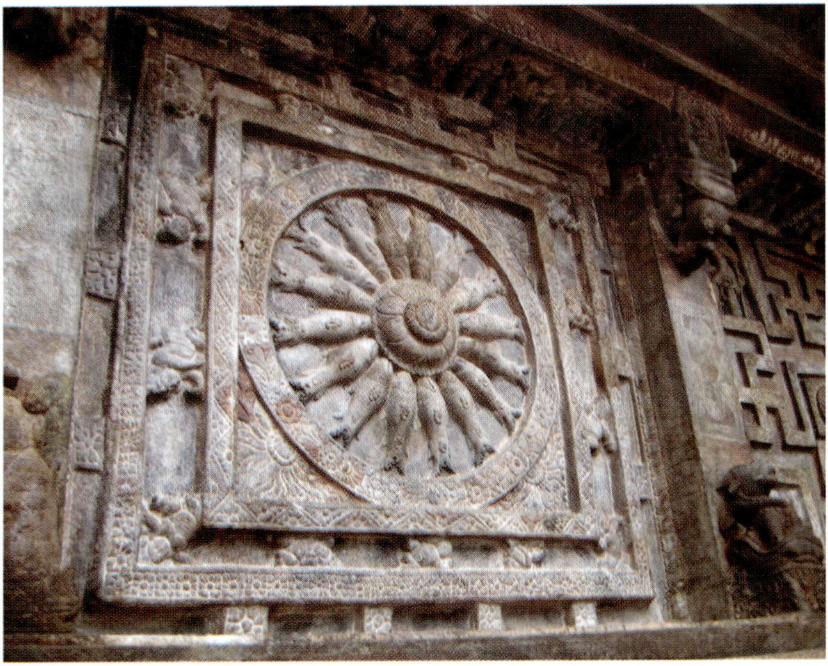

Pl. 13: *Matsya maṇḍala* at the cave temple of Bādāmi.

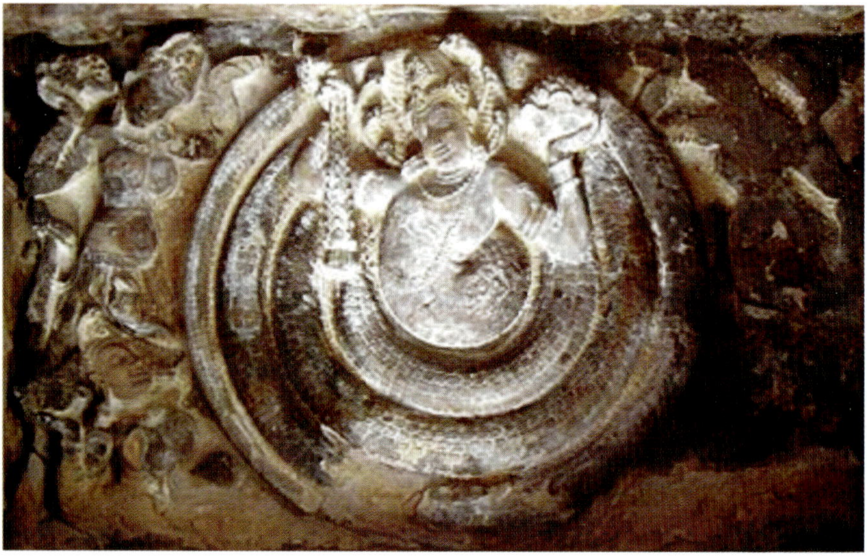

Pl. 14: *Maṇḍala* at the cave temple of Bādāmi.

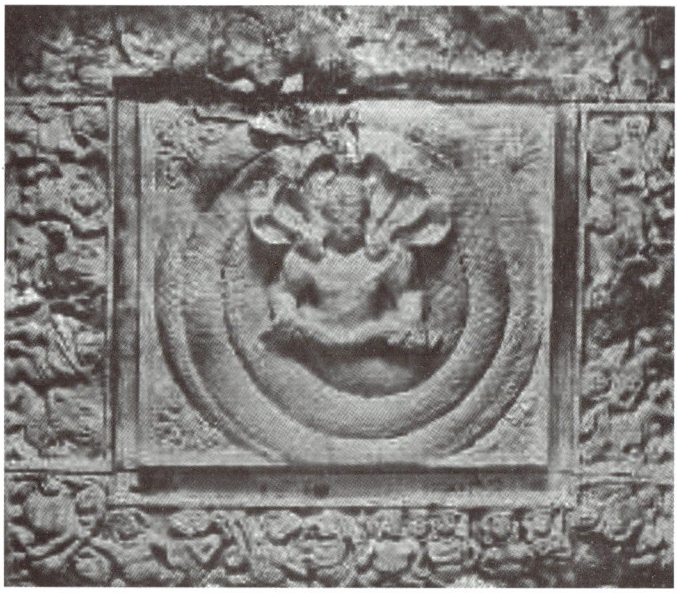

Pl. 15: Another *maṇḍala* of snake at Bādāmi cave temple.

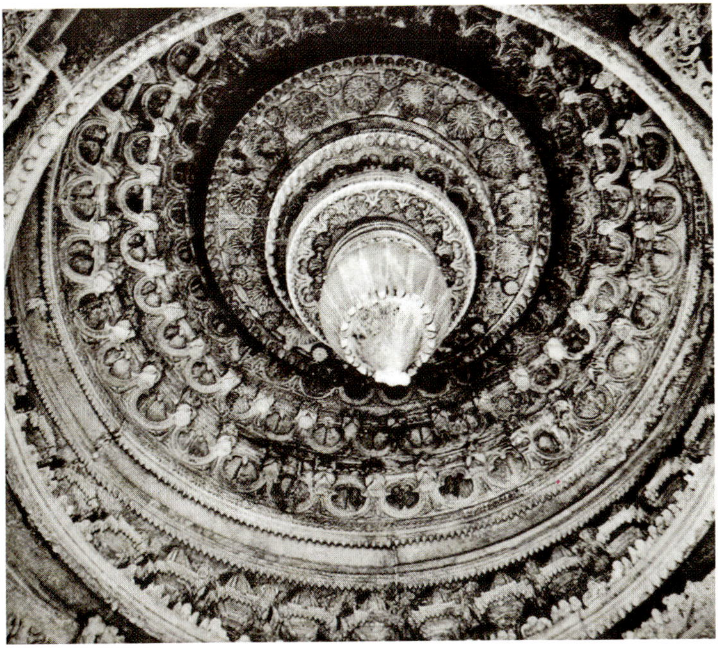

Pl. 16: *Maṇḍala* at the Somanāthpur temple.

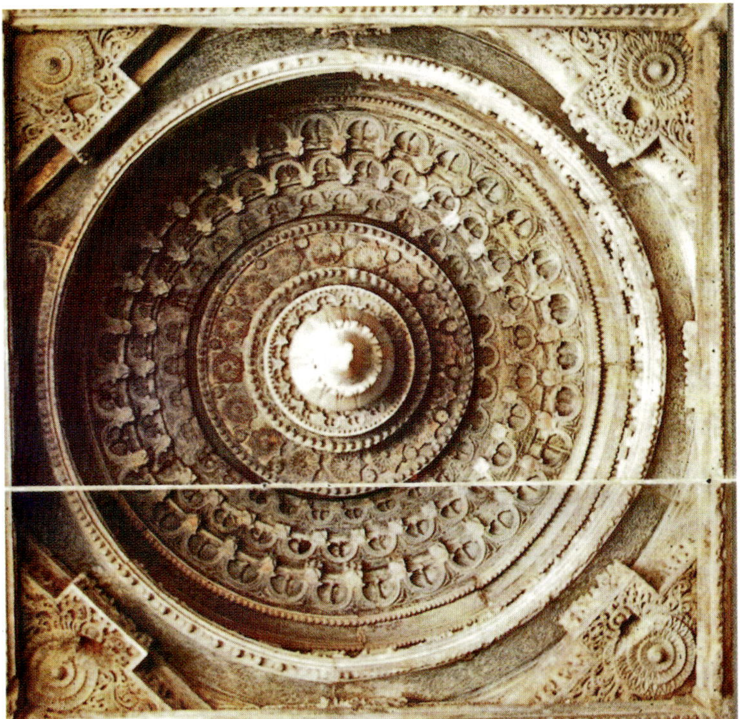

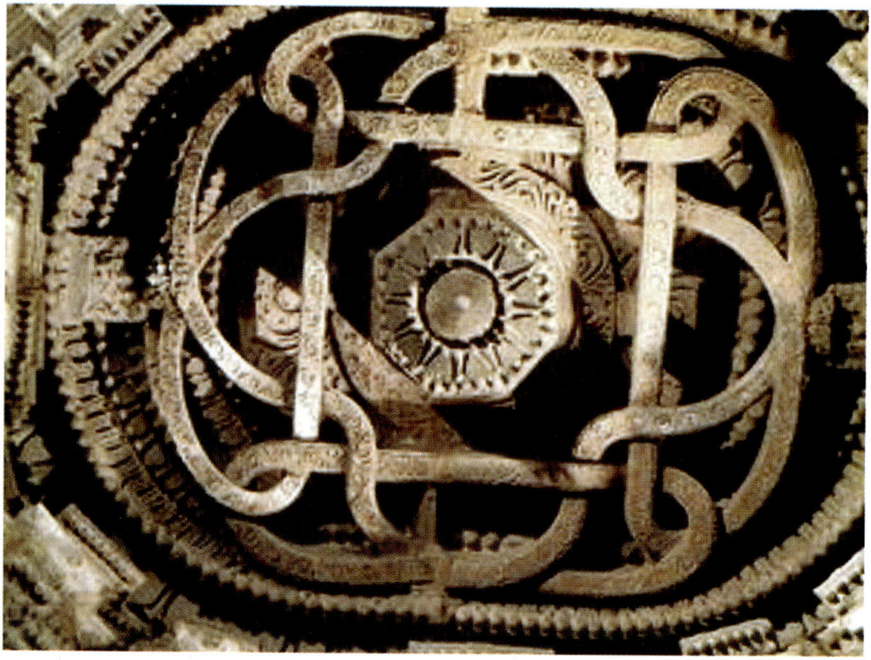

Pl. 17: Rhythm of life in the *maṇḍala* at the Somanāthpur temple.

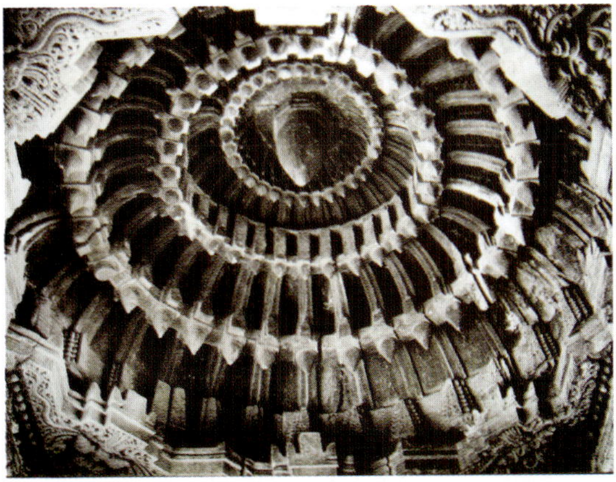

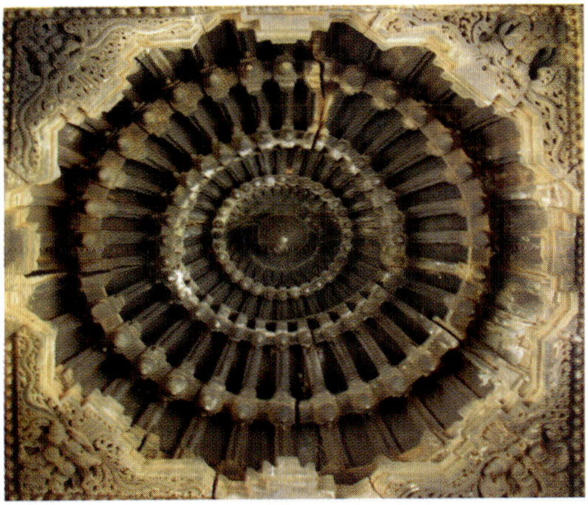

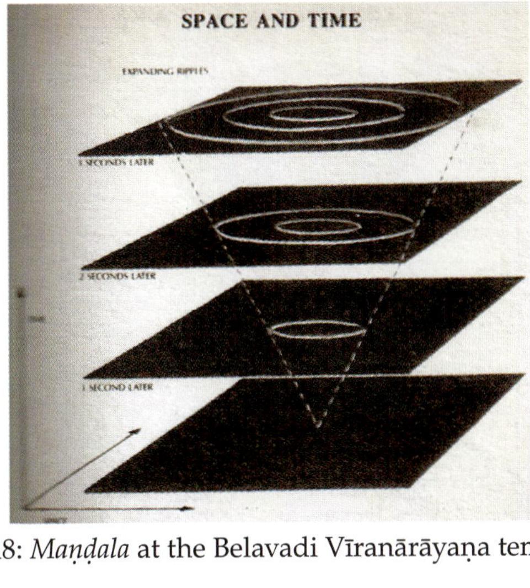

Pl. 18: *Maṇḍala* at the Belavadi Vīranārāyaṇa temple.

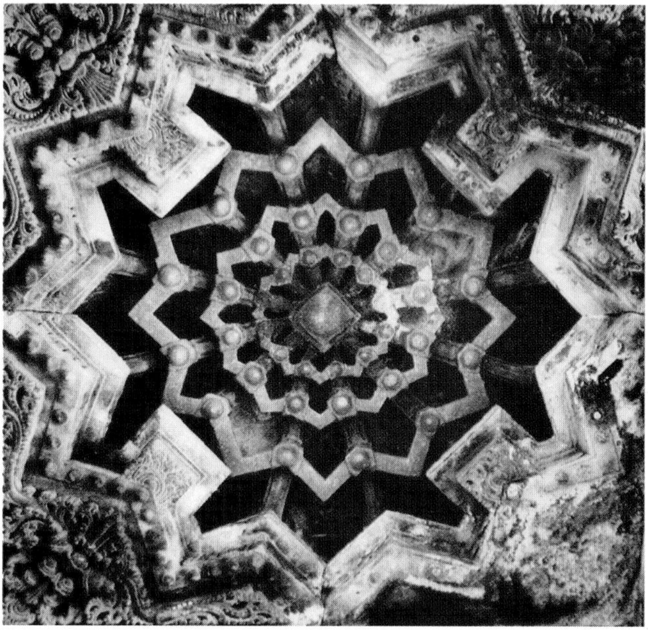

Pl. 19: The astronomical time cycles of ancient Hindu philosophy in the *maṇḍala* of Belavadi Vīranārāyaṇa temple.

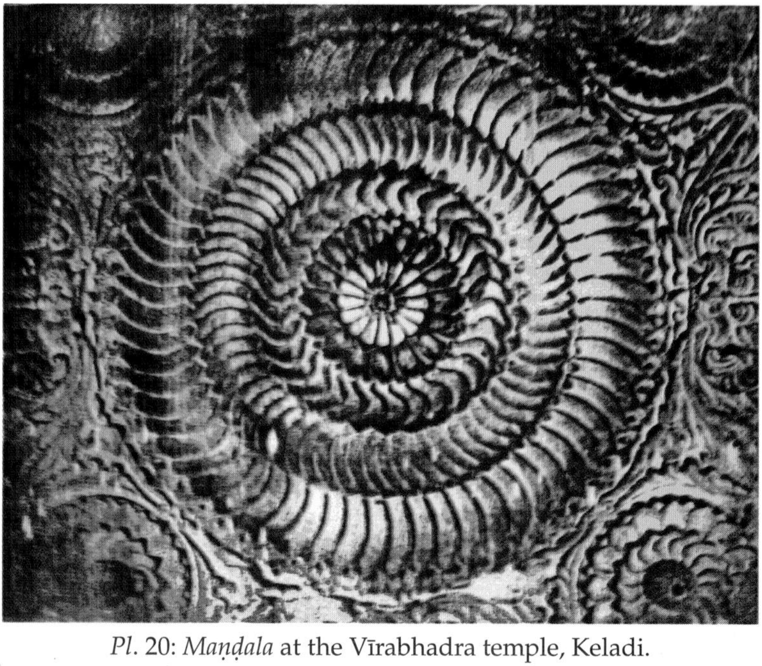

Pl. 20: *Maṇḍala* at the Vīrabhadra temple, Keladi.

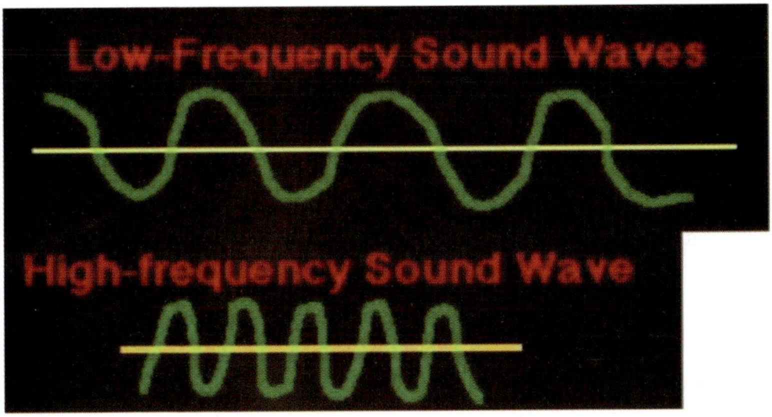

Pl. 21: Associated wave curves of low and high frequency sound waves.

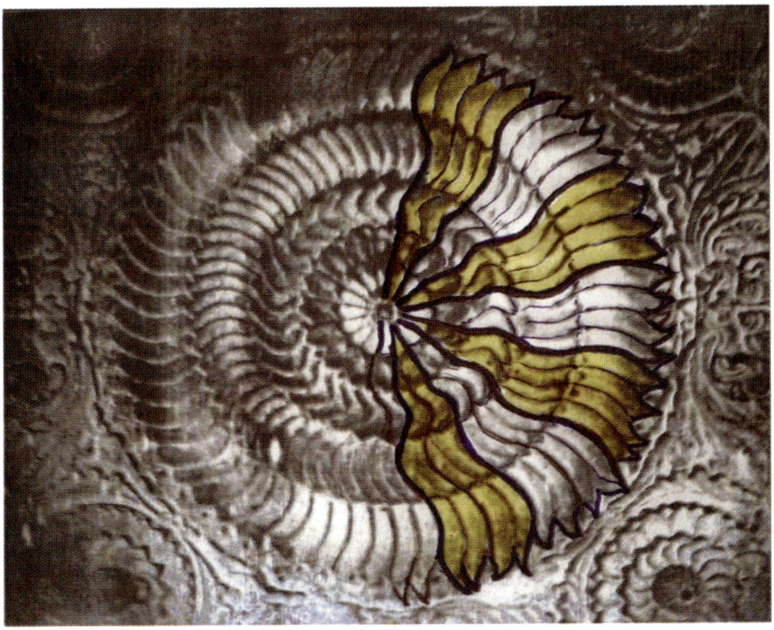

Pl. 22: Application of the ratio of the sound frequency.

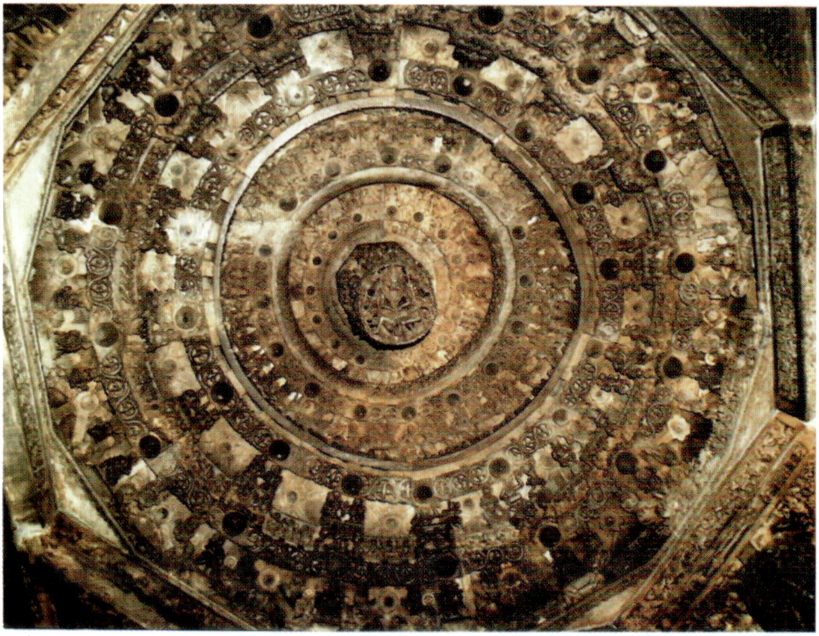

Pl. 23: The *maṇḍala* at Beḷūr temple,
the domical ceiling at the Basilica Santa Maria.

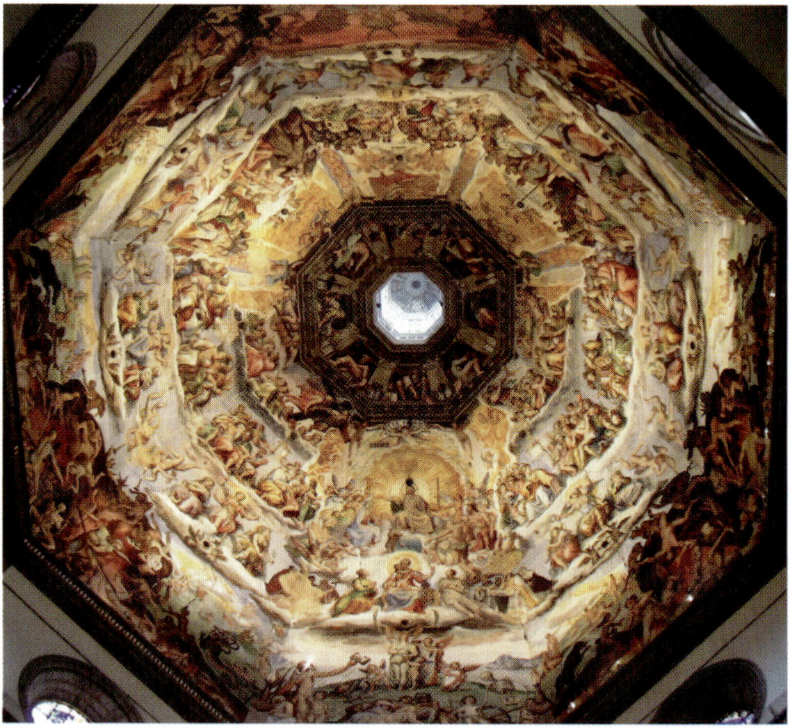

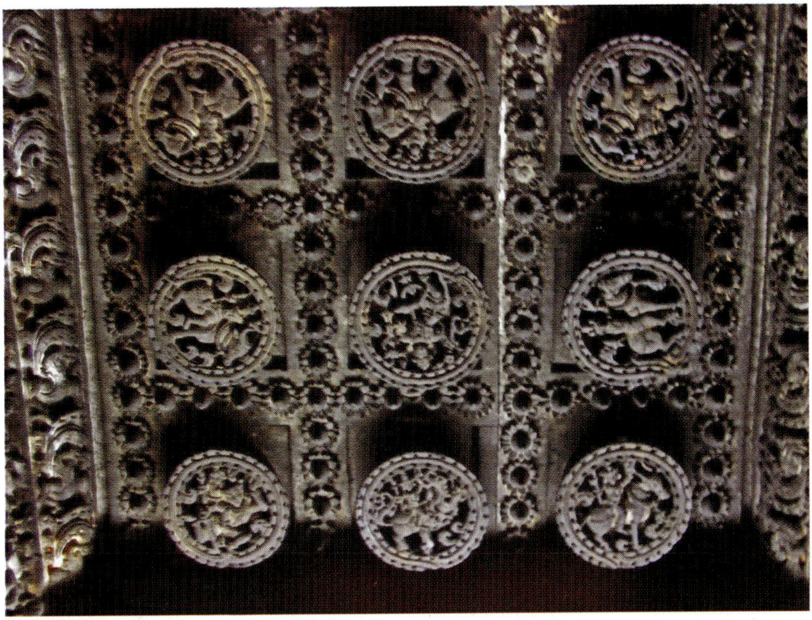

Pl. 24: *Aṣṭadikpāla maṇḍala* at Marale Siddheśvara temple.

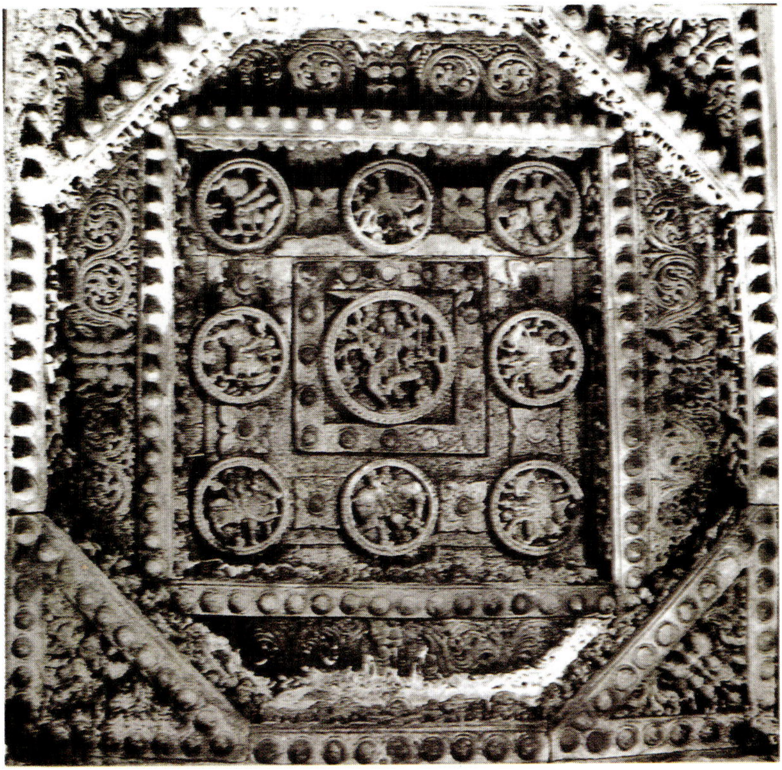

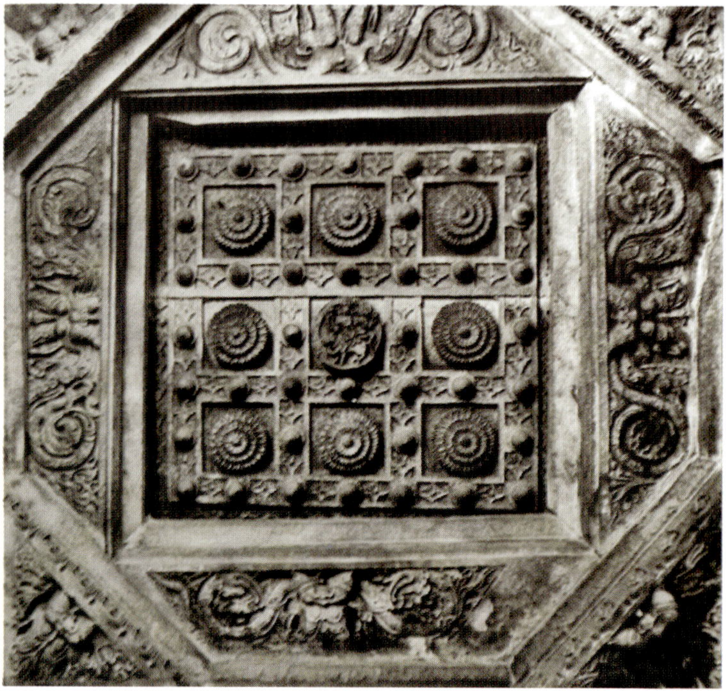

Pl. 25: *Maṇḍala* of square grids at the Marale Siddheśvara temple, and a varied version of *aṣṭadikpāla*s.

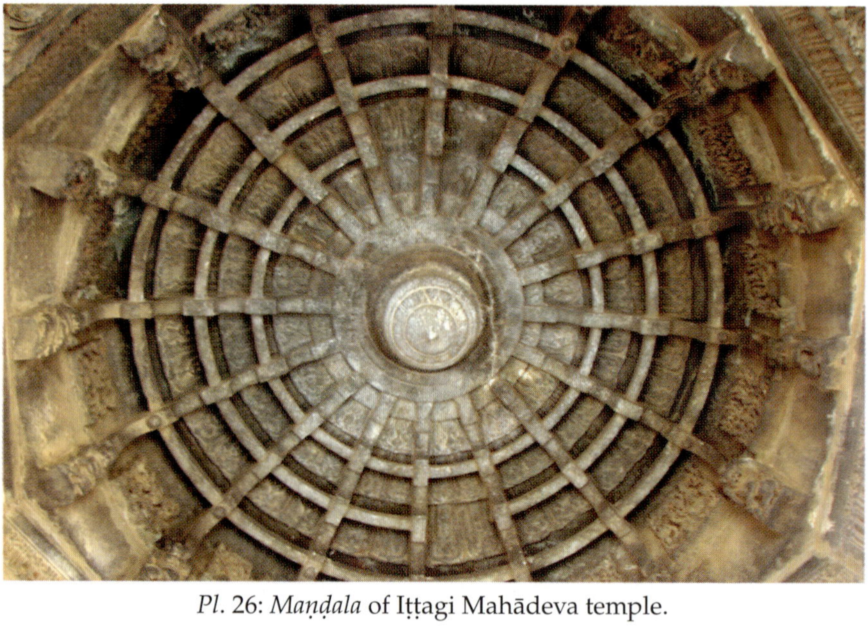

Pl. 26: *Maṇḍala* of Iṭṭagi Mahādeva temple.

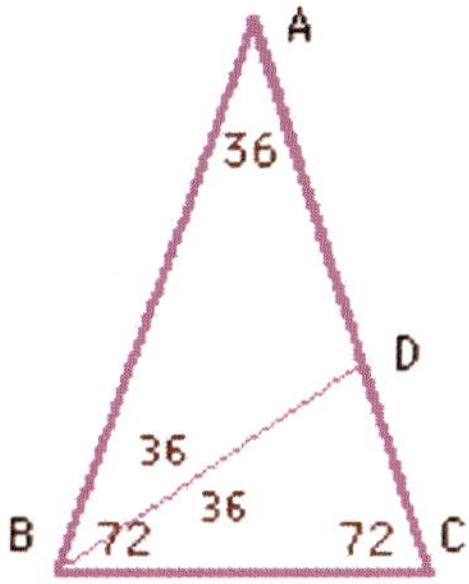

Fig. 1

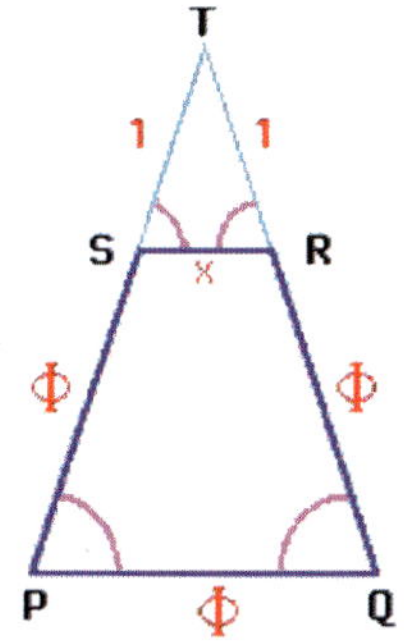

Fig. 2

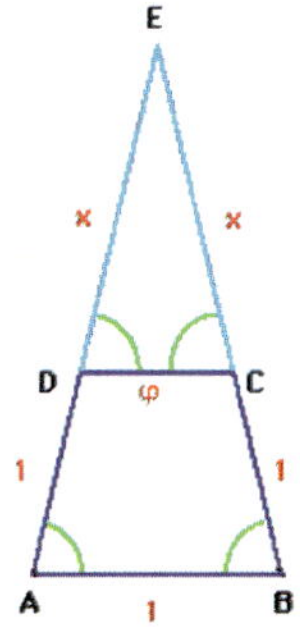

Fig. 3

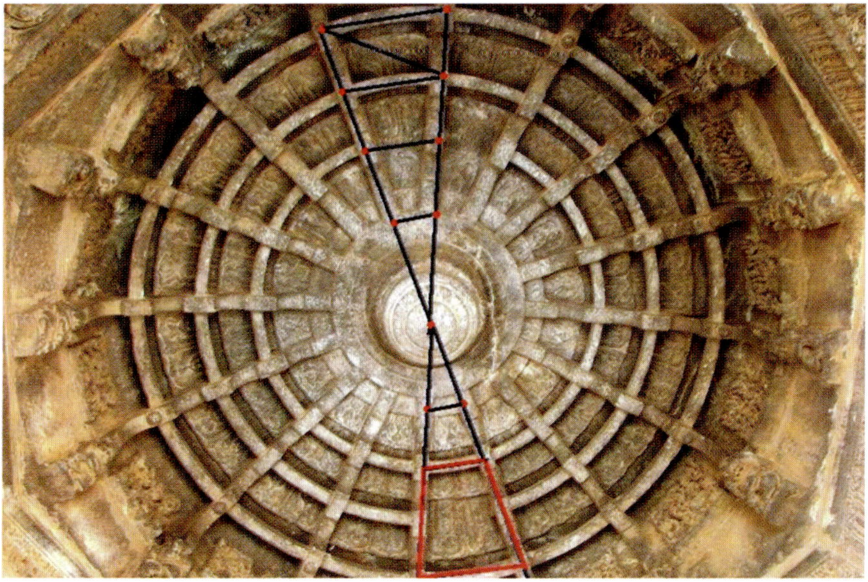

Pl. 27: Golden triangles and trapeziums.

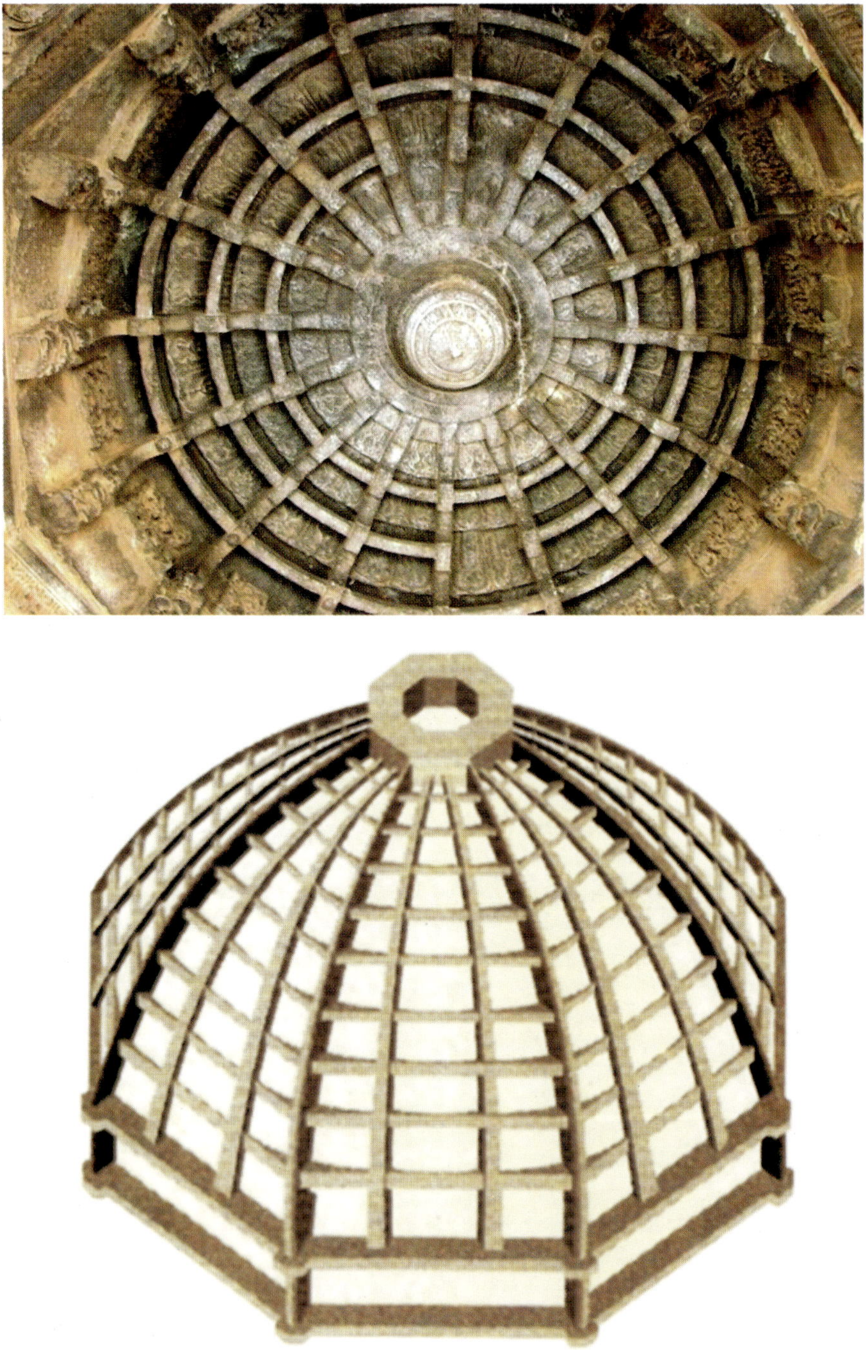

Pl. 28: Comparing the *maṇḍala* at the Iṭṭagi Mahādeva temple and the framework for a dome designed by Filippo Brunelleschi.

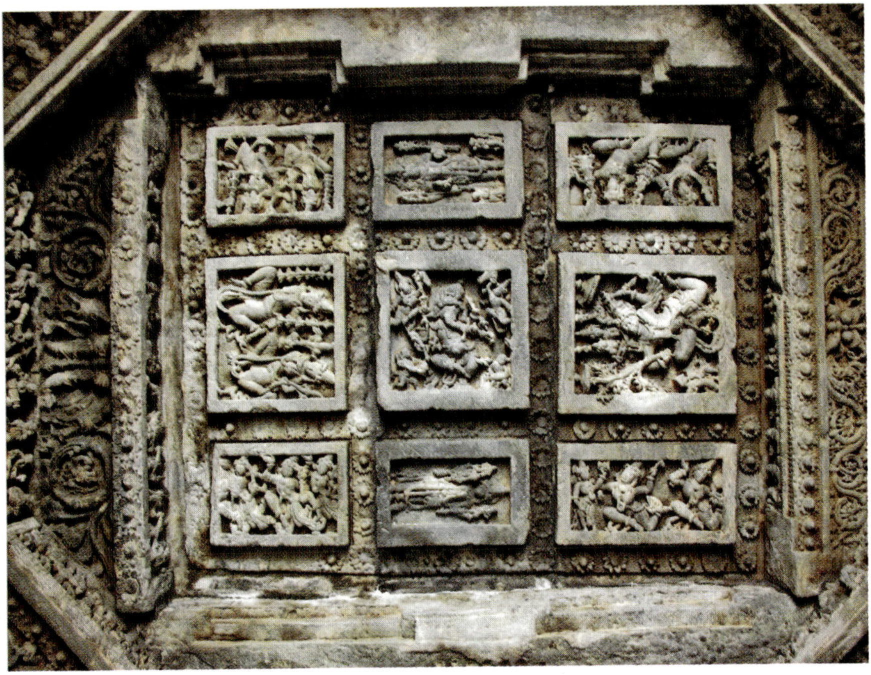

Pl. 29: *Maṇḍala* at the Hoysaḷeśvara temple, Halebiḍ.

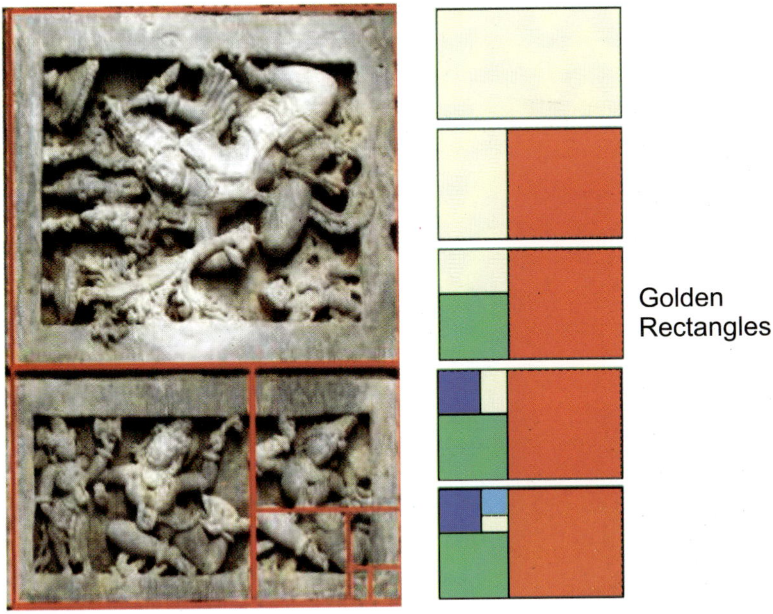

Pl. 30: A demonstration for the application of golden ratios and golden rectangles in the *bhuvaneśvarī* ceiling of Halebiḍ temple.

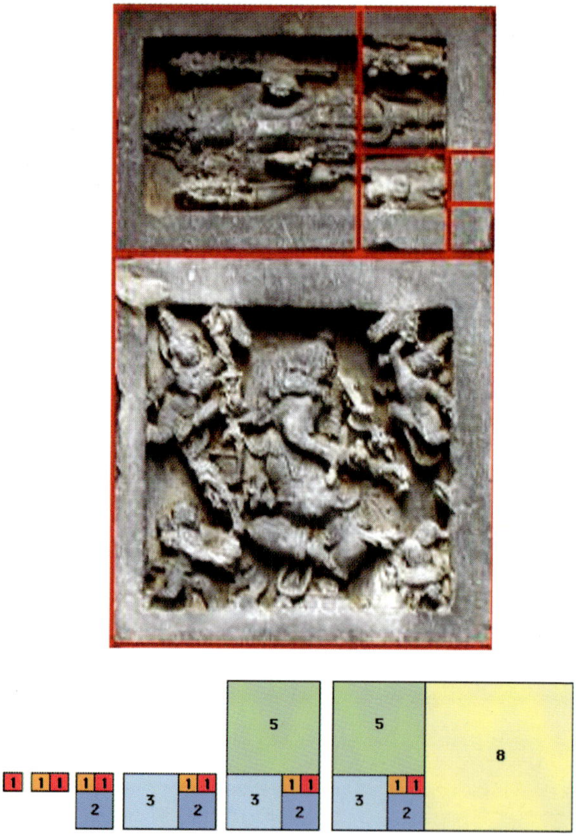

Pl. 31: A demonstration of the application of golden squares.

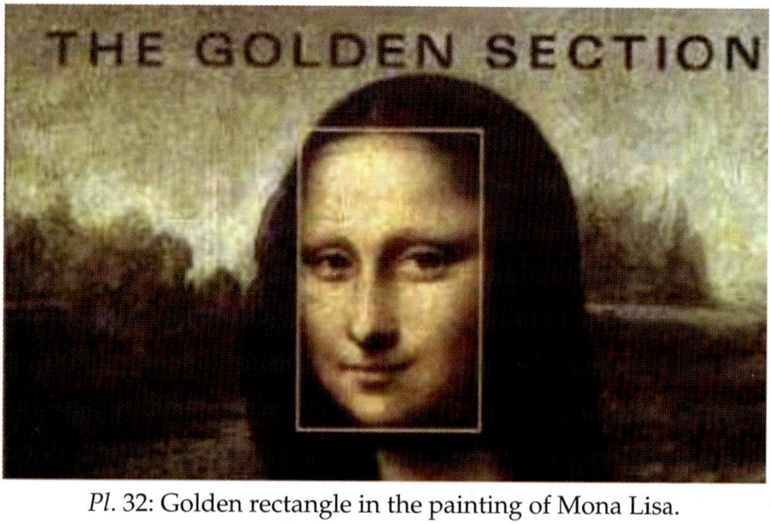

Pl. 32: Golden rectangle in the painting of Mona Lisa.

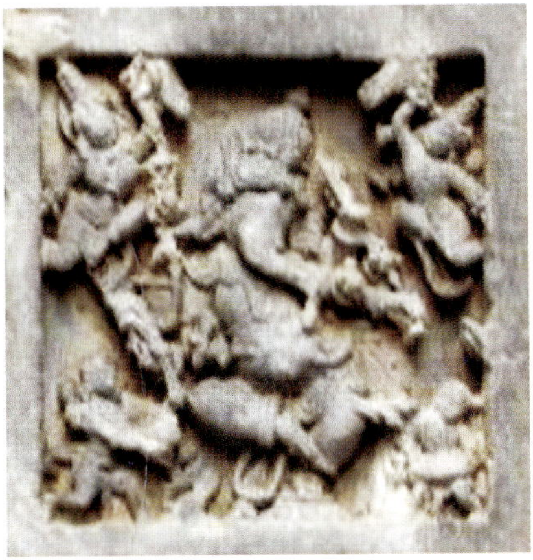

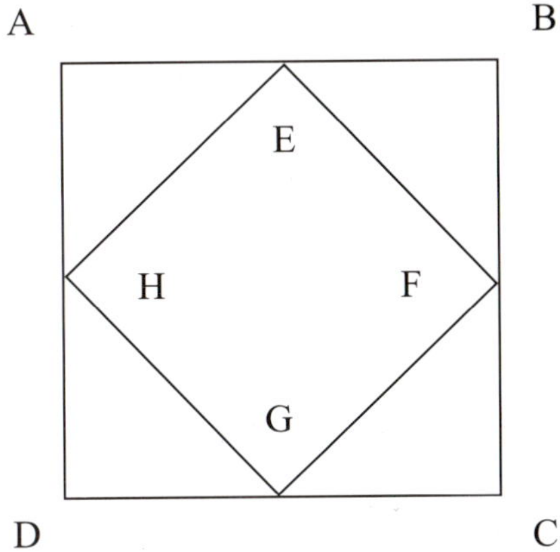

Grail geometry

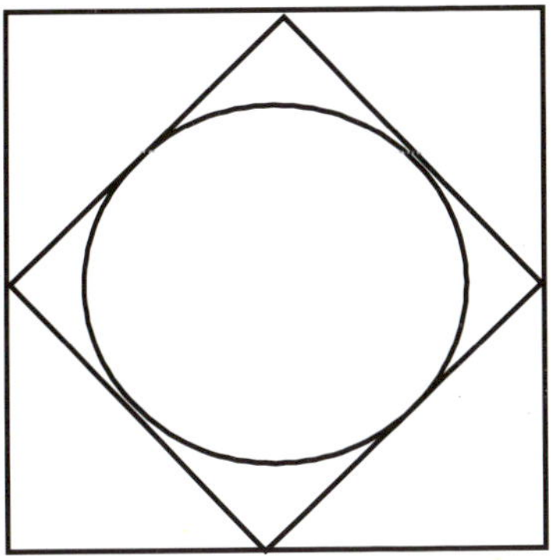

Templar variation

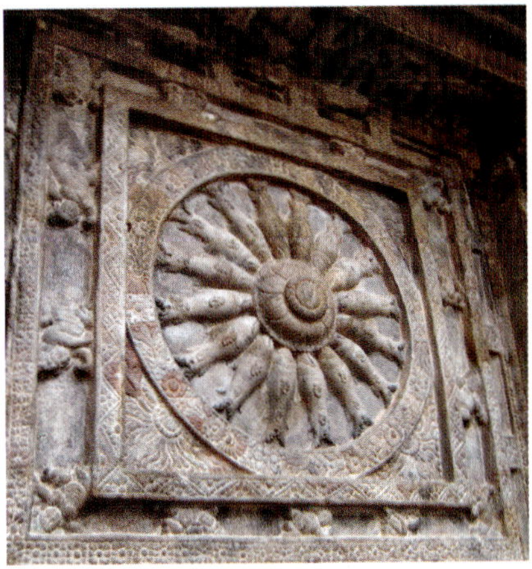

Maṇḍala in Bādāmi Cave

Pl. 33: Geometry of the Gaṇeśa panel.

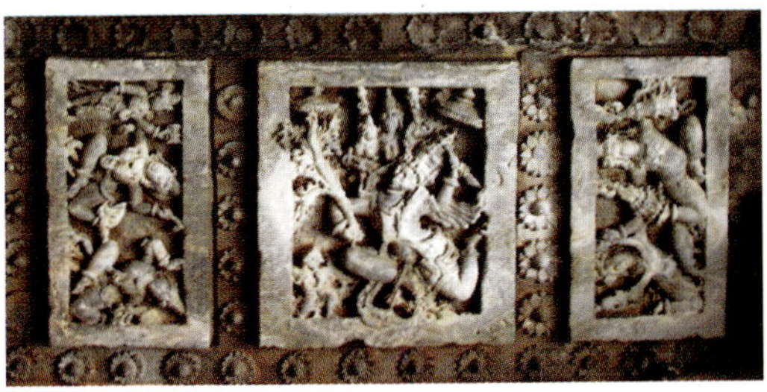

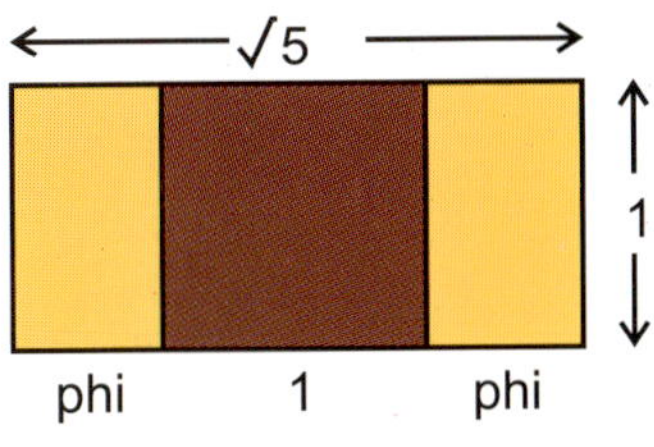

Pl. 34: Golden square and rectangles.

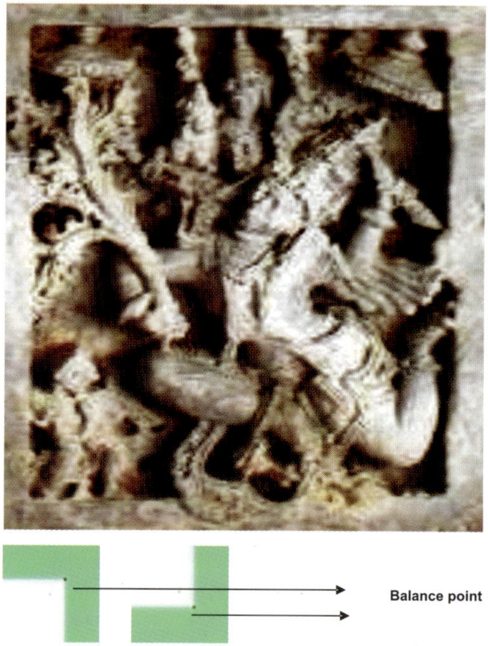

Pl. 35: Location of balance point in a square frame.

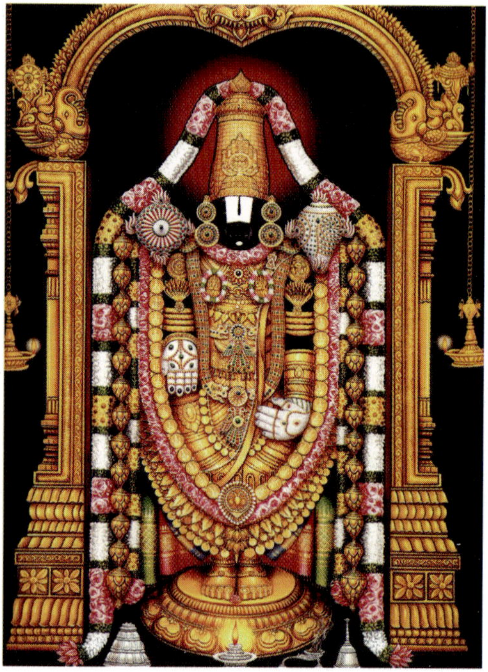

Pl. 36: Figure of Lord Veṅkaṭeśvara at Tirupati.

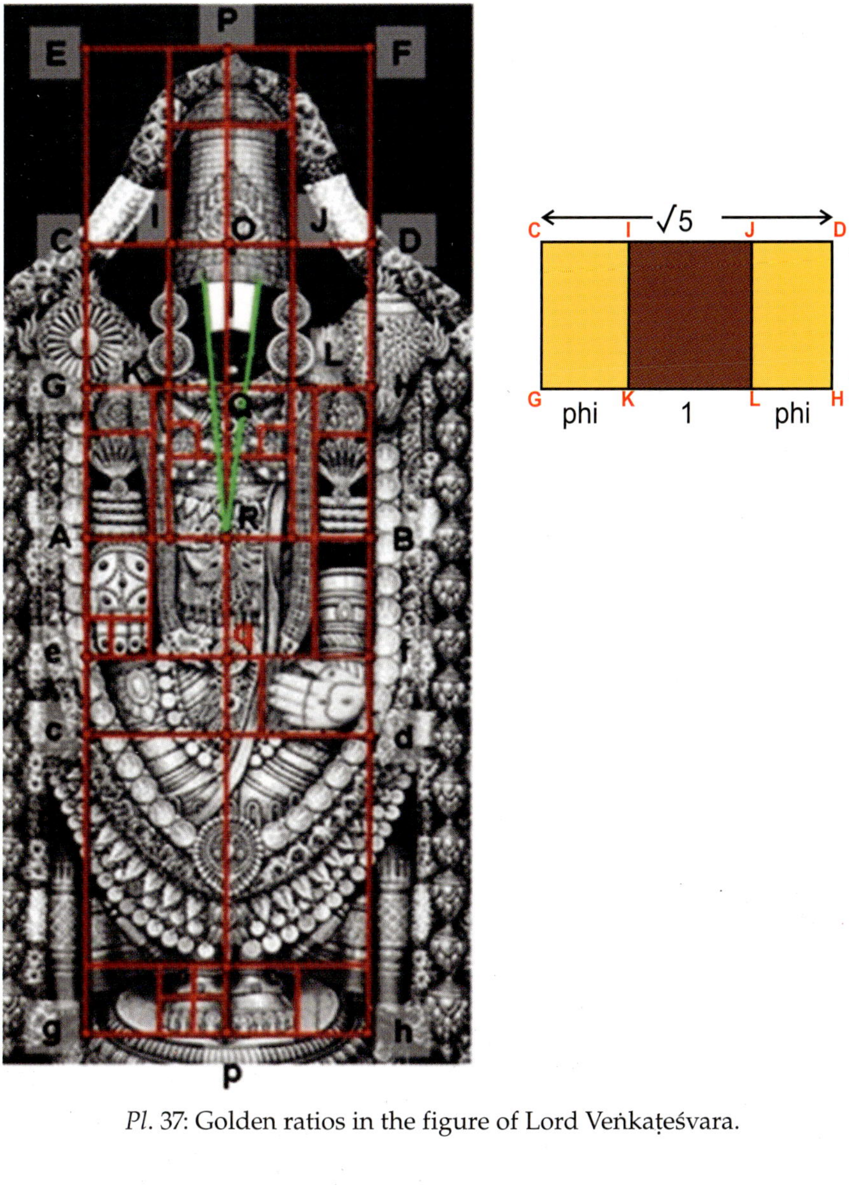

Pl. 37: Golden ratios in the figure of Lord Veṅkaṭeśvara.

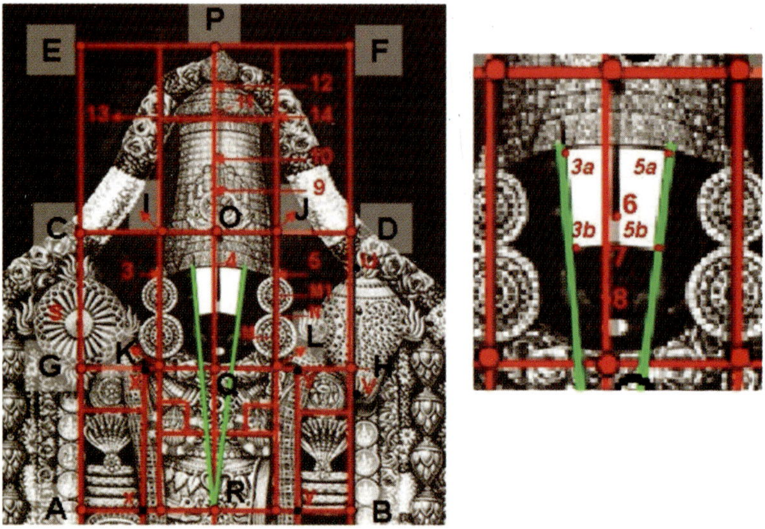

Pl. 38: The top rectangle and *Tiru Nāma*.

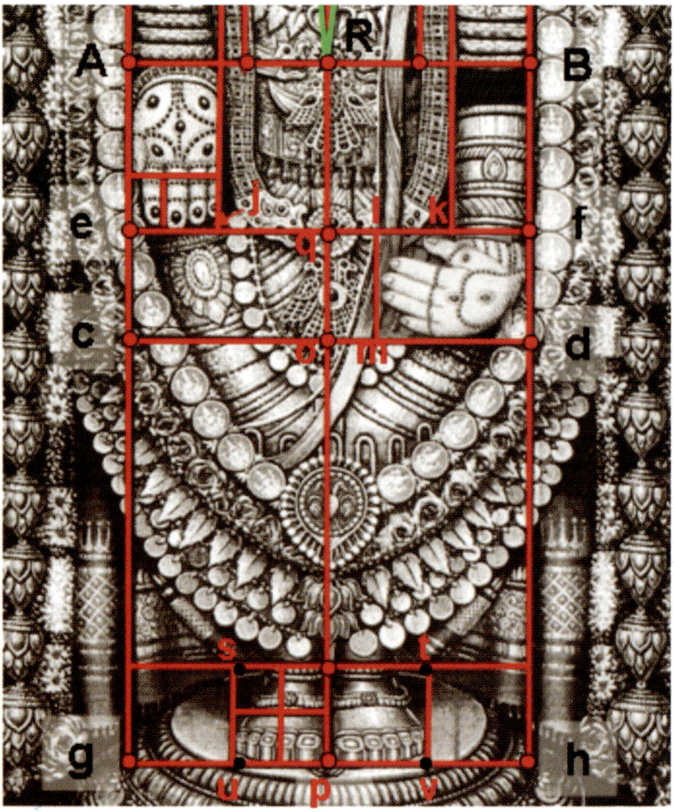

Pl. 39: The bottom rectangle.

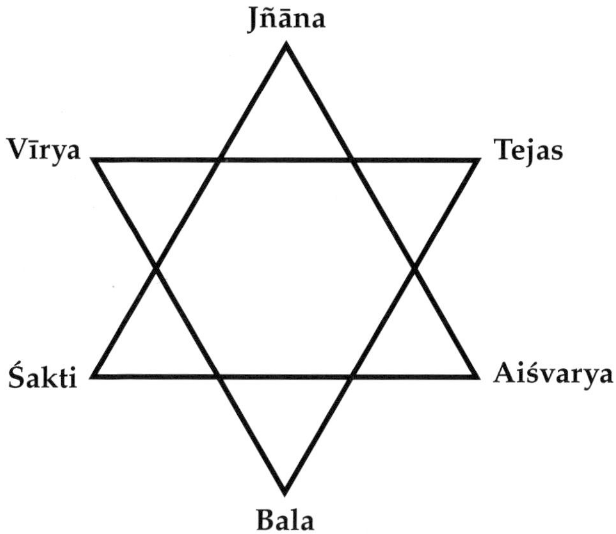

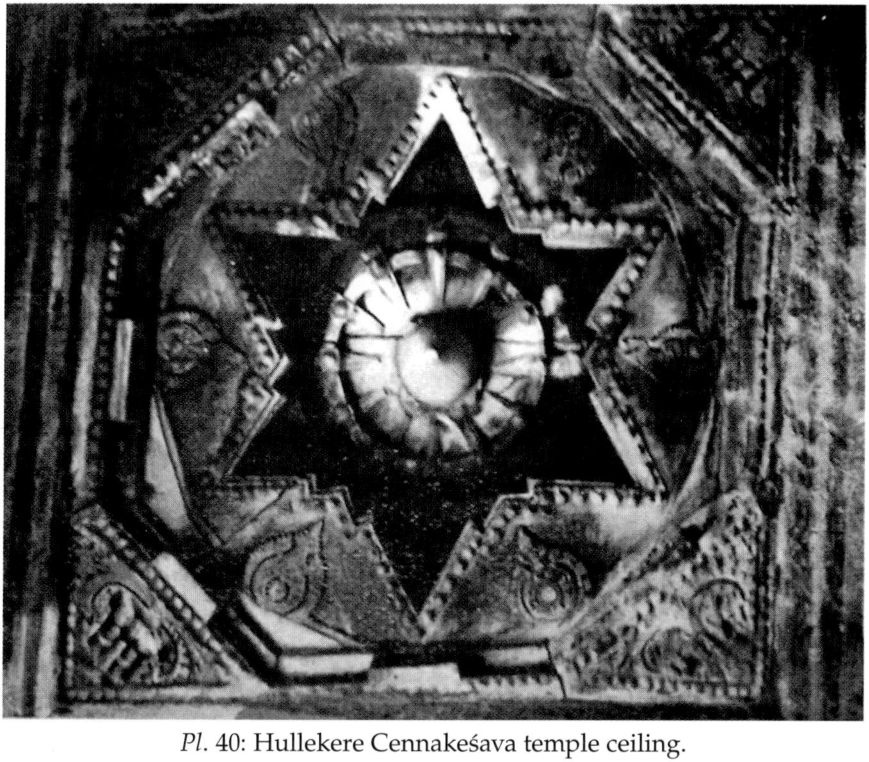

Pl. 40: Hullekere Cennakeśava temple ceiling.

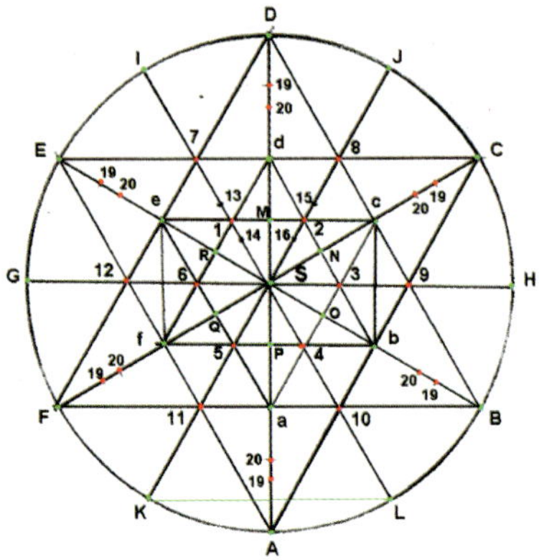

41: Frame of Naṭarāja sculpture.

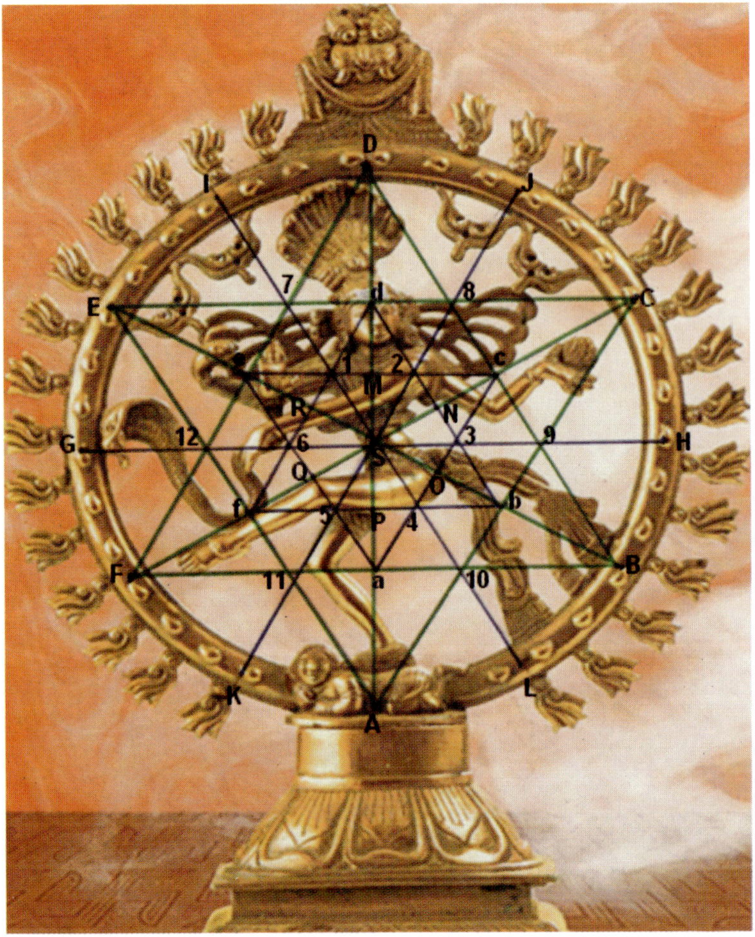

42: The sculpture of Naṭarāja with the frame superimposed.

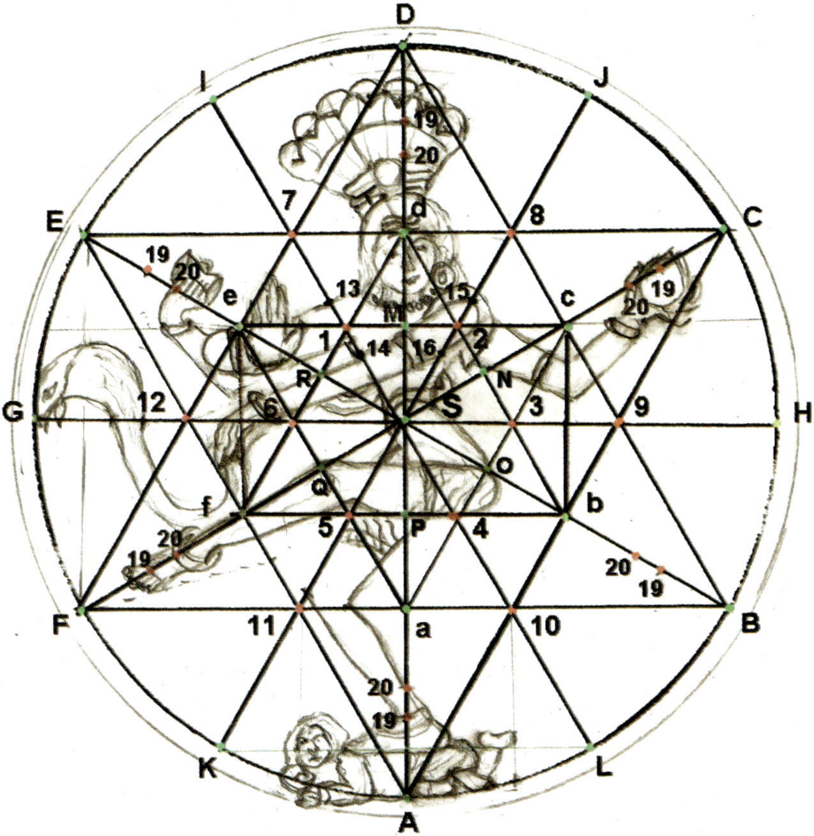

Pl. 43: The Trial figure of Naṭarāja drawn on the frame.

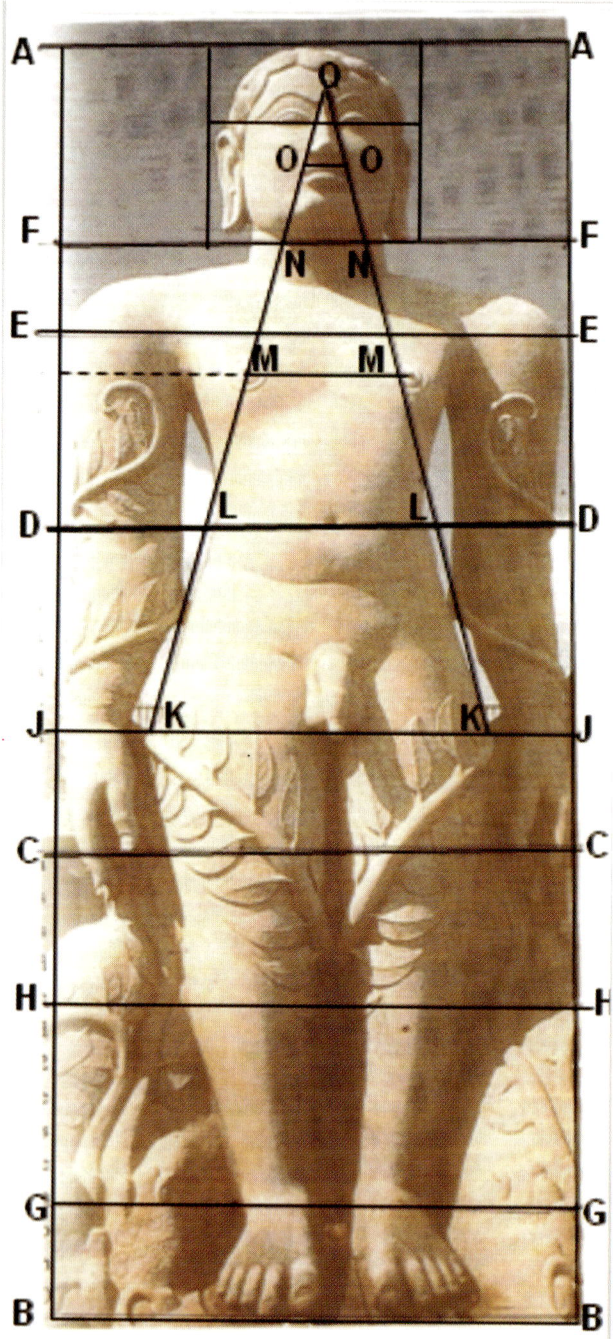

Pl. 44: Golden sections of Gommaṭeśvara.

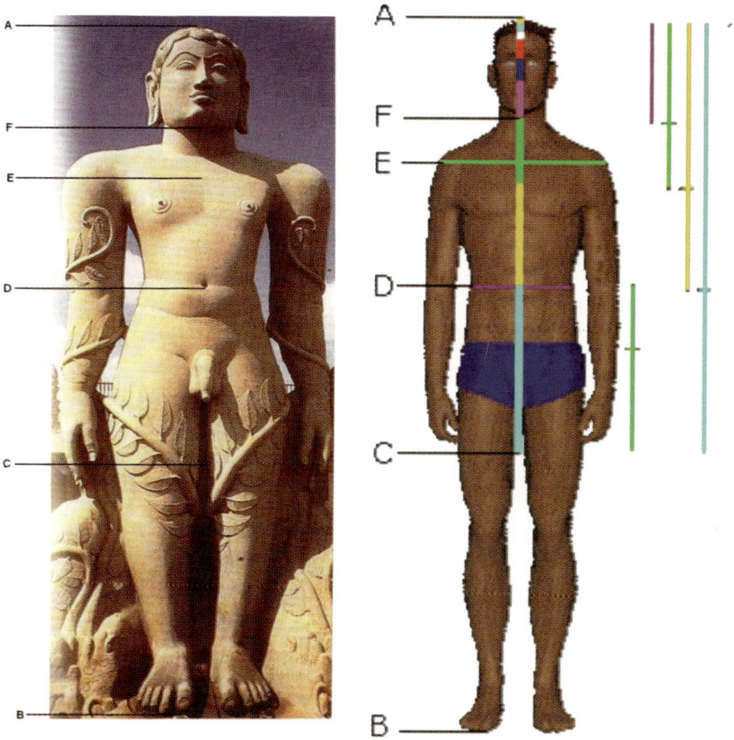

Pl. 45: Comparison of physical proportions between divine figure and the ideal human figure.

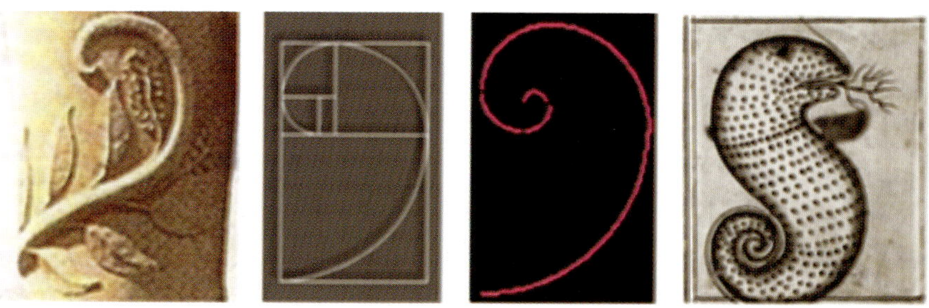

Pl. 46: Golden spirals.

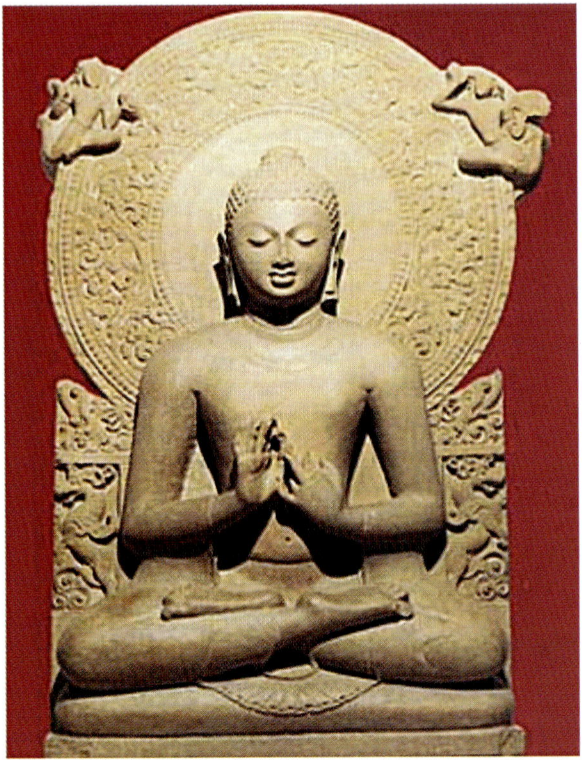

Pl. 47: Dhyānī Buddha at Sārnāth.

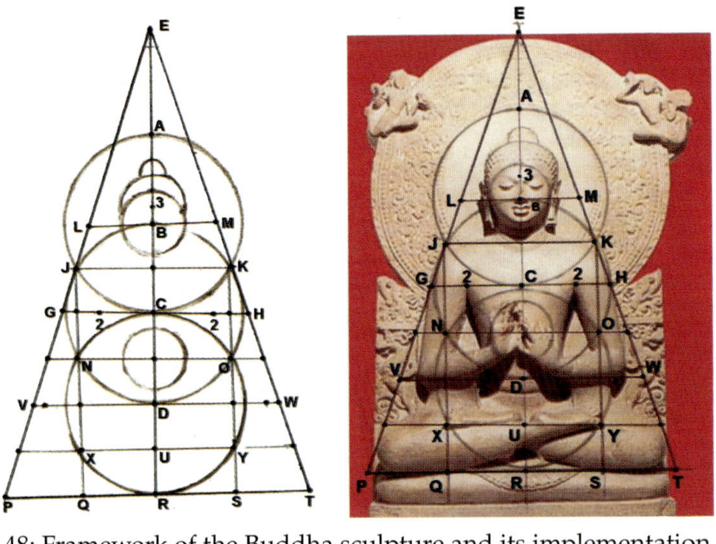

Pl. 48: Framework of the Buddha sculpture and its implementation.

Glossary of Sanskrit Terms

Abhaya-hasta	The hand gesture of protection.
Abhimānī devatā	A troop of benevolent gods.
Ādhāra	Support, power of sustaining.
Ādiśeṣa	The mythological serpent on the coils of which Lord Nārāyaṇa reclines.
Ādityas	Divinities of sun taken collectively.
Advaita	Non-duality.
Advitīyam	Without a second.
Agrahāra	A grant of land given by the king to brāhmaṇas for sustenance.
Aiśvarya	Sovereignty backed up by wealth.
Ājñā cakra	The wheel of sixth psychic energy centre.
Ahaṁkāra	Sense of self, one of the eight products of elements.
Ahirbudhnya	Serpent of deep sea.
Āmalaka	Cogged ringsstone on the *vimāna* of the temple, *āmlā* fruit of embolic myrobalan tree.
Aṁśumad	Luminous.
Anāhata cakra	The wheel of the fourth psychic energy centre of awareness.
Ānanda	Bliss.
Ānanda tāṇḍava	The blissful dance of Śiva/Naṭarāja in vigorous mode.
Ānandamaya	An abode of bliss.
Anantaśayana	Sleeping on the endless coils of the snake Ananta.
Animnonnatāgram	The sharp and pointed needle-like petals.

Aniruddha	Eternal creation.
Aṅkuśa	A goad used to guide the animal in the right direction.
Annamaya kośa	The sheath of psychic matter, the earthly body.
Antarāla	Interior, inner or the middle part.
Antarmayī	Omnipresent.
Aparā vidyā	Knowledge of the lower order.
Apsarases	Celestial beauties.
Ardhanarīśvara	The androgynous form of Lord Śiva representing the union of Śiva and Śakti.
Arthaśāstra	The science of political science.
Arūpa	Formless.
Aṣṭadikpālas	The guardians of the eight cardinal directions.
Aṣṭakoṇa	An octagon.
Aṣṭa-dala padma	Eight-angled or eight-petalled lotus.
Aśvattha	*Pīpal* or sacred fig tree.
Ātman	The self.
Avasthā	State of being.
Avatāra puruṣa	Descent of a deity, incarnation of a deity.
Avyakta	Unmanifest.
Āyudhas	Weapons.
Bala	Strength.
Bhadra	Auspicious.
Bhadramaṇḍala	A *maṇḍala* design that is secured and auspicious from all sides.
Bhū, bhuvar, suvar, mahar, jana, tapa and *satya lokas*	The seven worlds of awareness.
Bhūdevī	Consort of Lord Viṣṇu.
Bhūpura	The square courtyard of the *maṇḍala*.
Bhūtas	The elements.
Bhuvana	The world.
Bhuvaneśvarī	The domical ceiling in the assembly hall of the

	temple, the universe.
Bīja	Seed.
Bindu	Point.
Brahmānanda	Ecstasy of joy.
Bṛhadāraṇyaka	Name of an Upaniṣad.
Buddhi	Intellect.
Cakra	Wheel.
Cakravartī	Emperor.
Chāndogya	Name of an Upaniṣad.
Ḍākinī	Goddess of *mūlādhāra cakra*.
Dakṣiṇāyaṇa	Southward movement of sun.
Dalāgra	Tip of the petal.
Ḍamaru	The small percussion instrument held in the hand of Lord Śiva.
Daṇḍanāyaka	Commander-in-chief.
Danta	Tusk.
Darśana	Reveal.
Daśāṅgula	Ten fingers' width or height — a unit of measurement.
Daśāvatāra	The ten incarnations of Lord Viṣṇu.
Devālaya	House of God.
Devatā	Goddess.
Devatā yantra	A *yantra* — the divinity is in iconic form.
Dhāraka yantra	A *yantra* that is retained for protection.
Dhyāna śloka	Hymns giving the prescription for making divine figures.
*Dikpāla*s	Guardians of the cardinal directions.
Gadā	Mace, a weapon.
Gāṇapatya, Saura Vaiṣṇava, Śākta and Śaiva	The cult worshippers of Gaṇeśa, Sūrya, Viṣṇu, Śakti and Śiva.
Gaṇas	The troop of gods in second rank.

Gandharvas	The semi-divine gods of music.
Gaṇita	Arithmetic.
Garbha	Womb.
Garbhagṛha	*Sanctum sanctorum.*
Gati	Gait.
Gṛha	House.
Guṇas	Qualities.
Icchā	The will.
Icchā, jñāna, and *kriyā śaktis*	The forces of great will, knowledge and action.
Iḍā nāḍī	The nerve running up the left side of spinal column which is passive and feminine.
Īśāna	Lord of the north-east direction.
Iṣṭadevatā	God of personal choice.
Jagatī	Platform.
Jāgrat	Wakeful state of mind.
Janārdana and Veṇugopāla	Epithets of Lord Kṛṣṇa.
Jijñāsu	Seeker of knowledge.
Jina	Conquerer.
Jīva	Life.
Jīvātmā	Living soul.
Jñāna	Knowledge.
Jñāna śakti	Power of knowledge.
Jñānaloka	The world of knowledge.
Jyotirmayī	Related to light and sight.
Kailāsa	Mountain peak in Himalayas, the abode of Śiva.
Kāla, deśa, nimitta	Bound by time and space.
Kāla jñānī	One who has the knowledge of *mahāyuga* and Brahmā cycles of time.
Kālacakra	The wheel of time.
Kalaśa	The golden jar.

Kaliyuga	The epoch of Kali — the epoch of present time.
Kalpa	A day of Brahmā — a period of 4.32 billion years.
Kampana saṁkhyā	Frequency number.
Kaṭyāvalambita-mudrā	Hand gesture when it is placed below the waist.
Kesari	The stamens of the lotus flower.
Keśava	An epithet of Lord Kṛṣṇa.
Kīrtimukha	The face of a lion projecting religious symbolism, an ornamental expansion of glory.
Kīrtimukha	The face of glory.
Kośa	A closed flower bud, a sheath.
Krakaca	Sharp knife.
Kriyā	Action.
Kṣetra	Area.
Kuñcita ekapāda	A specific dance posture where legs are in bent position and one leg lifted up across the other knee.
*Kuṇḍalinī cakra*s	The wheels of awareness in relation to goddess Kuṇḍalinī.
Lalita	Beautiful.
Līlā	Blissful sports or pastimes.
Liṅga	The phallic symbol of Lord Śiva.
Lokapālas	The guardians of the world.
Mahākalpa	The 100-year span of Brahmā's one life.
Mahāpuruṣa lakṣaṇa	Special features adopted for Hindu divine sculptures.
Mahāyuga	One cyclic duration of all the four *yuga*s.
Manas	Mind.
Maṇḍala	Circular design.
Maṇḍapa	A decorated pillared hall.
Maṅgala	Auspicious.
Maṇipūra cakra	The wheel of the third psychic level of awareness.
Manonmaya	Pertaining to the mind.

Mantreśvaras	The troop of Śaivite deities of pure region in pacific form.
Manusmṛti	The code of laws ascribed to Manu — the father of human race.
Manvantara	A period of 71 *yugas* that is ruled by a Manu.
Māyā	Illusion.
Mayūkhas	Rays of light, brightness.
Meru	Mountain, mount Kailāsa.
Mīmāṁsaka	An investigator.
Mitra	The sun.
Mokṣa	Liberation.
Mukhamaṇḍapa	An entrance hall.
Mukti	Emancipated.
Mulādhāra cakra	The wheel of the first psychic centre of awareness.
Muṇḍaka	An Upaniṣad of *Atharvaveda*.
Muṇḍī	The blunt end.
Mūrtyāṣṭaka	The eight forms of Lord (Īsvara).
Muyaḷagan	The dwarf demon symbolic of illusion.
Nāgamaṇḍala	The coiling of the snake in circular form.
Nāgasūtra	A string or line in snake motif.
Nakṣatra	A star.
Nāma	Identification mark of Vaiṣṇavites on the forehead.
Nava-padma-bhadra	Nine lotuses of auspiciousness.
Navagraha	The nine planets.
Navaraṅga	The assembly hall of the temple.
Nirguṇa Brahman or *Paramaśiva*	The supreme spirit without any attributes.
Nirṛti	South-west direction.
Nitya śaktis	The eternal flow of forces.
Nṛtta	Pure dance movements.
Pāda-vinyāsa	The arrangement of square grids.
Padārtha	Objects.

Pādas	Square grids.
Padmanābha	Lotus-naveled, an epithet of Lord Viṣṇu.
Padma	Lotus.
Prakṛti and *Puruṣa*	The female and the male forces of nature.
Pakṣas	A fortnight.
Pañca	Five.
Pañcāyatana pūjā	The fivefold worship of the five Brāhmanical cult deities.
Pañcākṣara	Five lettered.
Pañca-tattvas	The five elements.
Pañcopāsana	The fivefold worship of the five Brāhmanical cult deities.
Paramaśiva	Absolute reality.
Paramātmā	The supreme soul.
Parameśvara	Supreme god — Śiva.
Parārdha	50 years' span of Brahmā's one time cycle.
Paridhi	Surrounding wall.
Paśupati	Epithet of Śiva, lord of animals.
Pātāla	The lowest region of the world.
Pātra	Role.
Pecaka	Square grid with four divisions.
Piṇḍa	Ball of flour.
Piṅgalā nāḍī	The motor nerve running to the right side of the spinal column, with rational and masculine energy.
Pīṭha	9 squares corresponding to the three divisions of a big square, pedestal.
Pitṛ	Forefathers.
Pradyumna	Form with dual forces.
Prakāśa	Luminous.
Prakṛti	The female power of nature.
Pralaya	Dissolution.

Prāṇamaya kośa	The sheath of vital breath.
Pratidhvani	Echo.
Pṛthvī, āpa, tejas, vāyu and *ākāśa*	The five elements of nature — the earth, water, fire, air and ether.
Purāṇas	Ancient scriptures.
Puruṣa	The male power, spirit.
Puruṣottama	The supreme man.
Rakṣā	Protection.
Rakṣā cakra	The wheel of protection.
*Rāśi*s	The zodiacal constellations.
Rati and Manmatha	The goddess and god of love.
Ṛgveda	The first of the four Vedas.
Rūpa	Form.
Sahasradala padma	Thousand-petalled lotus.
Sahasrāra cakra	The wheel of thousand petals, the seventh psychic centre of awareness level.
Śaiva	The followers of Lord Śiva or Śaivism.
Sakala	A square grid.
Śakti	Power, strength, energy.
Śāligrāma	The black round stone.
Saṁhitā	Treatise.
Saṁśāra	The course of worldly life.
Saṁśraya	Dwelling place, residence.
Saṁvatsara	A year.
Śaṅkha	Conch shell.
Sāṁkhya	Relating to number.
Śaṅkara	Epithet of Śiva, the curer of diseases.
Saṅkarṣaṇa	Art of drawing together.
Saṅkoca	To contract.
Śarīra	Body.
Sarūpa	A body with form.
Sarvatobhadra	Auspicious from all sides.

Śāstra	A sacred precept or rule.
Śatapatha	One of the Brāhmaṇa treatises.
Ṣaḍcakra bhedha	Knowledge of the six psychic centres of awareness.
Ṣāḍguṇaya yantra	A sacred diagram indicating the six divine qualities.
Satyayuga	The golden age.
Śata, Savīra	Hundred and thousand.
Saumya	Calm.
Śikhara	The peak of a mountain.
Siddhāntas	Formulae.
Siṁhāsana	The seat of honour, a throne
Ṣoḍaśa	Sixteen.
Soma	Moon, bestower of joy
Śrī	Wealth, honourific prefix used to the names of deities or eminent persons.
Śrī Devī	Consort of Lord Viṣṇu.
Śrī-Yantra	The sacred power diagram worshipped by Hindus.
Sthāna	Position.
Sthāpatya Veda	Indian traditional architecture.
Sthūla	Gross.
Stūpikā	The finial on the *vimāna* of the temple.
Śukla pakṣa	The brighter fortnight of the month.
Sūkṣma	Subtle.
Śūnya	Empty, void.
Sūrya	The sun.
Suṣupti	Deep sleep.
Svādhiṣṭhāna cakra	The wheel of the second psychic level of awareness.
Svapna	Dream.
Svarākṣaras	Vowels.

Svastika	An ancient and worldwide symbol, emblematic of Sun. The traditional and auspicious cross symbol of Hindus.
Tamas	Darkness, inertia.
Tantra	The framework of rituals, a regular order of ceremonies.
Tattvas	Elements, a primary substance.
Tattvābhimānī	Followers or lovers of true or essential nature.
Tejas	Brilliance, bright appearance.
Tirunāma	White coloured mark on forehead.
Trikūṭa	Triple-celled structure.
Trikūṭācala	A temple with three sanctums.
Trimūrti	The unified form of Hindu trinity lords — Brahmā, Viṣṇu and Śiva.
Turīya	The fourth state of the soul in which it becomes one with the supreme spirit.
Ugra	Terrific.
Upaniṣad	The ancient writings associated with the secret knowledge of Vedas, regarding the supreme spirits.
Uttarāyaṇa	The northward movement of sun.
Vāhana	vehicle.
Vairāgya	Renunciation.
Vaiśeṣika	One of the six principal systems of Hindu philosophy, founded by Kaṇāda.
Vaiṣṇavism	Relating to Lord Viṣṇu.
Vaiṣṇavites	Followers of Viṣṇu as the supreme God.
Vaivasvata	Name of the seventh Manu who is supposed to preside over the present age.
Vajra	A thunderbolt, the weapon of Indra, diamond.
Valaya	A ring, or a circle.
Vāṅmayi	Related to *śabda*, sound or speech.
Varada-mudrā	Hand gesture of God giving boons.
Vāstu puruṣa maṇḍala	The *maṇḍala* of Vāstu — the site of a building.

Vāyavya	North-east.
Vāyu	Air.
Vedāṅgas	Certain class of work regarded as the auxiliary to Vedas.
Veda	Sacred knowledge.
Vedānta	The end of Vedas (Upaniṣads).
Vidyeśvaras	Subordinate deities of Īśvara in the pacific form of pure region.
Vijñānamaya kośa	Sheath of intellect.
Vigrahas	Figure, form of the body, idols of deities.
Vimāna	Tall tapering roof of the temple.
Vimarśa	Deliberation.
Vīrya	Heroism, power of potency.
Viṣṇudharmottara Purāṇa	One of the celebrated Purāṇas.
Viṣṇu	The second deity of the sacred triad entrusted with preservation of the world.
Viṣṇu, Śiva, Sūrya Gaṇapatya and Durgā	The five cult deities of *pañcāyatana*.
Viśuddha	Purified, cleansed.
Viśuddha cakra	The wheel of the fifth psychic centre of awareness levels.
Vīthi	Road, lane.
Vṛndāvana	The forest near Gokula.
Vyañjanākṣara	A consonant.
Yajñopavīta	The sacred thread.
Yāḷi	A hybrid representation of *kīrtimukha* with parrot's body, with elephant's head and teeth of crocodile.
Yāmas	A three-hourly time division of the day.
Yantra	A power diagram.
Yoganidrā	The deep slumber (of Lord Viṣṇu).
Yoginī gaṇa	A troop of specific demi-goddesses possessed of magical powers.
Yuga	An age of the world.

List of Illustrations

Bibliography

Arguelles, Jose and Miriam Arguelles, *Mandala*, Berkeley & London: Shambala 1972.

Banerjea, Jitendra Nath, *The Development of Hindu Iconography*, New Delhi: Munshiram Manoharlal, 2002.

Buhnemann, Gudrun, *Maṇḍalas and Yantras in The Hindu Traditions*, New Delhi: D.K. Printworld, 2007.

Cornell, Judith, *Mandala, Luminous Symbols for Healing*, Wheaton, IL: The Theosophical Publishing House, 1994.

The Cultural Heritage of India, vols. I to VI, Calcutta: The Ramakrishna Mission Institute of Culture, rpts. 1991-2000.

Cunningham, Bailey, *Mandala Journey to the Centre*, A Dorling Kindersley Book, 2002.

Gopinath Rao, T.A., *Elements of Hindu Iconography*, vols. I & II, Motilal Banarsidass, 1997.

Greene, Brian, *The Elegant Universe*, New York, London: W.W., Nortan & Company, 1999.

Hawking, Stephen W., *A Brief History of Time*, Bantam Export Edition, 1989.

King Ross, *Brunelleschi's Dome*, Penguin Books, 2000.

The Holy Geeta, Commentary by Swami Chinmayananda, Central Chinmaya Mission Trust, 2002.

Kramrisch, Stella, *The Hindu Temple*, vol. I, Motilal Banarsidass, 1976.

Ramachandra Rao, S.K., *Yantragalu* (Kannada) Bengalore: Sriranga Printing and Publishing House, 2005.

Sadguru, *Sacred Space for Self-Transformation*, Isha Foundation, 2008.

Sagan Carl, *Cosmos*, United States: Ballentine Books, 1985.

Singh, T.D., Ravi Gomatum (eds.), *Synthesis of Science & Religion Critical Essays and Dialogues*, San Francisco–Bombay: The Bhaktivedanta Institute.

Tresidder, Jack, *Symbols and Their Meanings*, New York: Barnes & Noble, 2006.

Index